INTERNAL HEALTH

The Key to Eternal Youth and Vitality

by best selling author
RON GELLATLEY N.D.

1999
CARGEL PRESS INTERNATIONAL

ISBN 1 74018 041 0

Published by
Cargel Press International
Unit 3, 2 Frank Street
Wetherill Park NSW 2164, Australia
Fax: (02) 9756 0719
www.cargelpress.com.au

All correspondence to
PO Box 50, Horsley Park NSW 2164, Australia
email: info@cargelpress.com.au

Designed by
Wild & Woolley
Member: Australian Publishers Association/Publish Australia
16 Darghan Street, Glebe NSW 2037, Australia

Designed, printed and bound in Australia
Printed on acid-free, archival paper

2 3 4 5 03 02 01 00 99

Cover Design by
All Type & Art Pty Ltd

I dedicate this book to
suffering humanity searching for health
in a polluted world…

To Ella with love

from Teresa

Christmas 1999

DISCLAIMER

The information and procedures contained in this book are based on the personal experience of the author and are for educational purposes only. It is not a medical textbook, nor is it intended to replace your doctor or other health care provider. The publisher and author are not responsible for any suggestions, preparations, or procedures discussed in this book. All matters regarding your physical health should be supervised by a health care professional.

FOREWORD

If someone asked me this question: 'What is the most important thing anyone can do to ensure a long and happy life?', I would reply straight from my heart 'Internal Health'.

How can you or anyone else perform at a high level if your bodily systems are clogged up? How can you be full of joy if your liver is full of misery? How can anyone smile with a belly full of pain?

How can you be expected to have almost unlimited energy if you are not getting nutrition from what you eat?

I know from over fifteen years as a Naturopath if I can get a patient's digestive system, the liver included, in good shape I can do wonders.

I have seen it happen time and time again…

The change in a patient once his digestive system, his liver, his bowel are all in tip-top condition is absolutely amazing. It almost makes you believe in miracles.

Complaints seemingly unrelated disappear. Depression lifts. Energy lifts. Spirits lift. The joy of living comes back like a tidal wave…

When I wrote *How To Fight Prostate Cancer… and Win* hundreds of people wrote to me – men and women.

Apart from help with all sorts of cancer, not just prostate, I was often asked what could be done for sufferers with an Irritable Bowel, or what could I do to help someone with Diverticulitis…

This book is the answer to those hundreds of lovely people.

When you invest in this book on internal health you have taken a step that could change your life. In your hands you have the key to youthfulness, vitality and a vibrant life.

You will discover things you didn't know. You will get the secret keys to health. Your quality of life can only get fantastic!

I too have a dream.

I dream of a world free of pain. I dream of a world full of happy, healthy people. I dream of a world where laughter rings out down every street. I dream of a world without hate, a world full of love. I dream of a world where people act and feel young, regardless of their age! A world where everyone is vital and full of energy…

And I know the first step to realising this dream is showing people the secrets to good health. The way to good health is through the door of internal cleansing…

Trust me. You have spent your money wisely investing in my book.

Now it is up to me to show you the way.

Your part in making this dream come true is to follow the steps I show you…

Thank you for investing in my book.

I see you as a dear friend who shares a dream… Let us go out there and make it happen.

CONTENTS

INTERNAL
HEALTH
The Key to Eternal
Youth and Vitality

1

Something you don't want to talk about could be killing you!

Can I share a terrible secret with you?

Can you keep a secret? Of course you can… so I will share something with you. This is personal and I don't want the whole darn world to know about it.

But then… it may be something you can relate to yourself! Maybe you too had to suffer just as we did years ago.

The problem was with my Dad.

Dad was a Scot who believed we all had to have what he called a 'clean' bowel to be healthy… He used to dose us up with liquid paraffin regularly to 'clean us out'.

But here is the strange thing, the thing I could never figure out…

When my Dad went to the toilet it was like a gas attack in the First World War.

These sulphurous fumes enveloped the whole house. We would rush outside gasping and choking for air. Even the dog ran outside! And no-one could use the toilet for about two hours. It took that long to clear the air.

And Dad seemed totally unaware of the problem.

He believed he was fumigating the toilet because while he sat there, reading the daily newspaper and getting some peace from the rest of us, he was smoking away.

Far from disguising the horrible stink the tobacco smoke made it even worse…

That was his daily routine. He would grab the newspaper, trot upstairs to the toilet and squat in there for at least half an hour. He was very contented. I think he saw the toilet more like some other bloke would see his den – a refuge of peace and quiet. A place to contemplate the world and at the same time, evacuate his bowel.

And the stink was appalling. The only time I can remember a smell as bad was when we did chemistry at school and produced a mixture called hydrogen sulphide that had all the charm of a cupboard full of rotten eggs.

But Dad was so used to the stink he probably didn't even notice it.

We kids never got used to it!

How could a 'clean bowel' smell so bad?

The mystery was how could someone who was so dedicated to a clean bowel have such a stink when he emptied some of it?

In our house, back of the kitchen sink was a window sill. On this sill there was always a glass with this dirty looking brown liquid in it. It looked like some witches brew. All it needed was some bat's wings, dead toads and the other horrible ingredients that witches put in their potions to be the real thing.

What it was really was his Senna Pods brewing. He kept this glass full of Senna Pods covered with water. They sat there for days, stewing away. Now in case you don't know, Senna Pods make a very powerful laxative. Dad used to pour boiling water over them and let them stand for days. Sometimes even longer…

And to our never-ending amazement, he used to drink this concoction as though it was the finest wine you could ever taste. He would knock it back, lick his lips and say something like... 'That is good stuff, excellent for a proper clean bowel... can't beat it'.

We could never understand how he could drink the vile stuff with such apparent relish. Perhaps he was showing an example of mind over matter for the benefit of us kids! But drink it he did, every day.

My fear was that he would insist that we drank some in addition to the oily taste of the liquid paraffin, which was bad enough.

So Dad drank this laxative every day – day in and day out. Never missing... So how come his bowel smelled so bad?

LET ME TELL YOU... THERE IS NO SUCH THING AS A CLEAN BOWEL!

But my Dad was wrong.

What he should have been aiming for was a healthy bowel. His idea that you could clean out your bowel so it was free of bacteria was totally wrong... A clean bowel is an unhealthy bowel. It is a bowel that can cause you big trouble.

What my Dad was aiming for was not a clean bowel but a sterile one!

And the problem with the bowel is that by the time you can feel pain from it, it is often too late to do anything. Your bowel is not well served with nerves and it is nerves that signal something is wrong by causing you pain.

And guess what?

My poor Dad got bowel cancer...

I think this was in some part caused by his obsession with a sterile bowel and taking a powerful laxative day in and day out, year in and year out.

Doing this actually wrecked his bowel.

Did you realise that laxatives are one of the biggest selling products in any pharmacy after aspirin products? I bet they sell tonnes and tonnes of the stuff every week…

But laxatives may give temporary relief but in the long run they make your problem worse. Your bowel becomes lazy and goes on strike. It doesn't even work to rule. It doesn't work at all. Laxatives demand more laxatives… So instead of solving a bowel problem they disguise it… and under the disguise the problem gets worse!

IF YOU WANT TO BE FULL OF RADIANT GOOD HEALTH YOU MUST LOOK AT YOUR BOWEL… NO MATTER HOW DISTASTEFUL THAT MAY BE TO YOU!

Your bowel is an important part of your immune system.

So a defective bowel lowers your ability to protect yourself against disease. But we don't like to talk about it… even though an unhealthy bowel can be the biggest cause of disease in the world today.

It is a fact that your bowel could be sentencing you to a slow death!

I know you don't want to talk about it… but I'm your friend, and I want you to enjoy life. I don't want you to have Diverticulitis, Irritable Bowel, Bowel Cancer, Constipation, terrible-stinking stools, gas…

So we are going to have to talk about it!

And that's not all we have to talk about… we have to talk about your liver, your stomach, your digestion and all those systems that are quietly doing you in!

You are not a machine. The medical approach that takes the view you are like a machine has caused a lot of misery in the world. Your body organs and systems do not work independently of each other. You are a total person. Everything in your body works together for you or against you.

And for too many people their own body works against them.

How about this for a thought... 6 out of every 10 people die from what is called 'nutritionally induced disease'.

What this means is that 6 out of 10 people die before they should.

Here is a story for you...

This guy dies and goes to heaven. Well, not exactly to heaven, to the Pearly Gates. There he meets Saint Peter.

Saint Peter says to our friend 'And what is your name?'

To which he replies 'Arthur P. Johniston of Dallas Texas and elsewhere'.

So Saint Peter flips through his great golden book... looking for Arthur's name. Finally he finds it and looks at Arthur in surprise.

'Why Arthur,' he says 'we didn't expect you for at least another twenty years!'

To which Arthur replies... 'I know, but I ate it my way'.

Of course it is not a true story. I made it up. But it makes a very important point. Far too many of us dig out graves with our teeth!

Not only do we have a lousy diet, we also have poorly working stomachs, livers, pancreas and bowels.

Gosh, is it any wonder there are so many sick people around.

WHAT IS YOUR IDEA OF HEALTH?

I was talking to this lovely lady who told me she was in perfect health... except for the blood pressure drugs, the cholesterol drugs, the heart tablets and her arthritis pills.

And she honestly believed she was healthy.

Do you think she is alone in this belief? Not on your life! There are hundreds of thousands of people out there who think they are healthy. Never mind that they are on so many drugs it is like a second meal... They are functioning so they must be healthy.

But they are not healthy at all... no way!

However, we prefer not to talk about it. We like to pretend that all is well... Even if it isn't!

Because that is human nature. We all have a bit of the ostrich in us. We like to bury our heads in the sand. We are like little children who cover up their eyes in the belief that if they can't see you, you can't see them!

But we can see them and pretending that we are not there does not make us go away... And pretending we are well when we are not does not make us well either.

It makes the problem slowly worse...

And it can KILL us... and does!

Have you seen these girls on the television who are unlucky enough to have Anorexia? They look like walking skeletons but they insist they look like elephants. No matter how much you argue they cannot see themselves as they really are. They honestly believe they are overweight.

Everyone else can see these girls have a severe problem. But they insist their only problem is being overweight.

Well, there are a lot of people around like that.

No, they are not anorexic. But they do have a problem and get angry if anyone suggest they do have one. Alcoholics are a case in point. I know alcoholics who insist they are 'social drinkers'. However, these so-called social drinkers can't get through the day without alcohol. And if you can't get through the day without alcohol you are an alcoholic. Denying the truth does not make it any less truthful.

But here lies the problem...

Until the alcoholics admits there is a problem no-one can help them. It is everyone's fault but their own. Their marriages crash. Their kids don't want to have anything to do with them. And it is not their fault…

But it is their fault.

And in the same way, so many of us will not admit that our lifestyle is the cause of all our health problems.

Let me explain it this way…

This old bloke came to see me with chronic arthritis. He had bright blue eyes, almost white. One look into those eyes and I knew he was a great salt eater. And there was no doubt salt was a major factor in his arthritis.

Our conversation went something like this…

'Do you eat a lot of salt?'

'No, not really. Just on my tomatoes, my eggs and so on.'

'Mmmm… salt is not your friend and could have a lot to do with your arthritis.'

'Nonsense. I don't eat enough for it to be a problem.'

'Well, be that as it may, you will have to cut salt out of your diet.'

'What!! Cut salt out of my diet? Are you joking? I couldn't taste an egg without salt, I couldn't enjoy a tomato without salt. And what about my chips and dinner? Are you telling me I can't sprinkle salt on my dinner? Ridiculous. Salt has nothing to do with my arthritis. It must be some kind of germ or perhaps just because I am getting older.'

'Ah, well, then would you do me a favour?'

'What is it?'

'When you get home, find an adhesive label, draw a skull and crossbones on it. Write in black letters the word "Poison"… and stick it on your salt shaker.'

'What on earth are you talking about?'

'Well at least you will know what is causing your problems. You won't be able to blame your wife, the Government, the economy, your doctor or anyone else. You will see that you are doing it to yourself! You will see that you are responsible for your arthritis.'

He never took my advice, of course. He thought I was being sarcastic and never came back. I saw him limping down the street and someone told me he was having his knees replaced. Next year it will be his hips that have to be replaced…

A high price to pay for not admitting he had a salt problem.

We humans are a funny lot. We simply will not admit that we could have some part in our own downfall.

Another example is weight loss…

Grossly overweight people come to see me for help. They are delighted when I tell them that obesity can be a muscular problem. They are not so pleased when I tell them that it is probably the muscles of the jaw working overtime.

I tell them to do a great exercise called 'push aways'.

They have heard of push-ups but what are push aways?

You push yourself away from the table before you have eaten everything in sight…

I smile when they tell me the problem is the refrigerator.

'I cannot resist going in there and snacking on chocolate biscuits, ice-cream and such like stuff…'

I look at them and say 'Look, I have a really mind-bending idea for you. Something you have probably never thought of. And this will fix your fridge problem…'

This gets their attention so I continue…

'Who puts all that stuff in the fridge in the first place? I mean, is it God or do YOU put it in there?'

'Well, I suppose I do.'

'Well here's an idea for you to play around with. Why not stop putting it in!'

And I can see them wrestling with this idea. They are resisting it with all their might. The thought of going a whole day without a fridge to raid is appalling… and so we rationalise. We say something like we have to have these 'goodies' in the fridge, 'In case someone comes round for coffee or visits'.

Never mind that no-one has been around for two hundred years for a cup of coffee or a visit.

THERE'S NO PAIN... SO IT MUST BE ALRIGHT!

The other interesting thing about we humans is that if there is no pain we assume everything must be working just fine.

Never mind that the bowel only opens once a week. The doctor says that is fine. The person is certainly 'regular'... but hardly regular enough. But unless there is some discomfort we do not think there can be anything wrong.

How wrong can you be?

Simple arithmetic gives food for thought. If you eat six kilos of food a day for five days, that is 30 kilos of food, right? And if you only evacuate your bowel every two days... how much do you pass out?

Certainly not 12 kilos or more... So where is the rest of it? You are not going to like this... but it is sitting there rotting away!

Not digesting... oh, no, it is rotting away. Slowly decomposing like a dead body.

You are walking around with this horrible stuff in your bowel.

No wonder your stool smells like a gas attack.

Think of all those nasty bacteria breeding like crazy in this rotting mass of partly digested food.

And we pile more food on top of that... Not a pretty thought but it is the truth!

But worse is to come!

This rotting food poisons us.

It gives us headaches. It makes us nauseous. It robs us of energy. It lowers our immune system. It makes us constipated. It puts a coat on our tongue. It gives us bad breath. It gives us a poisonous body odour. It makes us feel off colour. It destroys our enthusiasm for life. It ages our body and leaves us open to degenerative diseases…

All because we are not digesting our food. All because we insist on eating processed 'dead' foods from packets or fast food outlets.

But mainly because we do not realise what is causing our misery.

We do not feel any pain… so what's the fuss all about?

Here's why you do not know you have bowel cancer… until it is too late!

My Dad got bowel cancer.

His was because of his obsession with laxatives. His food didn't get properly treated in his bowel because he pushed it through before it could be digested. He damaged the bowel wall with his constant daily purging.

Other people get bowel cancer because food, mainly meat, sits there and decomposes. It also damages the bowel wall.

And that is how bowel cancer starts off…

But did you know that the bowel is poorly served with nerves?

And it is nerves that tell you something is wrong by sending a pain message to the brain. But the bowel doesn't send any message about pain until it is really in huge trouble.

And all too often, it is then too late. The cancer has spread to the liver or to some other organ… They operate on the bowel… but this does no good. It has already set up house somewhere else in your body.

Where you feel the pain may not be the source of the pain!

This is hard for a lot of us to grasp.

Where you feel the pain may not be where the pain is coming from.

When you have toothache it is obvious where the pain is coming from. It is from that rotten tooth!

But my Dad had no bowel pain.

He had a bad back. They gave him deep heat to relieve the pain... They gave him anti-inflammatory drugs...

And they didn't work...

Because the source of his pain was the cancer eating away at his bowel!

Women come to me with backache, with headaches, with pains down their legs. They have taken aspirin but nothing relieves these pains. But the source of the pain is not in the back. It is not in the head. It is not in the legs... So treating these areas is really a waste of time.

The source of the problem lies in the uterus!

So unless you discover this, the pains will continue and will get worse. This is because no-one is paying attention to the real cause of the problems. The uterus!

So it is with your bowel.

You can have headaches. You can think you have chronic fatigue. You can have what seem to be heart problems. You can feel lousy most of the time... You feel depressed and lack motivation. You are bad tempered, irritable. Nothing pleases you.

You go to your doctor and he gives you headache pills. Or a tonic. Or anti-depression pills... And they don't work. I know people who have been on drugs for different complaints for years and years.

But look at it this way. If someone is on a drug, let's say it is for high cholesterol, for twenty years and they if they stop taking it their cholesterol hits the ceiling... Then that drug is not working for them.

It is not fixing the underlying problem.

Sure, it hides the cause and relieves the symptoms... but the problem is silently getting worse because nothing is being done about it!

And this is particularly true when we are talking about your bowel and digestive organs.

No pain, no problem is a deadly trap!

Here is the true secret of dynamic radiant health!

Very few people feel really well. Very few people know the joy of radiant health. Far too many people go to bed tired and wake up tired. Too many people drag themselves through the day. Too many people feel irritable. Every little thing annoys them. Too many people have unhappy relationships with their partners, children, work mates because they don't feel well. They are difficult to get along with… But if you ask them they will tell you it is other people who are difficult and cause them problems.

But your outer world is only a reflection of your inner world…

Bad news for some, good news for others.

Bad news if you believe you have no control over it… good news if you realise you can change your inner world.

And you certainly can change your inner world and by doing so, change your outer world.

Someone once told me how just one word has changed his whole life.

Yes, one word and it made his life wonderful from being miserable. This one word made him likeable, whereas before people reacted to him badly. This one word made him welcome where before he had been unwelcome.

I bet you would love to know this word… So I will tell you the story he told me.

This is what he said… 'When people used to tell me about themselves, and let's face it, our self is our most engrossing topic, I used to listen… and then I would say something like "Rubbish", "Nonsense", "Tripe"!

But then I learned my lesson. Now I simply say "Wonderful".

And that changed my whole life. I listen. I say "Wonderful". And they love me… that one word changed my whole life.'

And that is true. One word can change the way people see you.

And the same is true of the vital square in your body.

Change this square and your life can become radiant. You can become the life and soul of Life's party.

This square is the area below your ribs down to your pubic bone. This is the area below the big muscle called your diaphragm. It is the diaphragm that separates the lungs and heart from the organs below the diaphragm.

It is the square that houses your liver, your spleen, your pancreas, your stomach, your small intestine and your large intestine.

If the organs in this vital square are in good condition… so is your life… You will be always optimistic. You will be cheerful. You will find coping easy. You will be hard to stress… people will find you nice to be around.

You will not be plagued with an Irritable Bowel, you will not suffer from Diverticulitis, you will not suffer from heartburn or acid reflux, you will not have painful ulcers, you will not have a liver that makes you feel like death warmed up.

You will know, perhaps for the first time in your life, the wonderful feeling, the sense of joy, the feeling of boundless energy… that is total good health.

And total good health is rare in today's world…

But it is a gift I want to share with you.

That is the whole purpose of this book…

To open the door, to guide you, to encourage you, to reveal secrets to you… all to get you into that glorious feeling of wonderful, vibrant, radiant health.

I want you to die young… at a hundred.

I want you to be disease-free.

I want you to love life so that life loves YOU.

And if you read this book carefully… read it at least five times, write down the suggestions I give and make a plan for yourself, you will be amazed at the transformation.

You will feel you can do ANYTHING.

You will be like Superman… jumping mighty rivers, leaping over skyscrapers in one bound… unbeatable.

You will become irresistible.

Boy! what promises…

When this vital square is looked after you will feel better than you have ever felt in your whole life… trust me on this.

I guarantee it!

Few people realise the importance of this vital square… so let me tell you a bit more.

I don't want to thrash your mind with the big stick about bowel problems… Because it is not just your bowel that dictates your health…

It is your liver, your stomach, your pancreas, your small intestine and your large intestine. It is what you eat. It is how you think… your thoughts… your lifestyle.

Wait a minute! This sounds very complicated.

But it is not. It is simple.

You will discover how really simple it is to have boundless energy, be free of disease and have a wonderful life… by going forward with me in this book.

You know, I was once in a local shop and waiting for the girl to take my money. I stood there, staring into the middle distance… unaware that I was singing to myself. Let me tell you, my singing is a bit like a crow on a barbed wire fence.

The girl looked at me and said accusingly… 'You're happy, aren't you?'

I had to admit that I was indeed happy.

'Why are you so happy then?'

I told her that I was healthy, that is why I was happy. Healthy people tend to be happy people.

Her reply was interesting… 'I don't get the connection.'

And looking at her podgy figure, her pasty face, her spotty complexion, I could see why she couldn't get the connection between good health and good humour. She wasn't healthy. She had never been healthy. She had never known the glorious feeling of being vital and alive! No wonder she couldn't see the connection between health and happiness...

But she is not alone.

Try this little experiment some day...

Stand in a queue at the elevator in a department store... or in a hotel or other building... and start to sing to yourself. Loud enough for those near you to hear...

And watch what happens.

People will stare at you in amazement. They will move away from you... it will not occur to these people that you are happy.

They will think you are drunk. Or that you are on drugs. Or that you have just escaped from some asylum for the insane.

Because as a society we do not relate well to positive emotions like love and happiness. We will pass people arguing without a second glance... but if a young couple is embracing and kissing in the street we look at them with horror.

Funny isn't it?

But perhaps if we were one hundred percent fit inside, we would be full of positive emotions and would see happiness as normal behaviour... which it is!

It is my ambition to make you as healthy as it is possible for you to be.

I passionately want people to be free of disease. I want you to have a good life, full of happiness and joy. But it is difficult to be joyful if you are being attacked by billions of health-sucking parasites. It is difficult to be cheery if your liver is doing a number on you. It is difficult to be full of vibrant energy if you are not getting the best from your diet. A good diet is of little use with poor digestion! It is difficult to taste the joy of being alive every single day if your bowel is sludged up and you have a bad balance of bacteria down there.

And that is what this book is all about...

To let you in on the secrets which few people know about their own bodies... to reveal to you simple ways to get really healthy like never before. I want you to laugh at illness, to scoff at disease and to ridicule parasite attacks on you.

I take your trust in me very seriously.

You have trusted me enough to invest in this book and I want, more than anything, for it to be valuable to you. I intend for it to be worth far more than the money you invested in it... I want it to be the Magic Key to Eternal Youth and Vitality.

So let us go forward together, two friends on an exciting journey of discovery heading towards the goal of wonderful health... of ageless beauty... heading into an old age full of joy... without crippling diseases... just happiness.

Ready?

OK... Let's go!

2

Hey! No wonder you don't feel as well as you could!

Have you ever thought how great it would be if you felt like you were jumping out of your skin. Absolutely fabulous? Not just at the odd moment, but most of the time.

Boy, let me tell you how your life would change.

Fear would disappear out of your life. You would have a feeling of confidence. You would march forward overcoming any obstacle foolish enough to get in your way.

Your thinking would be clear and positive. You would be a lot more creative in your thinking. Ideas would flow more easily. You would be more willing to try new things, take more risks... make more gains!

Your relationships would flourish. This is because you would be more fun to be around. Healthy people are happy people. Their glass is always half full, not half empty.

You would not be going down with colds and flu. You would cope with stress without thinking about it. Life would be fun. Life would be exciting.

So how come it isn't?

THE TALE OF THE STUFFED UP MANSION...

Gather round, put a log on the fire, set the lamp and I will tell you a story...

Once upon a time there was this large mansion. Not your ordinary millionaire's mansion, but a mansion turned into a sort of processing factory.

From the outside the building was impressive. Impressive is the only word to describe such a magnificent residence. A beautiful structure. A joy to behold. Obviously created by a Master Buildcr.

One thing you noticed though as you got a bit closer was there didn't seem to be any lights on. As you grew nearer you realised that was because the windows were all broken and dirty. You also noticed that the stonework needed some repairs. You were sad to see the gutters were falling down and the drains weren't working, judging by the smell that hung over the place.

Anyone looking at this magnificent mansion would wonder why the owner would allow it to fall into such disrepair. It seemed such a pity that a building so magnificently designed and constructed by a Master Builder and Architect could be allowed to fall apart...

But you know from experience that people are 'funny' and seldom seem to appreciate how good they have things. People don't seem to appreciate their good fortune until they lose it.

Same with this mansion, as you cast your eye over it you do some mental sums and work out it would cost a fortune to restore it to its original glory. Probably cost more money than the owner could now afford. But the really sad thing was that the mansion was slowly falling apart. It was crumbling away and no-one seemed to notice. If they did notice they certainly weren't doing anything about it.

You realise that if the owner had taken care of the building... If he had done some repair work along the way, kept the gutters and drains clean, repaired and cleaned the windows... If he had taken just a few steps to preserve the building it would have cost very little and this magnificent building would be in excellent condition.

YOU DISCOVER THE SECRET OF WHY THE MANSION IS FALLING APART...

Undaunted, our hero, You, approach the house and get to the front door. At one time this was obviously painted a glistening white, but is now a dingy yellow with some panels missing.

The front door opens into a fairly large room with what appear to be cutting machines. There is quite a bit of activity going on, which you find a bit surprising considering the state of the mansion.

And there are people carrying all sorts of stuff into this room and feeding it to the cutting machines. A conveyor belt carries the stuff from the cutting machines down a long corridor to another room.

As you gaze down this corridor, the door to the other room is open, you see more passages further down and dimly, in the distance, you notice there is a back door barely visible.

You suddenly notice there are trucks parked in the courtyard of the mansion and people are busy unloading them. They truck this great assortment of goods into the front room and tip them into the cutters. But like the rest of the house, you notice that these cutters are not very efficient. A lot of the stuff gets onto the conveyor belt and it has not been crushed properly... but still, the conveyor belt carries it along the tunnel.

Down it goes into the room further down. You can hear the

noise of machinery down there and it appears that more processing is going on. The goods are being crushed, mashed, battered and reduced to pulp by machinery you can't see, but can hear.

To your surprise, you notice that the passageways beyond the second room are stacked to the ceiling with partly processed stuff. You can't imagine what kind of people would be running this show. Everything is so inefficient. Stuff piling up everywhere. And still more stuff is being brought in, sent down the conveyor belt and piled on top of the great heaps already clogging up the passages.

It seems like lunacy. Here you have corridors jammed up with partially processed stuff and no-one is doing anything to fix the machinery. No-one is reducing the constant in-pouring of goods through the front door…

And now you notice something else!

This is really 'Oh, Yuk' country. You can hear rats and mice scampering about in these piles of partly processed goods. You can see the piles are crawling with cockroaches. There are beetles, slimy worms, fungus, and noxious growths on the stuff piled up there. It looks like some nightmare scene from a horror movie.

Oh heavens, now you notice something else that you hadn't seen before. There were sounds that the rats, the mice, the cockroaches, the beetles, the worms and various fungi had migrated from these downstair corridors into the rest of the mansion.

Now it was rotting away from the inside too.

'What a tragedy' you think to yourself. 'This wonderful mansion, clearly designed by a Master Architect, built by a Master Builder, allowed to rot away. To be allowed to decay, to fall apart. A mansion that should have been a monument for hundreds of years will be a broken shell long before its time.'

What a terrible waste. And all because someone allowed these things to happen.

Someone just didn't find out how to repair the gutters, to fix the drains, to clear the passageways, to stop piling goods in on top of other piles… To keep the passageways free so mice, rats, cockroaches, beetles, worms and so on could not make their homes there.

But there is a happy ending.

You found the owner asleep in the back garden in a hammock between two stunted apple trees. His hammock was surrounded by empty beer cans… and he was snoring disgracefully.

You were so furious at the way this guy had neglected this beautiful home you tipped him out of his hammock… Shocked, he listened while you gave him what for. You really gave it to him… And as this is just a fairy story, he listened, he learned and he decided to do better.

So he fixed the front door, it is now glistening white again. He had the gutters repaired and the drains fixed. The crumbling stonework was rebuilt. The broken windows replaced and cleaned. The lights now shone brilliantly.

Awakened to what he had been doing to this handsome house, he stopped the indiscriminate inflow of goods. He became very selective about what he permitted to be brought in.

He repaired the cutting machines and made sure they chopped up the goods to a fine powder. This took a real load off the conveyor belts and his energy bill dropped dramatically. He cleared all the passageways of the piles of rotting rubbish. This helped to get rid of the rats, the mice, the cockroaches, the worms and other horrible nasties that had taken over his home.

Now everything flowed like a dream.

The dismal smell that had hung over the place went away.

And guess what? With this mansion gleaming like a beacon it attracted a passing princess… and this bloke married her and they lived happily ever after… I told you this was a fairy story!

Wasn't that a nice story?

But the brutal fact is you see this story enacted before your eyes thousands of times a day… in fact, it is likely YOU are one of the owners of one of these magnificent homes allowed slowly to fall apart.

Of course, as you have probably realised, the mansion is your body. The front door is your teeth and the opening room with the cutters is your mouth. The conveyor belt is your throat leading to the second room, your stomach.

The passageways are your intestines, both small and large.

And the rats and mice, the beetles, the worms are the bacteria, worms and fungi thriving in you bowels…

No wonder people are nothing like as well as they could be.

No wonder people are not as well as they should be.

And no wonder they don't attract princesses and princes along the way!

Keep reading and in a few minutes you will be an expert!

Let me tell you another story, a true one this time!

This lovely man came to see me and he told me he had a liver problem. To prove it he pointed to his left side and said that was where his problem was… in his liver.

Only one problem with this… your liver is on your RIGHT side and not your left!

I gently remarked that I believed his liver was on his right. I do this gently because people have been known to die to prove they were right, even when they were hopelessly wrong.

He glared at me indignantly and exclaimed 'It is there! I know it is there! Because that is where my doctor told me it was.'

And who was I to argue with his doctor?

But the fact is your liver sits under your right ribs… if you cup your hands, heel of palm to heel of palm and place your hands so that your fingers lie along the front and the back, you will get an idea of where your liver is. A bit hard to describe. But your hands are just under your ribs at the front and back of your body. One hand at the front and the other at the back. Quite a large organ…

But back to our friend with the migrated liver…

You may be very surprised to find out that people don't always hear what is said to them. I know you always hear what is said to you, but you must have had the experience when you explained things to someone and they obviously didn't hear. You can tell that from what they did after you spoke with them!

So it could well be that this man misheard his doctor.

The other thing is this. As a practitioner I get into the habit of pointing with my left hand to the patient's right side to indicate where their liver is… And I have been known to carelessly use that same left hand to indicate where my liver is when talking to someone else. I usually realise my error and quickly change sides…

So it could have been the same with this guy's doctor.

If his doctor really believed the liver is on the left, which I am sure he didn't, I would advise changing doctors!

But the point of this story is that few people know much about their own bodies!

People often come to me complaining of the stomach ache. They have a pained expression on their face. They are in agony. Their stomach is giving them hell, they tell me.

But they are not clutching their stomach, they are clutching their bowel. So either their stomach is badly prolapsed, it has dropped down from where it is supposed to be into their bowel… or, dare I say it? They don't know where their stomach is!

I sometimes wonder if kids are taught biology anymore at school.

Most people don't really care anyway. And why should they? The only time they care is when trouble comes… and it does!

Most people have little idea of what goes on inside their body. You chomp your steak and ketchup, you wolf down your ice-cream and biscuits, you pour hot coffee down your throat… and forget about it!

Down it goes into the hidden depths never to be seen again… and for a lot of people with constipation, that is true too. It is never seen again, well, not much of it!

We tend to eat what we have always eaten. I am Scottish and I like simple food. I was brought up on simple foods. My mother made everything. Good wholesome broth. She made her own cakes and scones. She made her own lemon curd. We could not afford fancy food when I was young. We never had bread, butter and jam. We had bread and jam. Putting butter on the bread as well as jam was seen as a terrible waste. In fact, when I went to a friend's house and they gave me bread and jam, with butter… I didn't like the feel of the butter in my mouth.

But when a man gets married he then finds he is eating the meals his wife was brought up on. In my case, away went the broth, the oatcakes and so on… I have had to insist over the years that I really prefer broth and soup to some carefully prepared dish I see as fancy. My dear wife is quite adventurous in her eating. She will try new dishes when we go to a restaurant… whereas I am very timid that way. I used to ask my wife I would like some fancy dish on the menu…

Because she was brought up on a different sort of diet from the one I was brought up on.

My dear friend, Frank Caruso, is Italian. Well, he is actually born here but his Mum and Dad are from Southern Italy. So when we go out guess which restaurants he loves to go to? Italian, of course! To get him into a 'regular' restaurant takes a lot of friendly persuasion on my part. You see, he inherited his tastes in food just as I did… his taste is Italian… mine is Scottish!

But neither of us ever sat down and thought this all out.

And it is probable that you haven't either!

Hey, have you noticed something? I don't want to be unkind,

because that is not my nature… but have you noticed that fat people have fat children? And have you noticed something else? They even have fat dogs!

That is because they all eat the same kind of foods and pity the poor dog because they feed him the same foods too!

And here is another thought for you to hold on to…

We continue to eat the same kind of foods as we grow older… even though our digestive system is no longer anywhere near as efficient as it once was!

And we are surprised we get gas. We are surprised we have stomach upsets. We are surprised we don't have the same energy we once had…

But it never occurs to us that it could be what we are shoving in our mouths that is causing us most of our problems.

Doesn't seem fair does it?

I remember when I was quite small running to my Dad and crying 'It's not fair! It's not fair!'

Dad just looked at me and said 'I'm glad you've found that out. Get it into your head once and for all, Life is NOT fair! Now run away with you and don't bother me with this nonsense about Life not being fair!'

And he was dead right.

Life is not fair. But let me tell you, Life is just.

Mother Nature thought of 'play now, pay later' long before anybody else did. We pay for our indulgences. The problem is when we get the bill we don't realise what it is for. When we overeat, cram lifeless food into our bodies, we do not fall over. We keep on functioning… and we do not realise we are creating a debt.

But the debt keeps piling up and one day we are called upon to pay it.

Oh, not in money, you understand. But in health!

We get high blood pressure. We get heart problems. We get memory problems. We get arthritis. We get digestive problems…

ulcers, Diverticulitis, Irritable Bowel, acid reflux and heaven knows what else. We limp where we once ran. We become stiff where we were once supple.

We are being asked to meet the account that Nature has stored up and is now presenting us.

Doesn't seem fair… but it is.

When you go through life you remember certain mind-shattering occasions. I remember the intense disappointment I suffered when I was young when someone unkindly told me sex produced babies. I thought sex was too good to be true. I thought it was all for fun… It never occurred to me that this was the way people got babies. I thought babies were brought by storks or found abandoned in cabbage patches or gooseberry bushes.

I thought sex was just for fun…

Same with politicians…

When I was a young man I had the quaint notion that people in high places were the kind of people we should look up to. I saw them as people of exemplary natures. People who were role models for the rest of us… I thought they were all honest, hard working, God fearing.

So it was a bit of a shock when I read the autobiography of one of Britain's pre-Second World War ambassadors… and it really shook me when he revealed how they tell the public outright lies… and all the shenanigans they get up to.

I tell you this because you may be in for the same kind of shock when I tell you the diet you have grown to love is actually doing you in!

Despite my claim we inherit our diets there have been considerable changes over the past couple of hundred years. At one time the peasants were healthy and the rich were decadent… The poor had the monopoly on poverty but they tended to be healthier than the rich who had the monopoly on money… they tended to have the most disease.

In those days only the rich could afford white flour and sugar.

The poor had to get by on flour that still had all the goodness in it. The wheat germ was still in the flour. The husks were still in the flour. Sure, the bread tended to be black and coarse but it was packed with nutrition. None of this rubbish about adding a couple of vitamins and a bit of iron... after robbing it of everything else! They got the lot!

In those days, when a farm labourer had a pint of beer and a cheese sandwich he got a lot of good nutrition. The bread was from flour his wife had ground herself... from wheat grown in good, rich soil. No pesticides, fertilisers, herbicides... they used cow manure. They let one field lie fallow every year. They rested the soil. They cared for the soil. So the wheat was rich in goodness.

Not for them... quantity at the expense of quality. That came later with 'progress'.

The cheese was from their own cow... a cow that grazed contentedly on grass full of nutrients from the rich black soil. She wasn't fed on processed pellets or reinforced cow feed (with a good whack of female hormones or stuff like that). No, just good old-fashioned grass!

Her milk was not boiled, skimmed or treated so it would last for months without going sour. It was fresh, rich and straight from the cow.

And his beer... This was made from hops, barley and pure water from unpolluted streams (not rich in chemicals and froth-making stuff). The head of the brewery was a Brew Master not a Chemist.

Contrast that with today. If you have bread, cheese and a glass of beer for your lunch you will probably suffer from malnutrition.

The bread will be white, devoid of nutrition. In fact, your body will have to drag vitamins from somewhere else in your body to digest the stuff. The cheese will be pre-packed in thin slices. Looks and tastes like rubber… and about the same nutritional value. And the beer! Well, this is a long haul away from the beer your great granddaddy drank, I can assure you.

Can you guess what is the fastest growing disease in the so-called civilised world today? No, it is not heart disease and it is not cancer… It is diabetes.

And diabetes my friend is the number one cause of blindness in our society. It is responsible for more limbs being amputated than you can possibly imagine…

And why is it growing so fast?

Because in the olden days we ate about a pound of sugar a year…

And today we eat over a hundred pounds of sugar a year.

Sugar has been described as pure, white and deadly… with good reason.

SUGAR BRINGS NOTHING TO THE TABLE
EXCEPT TASTE

It does not give you long lasting energy, no matter what the advertisements say. When you eat sugar there is an insulin response and the sugar goes down… But you use up a lot of internal energy to process it. So you find that people who eat a lot of sweet things often have a low level of energy, not a high one.

You also find that these people go to bed tired and wake up tired. They can be moody, their moods swing up and down all day. They can be irritable. If they don't eat they feel spaced out. They also tend to be tired in the afternoon. They fall asleep easily through the day.

This is because they now process the sugar very quickly. The sugar level in their blood drops dramatically and with it their mood and temper. Here is their daily pattern, does it fit anyone you know?

They wake up tired but they buck up when they have their first cup of coffee and perhaps a cigarette. Then down they go until the next cup of coffee. These people think they have to drink coffee all day just to get through the day. They flop into bed bone tired and often can't get to sleep. When they wake up they are still tired and can't get out of bed.

What is happening is their blood sugar level is going up and down like a yo-yo.

In the olden days, doctors would tell these people to go out and eat a candy bar. Got to be the worst advice in the world! The last thing these folk need is more sugar.

The condition is called 'Hypoglycemia' which simply means low (hypo) blood sugar (glycemia means sugar). So you have hypo… glycemia. Low blood sugar.

It doesn't mean your blood sugar is continuously low. It means that when you eat sugar your blood sugar levels goes up and then drops far too quickly…

And guess what is the next stage after hypoglycemia?

You hit it in one… diabetes.

ATTENTION DEFICIT DISORDER… AN
INTERNATIONAL PROBLEM

There are now hundreds of thousands of children around the world who suffer from what we call ADD or Attention Deficit Disorder. These kids are usually bright kids but who cannot keep focused on one thing for more than a few seconds.

Their behaviour patterns are similar. They are usually the 'class clowns'. Full of disruptive actions. They will trip up another child and then deny doing it. They will deny it even if they know you saw them doing it. They can, and do, drive their family to distraction.

You will often find these kids also suffer from dyslexia. When they try to read anything, the letters can be reversed or jumbled. Naturally, this makes for big problems for the child. They cannot read what is written on the blackboard and so fall behind. At one time these children were classified as stupid. Only recently it has been recognised they have a physical problem.

What should alarm all parents is that there are still plenty of people in the school system who have no idea about ADD and even if they have heard of it they have no idea of what to do about it.

NOTE THIS POINT… IT IS IMPORTANT!

Testing has shown that most of these children are Hypoglycemic. They have a sugar problem… And sugar makes these kids hyperactive and also affects their capacity to think. By the way, white sugar affects YOUR capacity to think too.

No wonder we have so many people who have memory problems… look at what we eat!

Getting back to our kids who cannot concentrate and who have behaviour problems. Hey, have you ever sat down and looked at what kids really eat these days?

We hear all this stuff about balanced diets and stuff like that. A lot of rubbish, in my opinion. Certainly it is true that a balanced diet would be a good thing.

Only a couple of problems here though. One man's meat is another man's poison… so what is a balanced diet for one person is not for another. I will go into this in more detail a little later… And the other problem is that only dieticians recognise a balanced meal when they see one. Most people wouldn't recognise a balanced meal if they fell over it. That is not meant to be unkind. It is simply the way things are with us!

What so many kids eat could not be called 'balanced' in a fit.

Come on, get real folks… Not unless you call a hamburger in one hand and a bottle of coke in the other, balanced!

How about corn flakes for breakfast… covered in sugar! Milk on them… and more people than you realise are allergic to milk. Never mind the clever advertising, milk is NOT good for you.

How many kids drink pure water with their breakfast? Not many! They are more likely to want orange juice or cordial. Did you know they can call orange juice unsweetened and still put in up to five percent sugar? It's like jam. You can't call any preserve 'jam' unless it has 25% sugar in it. That is why you see these naturally sweetened jams called 'spreads' rather than straight out jam…

As my Dad said, 'Life ain't fair!'

If you looked at the amount of white sugar the average child gets through and looked at this from a body weight point of view… they are getting through the equivalent of tonnes of the stuff.

Any wonder we have problem kids…

Have you ever thought of this… now hold on to this one… what we are seeing today are the junk food kids from junk food mothers. And boy, are we paying a price!

And as these new Mums are hooked on sugar and snacks, guess what they give their own children? I have seen babies in their prams with a bottle full of coke… and even coffee. Heavens above! No wonder we have problem children.

And what is the favourite drink of so many kids? Cordial!

Have you ever looked at the ingredients in cordial? First on the list is water… I wonder if this is purified or out of the tap with all the chlorine and other goodies we get in our water. Next comes sugar… heaps of it. Next comes artificial flavouring. Note that it is artificial and not natural and then comes colouring.

This is not a formula for radiant health… it is destructive. It does not build healthy tissue. This stuff breaks down healthy tissue. Give your child a break and wean them off cordial.

It is not surprising that so many kids are Hypoglycemic… And remember what I told you about Hypoglycemics? Mood swings, irritability, getting spaced out, loss of motivation, going to bed tired, getting up tired… difficult to live with. Do you know anyone like this?

If you do, then have a look at what they are putting in their mouths!

YOU WOULDN'T DO THIS TO YOUR DRAINS, NEVER MIND YOUR BODY!

Can you imagine someone pouring stuff down the drain knowing it will block it up? Can you think of anyone who would set out to clog up the drains to and from their home?

No, of course not. No-one would be that stupid, would they?

But we do it all the time to our own drains… our elimination organs.

And what is the most common way we do this?

You won't love me for saying this… it is white flour.

When I was younger we used to make wallpaper paste out of white flour and water. Before there were packets of ready-mixed 'slip' glues for wallpaper, people made their own. And it was from white flour and water.

This stuff is potent glue. You had to be quick and accurate when putting the wallpaper on the wall. There was no room for error with this stuff. It stuck the wallpaper on the wall on contact. Slap, bang and it had to be dead on. None of this ability we have with modern glues to take it off and have a second attempt.

And I tell you what else… Getting the wallpaper OFF the wall the next time it was time to re-paper it was hell. This stuff really sticks. You had to soak the old wallpaper and use a lot of muscle to scrape the old paper off.

Yes sir! White flour and water makes a really powerful GLUE!

And we eat this stuff every single day of our lives.

Is it any wonder we have so many people with bowel problems? What do you think? I mean, how can you operate if your bowel is glued up? All that sticky stuff clinging to your bowel wall… Wholemeal flour doesn't act that way in your body. Only white flour.

Doesn't this suggest something important to you?

Yeah! Stop eating white flour (never mind Auntie Martha who is mumbling with a mouthful of white toast and jam that I don't know what I am talking about).

When I was a kid they used to deliver bread right to your front door. Imagine that, delivering bread. They also used to deliver milk, actually knock on your door and would even ladle it out into your container. The mail was delivered twice a day and once on Saturdays.

In those days, people at home alone had lots of visitors… the breadman, the milkman, the butcher boy, the postman... and they all had time for a chat. Now we have progressed, if that is the right word, to the stage when you can be at home for weeks and never see anybody! And they call this progress. May I remark that I consider the word 'progress' to mean movement. And as you know, you can have movement backwards as well as forward. Too much of what we term progress is a big leap backward, if you ask me.

But as kids I reckon we knew a thing or two people have forgotten today.

Let me tell you what we did as the horror gang of urchins in the 1930s.

A firm called Dobson's used to deliver bread. This was in the days when working class people didn't own motor cars, despite Henry Ford's efforts to bring cars to the working man. We still had men with a horse and cart doing deliveries. Hard to believe, but nonetheless true. This firm delivered their bread in a chocolate-coloured closed-in van, with Dobson's Bread in gold leaf along the side and back. The horse was well turned out with a driver/delivery man up front.

In those days they didn't have the knowledge about bread so all the bread was white in a variety of loaf shapes. Anyway, we kids used to walk behind the cart and we had a special chant for Dobson's that went like this...

> *Dobson's Bread*
> *Shit like lead,*
> *Fart like thunder,*
> *No bloody wonder...*
> *Dobson's bread*

Can you imagine the scene? All these scruffy little ten-year-olds marching behind the bread cart chanting this doggerel at the top of their screechy voices? The driver used to have a long whip and he would flick it back in a futile attempt to make us shut up.

But the point is this... whether we knew it or not, we were telling people exactly what white bread would do to them...

Constipate them. Give them gas.

And your favourite additive is no better. Listen to this...

If you are having problem remembering people's names then cut down on white flour and sugar. I hate to tell you this, but this means biscuits and especially chocolate biscuits! They are not helping your case no matter how delicious they taste.

Alzheimer's Disease, Short Term Memory Loss... white sugar does not help. In fact, some scientists and memory experts believe that the enormous intake of white sugar these days contributes to the problems people are having with their memories.

So think about that one... it could be that if you keep whacking into the sugar you won't be able to remember what I have told you about the damage it could be doing to you!

Oh dear, for many of us Life without cakes and biscuits has no meaning.

Ah well, we can get used to living without them. I used to eat heaps but now I don't… And Life goes on very happily as I now have more energy and I can remember people's names very well. So there!

And if I can do it… so can you!

So what **REALLY** happens to what we eat?

I guess I have wandered off the point as usual. I was all about telling you what happens after you chomp your food and send it down the conveyor belt to your stomach.

What is supposed to happen is we start our digestion in the mouth by chewing our food. Remember how we were told to chew every mouthful 32 times. I think this was one chew for every tooth!

But in this modern, fast-paced, no-time for anything Life we all lead, chewing our food thoroughly has vanished for many people. I mean, who has time to chew every mouthful 32 times? Goodness sake, you'd be sitting there at the table, or in front of the TV set, all night! If you are old fashioned enough to eat your meals at a table, you would end up sitting there all by yourself chewing away.

And if you are a mouth breather, you would be taking in a lot of air with your dinner!

Hey! And if you have gas you would be adding to the supply… more air!

No matter, digestion does start in your mouth. This is true for meat as well as for bread. Carbohydrates, that is starch foods, start digesting in the mouth. In your saliva are enzymes that start to break down the starch to sugar.

Want to try a little experiment?

Take a dry biscuit and chew it… and chew it… and chew it.

Guess what? It will start to taste sweet. This is because the digestive enzymes in your mouth are breaking the starch in the biscuit down to sugar.

But for most people the digestion in the mouth is not done properly. This is because we are in such a hurry we tend not to chew our food for as long as we should.

Ah well, that's life I guess... (It could be the steps we are taking on the road to a premature death too, by the way. I just thought I would throw that in to make you think!)

The same applies to meat except here we are not predigesting it. What we are doing with meat is breaking it down into manageable portions. The digestive acid in your stomach works far more effectively on a lot of small pieces of protein than it does on large lumps. That makes a lot of sense, doesn't it?

Anyway, down we go into our long suffering stomachs.

Here's something I bet you never thought of... your digestive tract, as they call it, goes from your mouth right down to your anus. It is the one same tube all the way... with a few bulges for your stomach and loops for your intestines. It is IN your body just like a copper tube through a concrete block. In it but not part of it, if you get what I mean. And I am sure you do.

YOUR STOMACH IS PROBABLY TWICE THE SIZE IT OUGHT TO BE!

Pity your poor stomach... Can you possibly imagine what it must be like down there?

There is this constant, non-stop avalanche of food and other stuff pretending to be food pouring down. In some people it is almost non-stop. Flop, slop, crump, slither, splash, bump, down it all comes...

And your stomach is supposed to handle this lot in its stride. Well, quite often it doesn't!

Let's be fair. What if someone kept chucking things at you

non-stop and expected you to catch them? How well would you do? You might do alright at first when your wits were a bit on the sharp side. However, once you got tired your co-ordination would go off and you would drop some, miss some... and if they kept on coming and coming you would probably want to quit catching. Hey, man, enough is enough!

But your stomach is expected to go on performing no matter how much and how often we load stuff into it!

In fact, some people load so much in their stomachs that it is twice or even three times the size it ought to be. It has been known for people to have their stomach reduced in size. They do this by stapling it... 'Nurse, pass me the stapling gun... I'm gonna get this stitched up in no time flat!'

But guess what. Very often these operations fail.

Why? Because the person who has had the operation goes on shoving stuff in until the staples pop out... And their stomach flops back to its former outlandish size.

Not good!

It takes a lot of energy for your stomach to contend with the constant flow of stuff we send down. No wonder so many people fall asleep after lunch. All their energy has gone into their stomach. Left their brains, left their muscles... all cranking away down there in your stomach.

WORLD WIDE ENERGY CRISIS ALARMS EXPERTS

There is a world-wide energy crisis. But it is one you don't read about in your daily newspaper. It is the low energy level of most people these days.

You don't often meet someone who is vital, alive, brimming with unstoppable energy. How many people do you meet who impress you with their incredible energy?

Not many, I bet.

Most people we meet are limping through their day. They

rely on coffee and other stimulants to get them through. I was surprised to get a phone call from a coach for a junior football team to ask me if Guarana was harmful to kids.

In case you haven't heard of Guarana, it comes from South America. The Indians down there get it from a vine and chew the seeds. This gives them all-day energy for running through the rain forest looking for something else to chew on.

I was amazed to hear that some of these kids had eaten over twenty tablets to get energy to play football. There is something wrong here, folks!

This is part of a trend.

Too many kids think they need drugs to have the energy to enjoy a good night out. When I was a kid I could play football all afternoon and taking something to give me energy would never cross my mind. And why wouldn't it? Because I was loaded up with energy.

Same with the good night out. We used to dance for hours. Ballroom dancing at first and then good old Rock and Roll. We didn't need artificial stimulants. The band, the music, the atmosphere, the girls… who could ask for anything more?

So what is wrong with the kids of today?

They are using up too much energy trying to digest all the junk they send down to their stomachs disguised as food!

And I will say it again, even if you are sick to death of me saying it… sugar does NOT give you 'all day energy', it really saps your energy.

HANDS UP THOSE WHO KNOW WHAT IS GOING ON DOWN THERE…

I bet there are very few people who really know what is going on down there in the darkness of their stomachs. We eat it, we forget it. We are only reminded that there is any action when something causes us bother.

For all most people know there could be a team of elves down there shovelling the food out of the stomach somewhere else. Where that 'somewhere else' is we are not sure, but out of the stomach anyway… We take digestion for granted.

And we shouldn't.

Death starts in your digestive system. So does disease. So does misery and despair… but we don't realise it!

Have you ever noticed what goes on in restaurants? People finally get what they thought they were ordering. The plate is plonked down in front of them. Without even thinking about it they reach out and grab… no not the knife and fork… they reach out and they grab the salt and pepper shakers.

Yes, they do, I watch them do this all the time. I bet you are one of the people I have seen doing this. And they shake the salt shaker with a will they seldom show in any other area of their lives.

Without even tasting the food!

You can bet your boots that the chef lashed plenty of salt into the meal before it arrived in front of you… And there you are, adding even more poison to your food.

Now hang on, Ron, poison, that's a bit much.

But salt IS poison.

They force it down people's throats to make them vomit. Your body knows better than you do what is good and what isn't. If you put enough salt in your mouth in one hit your stomach will, very sensibly, reject it.

Eating salt is a bit like smoking and getting drunk. Our body tells us it doesn't like it… If you have smoked, can you remember what it was like when you puffed your first cigarette?

Your head swam, you felt sick, dizzy… but bless you, you persevered until you could inhale without those effects. This was because your body was doing its best to adjust to the insults you were piling in!

How many people with a hangover promise themselves they will never booze themselves over the top again? A hangover is simply your body complaining about the poison you have poured into it. And, sad to say, alcohol is poisonous. The amount it takes to poison us varies from person to person. But poison us, it does.

A doctor friend of mine, a very nice man, once told me after he had done his rounds at the local hospital, that at least 40% were there by their own doing. They were in there as a result of a poor lifestyle. Heart attacks, by-pass surgery, strokes, bowel problems from Irritable Bowel to cancer. And on and on…

He made the point that one day people will have to pay money to repair the damage they have done to themselves. His point was simple. Why should the 'Health Care' System have to pay? I put health care in inverted commas because I was being sarcastic. Disease Response System would be a better way of putting it. Very little encouragement is given to people to take care of their own health… And the system of medicine we have is sickness-response, not health-inspiring.

Gosh, I've done it again… wandered off. Well I told you this book is more like a conversation between two friends, you and me, than a textbook.

He went on to say the system will not be able to afford to cater for people who really could have avoided going to hospital. With a sensible lifestyle they wouldn't have had lung cancer and bowel cancer… they wouldn't need by-pass surgery and so on.

Makes you think… Think of the billions of dollars spent on fixing up people who have eaten, smoked and drank their way into a hospital bed!

Don't you be one of them… I know you won't, because you are reading this.

Let's get back to what should be happening in your stomach while I am chatting away with you.

When the food drops down into your stomach it signals 'Action Stations' to various cells on the stomach wall... Rush out the starch enzymes... Rush out the protein enzymes... Release the acid.

An enzyme, by the way, is something that makes everything else work like mad. A bit like your boss at work. He sits there and makes everyone work hard. (That's the theory, anyway, so don't blame me if that isn't how it is in real life!)

Enzymes speed the process up. If it weren't for enzymes everything would work so slowly we would all be dead waiting for it to happen!

So, as you can see, they are very important. Whole diseases are caused where enzymes don't work, or work too hard.

Enzymes speed up the process of breaking down starch to glucose. The acid breaks down the protein so it can be further broken down into its basic amino acids.

If it all tried to get into your bowel without being broken down... you would be in pain and in trouble... and sick!

Let's go to the next chapter to explore the tunnels, the sub-tissue labyrinth, we call our intestines.

Come on, it's not that bad. You will learn a lot and this will encourage you to live to be a hundred. Not a creaking, stooped, stiff, drugged up invalid...

But someone who enjoys being older... Someone who knows the secret of staying young all his or her life.

Think about that... sex at ninety... something for some of us to look forward to... especially if you are not getting much right now.

3

Don't bring your canary down here, please!

If you love birds you wouldn't want to bring your canary to where we are going.

You will recall that in the olden days they used to take canaries down the coal mines. If the poor old canary dropped off its perch and lay at the bottom of the cage with its toes turned up, you immediately knew two things. One was your canary was dead... and the other was, get the hell out of where you were as quickly as possible. The air was loaded with Methane gas!

Yeah, well here's another thought to get hold of. You have heard about the Greenhouse effect? The way we are heating up the planet with our free-booting ways with fossil fuels? Did you know that one of the biggest contributors to the Greenhouse Effect is Methane Gas? No, it isn't escaping out of the coal mines. It is coming from the millions of cattle we have grazing these days to satisfy the taste for hamburgers!

We are allowing the rain forests to be bulldozed away at a rate that is amazing. You can only admire the efficiency with which we destroy our planet… and deplore the effect it is having now and the future. I sometimes wonder if our grandchildren will have a planet to live in at all.

Can I do a little mind wandering yet again? C'mon, we're friends!

OK. At school, one of the few subjects I did really well in was History. It is a pity that so many of our politicians obviously didn't. I say that because every time I hear these characters make their pronouncements I think of a song that went something like 'When will they ever learn'. History repeats itself, so they say, the reason being our politicians obviously didn't do all that well in it when they were at school. The definition I like for stupidity is doing the same thing again and again… and expecting a different result. A bit like my golf game!

We are chopping down the forests to provide very inferior grazing land… and like all the civilisations (I use the word 'civilisation' loosely) we think we are immortal. All the other political empires faded away. At the peak of their power they really believed their system would go on forever. We are happy in the thought that we have conquered Nature… But bless us, how wrong can we be!

And most of them disappeared without trace

Now gentle reader, what makes us think we will be any different?

They too conquered their known world just as we have. But they disappeared just the same. And here we are… but we are different.

Those poor souls knew no better. But we do. Anyone with half an eye can see what we are doing to the planet… but no-one in power seems to think it is important.

One voice can make a difference, so add yours to the cries for help before everything goes…

Do you ever get the feeling that humanity is a bit like a virus plague? The Black Death swept across Europe killing thousands and thousands of people… eventually it went away… leaving death and destruction behind.

What has that got to do with us? Well, we are much the same. Wherever we go we too leave death and destruction behind.

We kill off all the other animal species… it used to take bison weeks for the herds to gallop past one spot. Now you have to gallop all over America and Canada to find any!

We poison the air, we poison the water. With our wasteful agricultural methods we are destroying the soil. We have the strange notion that it will all be fine… just pour more fertilizers into it. But now that isn't working… And let me add, we concentrate on quantity, increasing the yield from each acre… but never mind the quality.

More of inferior crops means a lot less nutrition.

Hey and get this for innocence…

When I tell people of my fears they say 'Don't worry, they will take care of things. It'll all work out in the end.'

Who 'they' are who will look after the planet, I have no idea. Whoever 'they' may be, they are not doing much of a job right now… 'They' put profit before everything. So I do not put any of my faith in 'they'. And neither should you!

People who are concerned are labelled 'Environmentalists' or 'Greenies' and are seen as people who stop other people from having jobs. Never mind that most of these jobs are self-limiting. Having worked hard to destroy the source of the jobs, there will be no jobs!

Like the virus, we are killing our host, Mother Earth…

But she will get her own back. Can't you hear Her whispering?

She is saying 'Don't worry… I'll get you in the end!' And she will.

BUT LET'S GET BACK TO YOUR ENVIRONMENT

Let's get back to the environment that is most important to us at this moment.

Yours!

It's not a bad idea to be an inner environmentalist… could save your life, could save you a lot of discomfort and pain.

Gosh, I almost forgot… Talking about Methane, take this thought to bed with you… If we could harness all the Methane humans blast out we could light up whole cities with it!

People are breaking wind all day long… millions of them.

We used to sing this song, along with all the other songs I learned at Burnage High School… 'He could fart anything, from God Save The King, to Mendolsohn's Moonlight Sonata'.

It's a funny thing about wind, gas and farting. We all pretend we don't do it!

You are with a group of people and one sneaks out on stocking feet, as we used to say, and boy, does it stink! Everyone looks the other way. No-one wants to be held responsible.

I was once at a function and some bigwig was giving a speech. And horror of horrors, just at the moment when he paused for effect, someone let out a rip roarer. It whined… it grew in volume to a crescendo of sound.

A voice said 'What was that?'

A voice said matter of factly in a rich Irish accent… 'Sumwun forted!'

At this comment the whole room cracked up. People laughed until they cried. The more polite were stuffing handkerchiefs in their mouths so they could laugh privately… wrecked the poor guy's speech totally.

Isn't it strange how we find breaking wind so humorous?

Believe me even nice people fart away with the best of them!

Why?

That is the question. Why do we have so many people who are so full of gas they could run their car on it?

Let's get back to your stomach… and then you will see why!

You were intended to chew and digest so well that all the food in your stomach is broken down into a sort of juice. We call this 'Chyme'.

It is this Chyme, this now liquefied food that leaves your stomach and begins its long journey on the human underground railway to its destination. The toilet… and to nurture you along the way.

But, and I hate to remind you again of this, we are far from perfect. We are what we choose to call 'human'. When we say someone is 'only human' we mean they don't learn from experience and are always making mistakes. A mistake being an error of judgement.

Oh, I know, you think I am very unkind. Some may think I am harsh in my judgements… But we humans specialise in believing hope will always triumph over experience. I don't want to discourage you… but History tells me it won't!

One of the problems we have is that we send partly or undigested food down the conveyor belt. Sure, a lot has successfully been turned into the juice we call Chyme… but there is also a lot of stuff in it that shouldn't really be there…

Seeds, nuts, lumps of meat, carrots and so on.

Now this stuff has to somehow be broken down in the intestines instead of the stomach. The small intestine has to work harder.

Another reason for poor digestion is so obvious I feel the need to point it out to you. (We seldom see the obvious, it is too close to our noses!)

This is a new thought for most people, so I will take it easy…

Someone once said to me 'You learn something new every day'.

And my response was 'Only if you are not careful!'

Because, the truth about us is, we resist new thoughts with as much energy as we have at that moment…

But be kind. Listen to what I have to say... see if it could possibly apply to you.

As we age we don't do things as well as we did when we were younger.

Well, you could be justified for asking me what's so new about that idea.

The answer is 'Look around you'.

You can watch bewildered as people at an age when they should know better are bashing away at a squash ball... and quite often, dropping dead! You see people driving fast cars fast! But patently not aware that they don't have the reflexes to drive such a car... and away they go... Crash!

And the biggest joke of all... You see elderly men hoping that sex with a young woman will somehow give them the elixir of eternal youth. These hopefuls leave their wives of thirty or more years and run off with some young woman. The promise may be of eternal youth... but that is not what they often get.

There is an old Arab proverb I commend to wives whose husbands have done the dirty on them and ridden off into the sunset in their new red sports car with some young hopeful. It says 'When an older man goes off with a young woman... Death smiles!'

But I don't want to be offensive. I know it is different with you...

BUT IT'S JUST THE SAME WITH YOUR DIGESTION!

It is hard to believe, but your digestion also slows down as you age. You don't push out as much Hydrochloric Acid as you did. Never mind the fact you get more acid reflux these days than you could ever remember.

What this means is you don't digest those steaks as well as you once did...

But you still eat them!

And you suffer because of that…

These undigested lumps clog up in your intestines. They slow down the flow. They block up the works…

And in a lot of cases they are not digested at all.

Here is a horrible thought… they sit there and they rot. They decompose just like a dead body decomposes.

Any wonder people get gas!

And get sick. And get bowel cancer!

Not to mention Constipation, Diverticulitis, Colitis, Stomach Ulcers, Bloating… you get the picture, I am sure.

I heard someone ask about acid reflux.

If it isn't digestive acid then what is it? What is that burning acid that gushes up from the nether regions up into your mouth… that stuff that burns all the way up as it rushes into your throat? Well, it is usually phosphoric acid rather than the digestive acid, Hydrochloric. We tend to get this from our meat eating diets. Not only dead cow, but also dead chickens, dead pigs, dead fish and any other parts of dead creatures that we eat with relish… This flesh has a lot of phosphorous in it and we make acid from that. And don't forget this, and I don't want to put you off your lunch, but flesh starts to decompose from the moment the creature dies.

In the case of animals, where they die brutally full of fear and terror, they secrete adrenaline and other poisons. This also affects the meat you eat. Think about that for a moment… Let it sink in.

No wonder I am a vegetarian!

YOUR INTRODUCTORY INTESTINE IS OVER TWENTY FEET LONG…

And your response to that is probably 'So What'. I found it mildly interesting but certainly not fascinating to be told how long my 'small' intestine was. And I found it odd that the first part of my intestines should be called 'small' when they were so much longer than the large intestine.

Life is full of these little paradoxes, isn't it?

When they say 'small', they are not referring to length but to circumference. The tube is smaller, not the length. See, you can learn something new every day after all!

Now the next bit I found interesting…

When the Chyme trips through from the stomach into the small intestine the pancreas whips into action. If you place your finger on your belly button, your pancreas is hiding somewhere behind it (your finger or your belly button, it doesn't matter which).

This is one smart little organ.

When the Chyme arrives it triggers off an instant response. Your pancreas releases the equivalent of bicarbonate of soda. It does this to reduce the acidity of the Chyme. Your small intestine doesn't do its job properly if it is acid.

Your pancreas also has the job of releasing insulin when you have put a load of sugar on your cornflakes. It does this to carry the sugar out of your bloodstream into the cells where you burn it up. If you don't burn it up, it deposits as fat.

And here is yet another gruesome thought for you… If your body appears fat on the outside it is nothing to how it appears on the inside! There will be fat deposits all over the place. In your arteries, in your tissues, in your liver, packed around your heart… not the best situation to be in.

It is similar to those brown spots people get on their skin. Unkind people who don't have them call them 'age spots'. Have you noticed that it is always younger people who refer to them as 'age' spots? Why not simply call them brown spots?

What these brown spots are, is fat. Undigested fat. Some people call them 'liver spots' and that is logical. A liver that is not doing its job properly has a problem breaking down fat. So when you see these brown spots you know straight away there is a problem with that person's liver. I hope to high heaven that YOU don't have any of these spots.

Good heavens, it's enough to make a person go on a diet… I will chat with you about diets in a later chapter.

But what does the small intestine DO?

We now know the small intestine isn't exactly small when we talk about length. We now know the pancreas shoots in loads of bicarbonate… Other enzymes are also shoved into the food mix as it is moved along.

Most of the nutrition, if there is any, in your food is absorbed in the small intestine. More digestion takes place here too.

Imagine a writhing, wriggling, squirming snake. Well, that's a bit like the appearance of a healthy small intestine doing its stuff. The contractions, the wriggling and the squirming mix up the Chyme even more. The acid mix is rendered alkaline by the bicarb from the pancreas. The gallbladder sends in bile to digest the fat. More juices break down the stomach's contribution even more.

This is so your body can grab whatever nutrition there happens to be present.

Another mind-boggling statistic to amaze your friends…

Your small intestine, just to prove even more that it is not small, is in folds. If you opened it up and spread it out it would cover about two hundred square feet. I told you there is nothing small about your intestine.

You can use this fact as a conversation starter when you are with a group of people. Just drop into the conversation… 'Hey, did you realise that your small intestine, if opened out, will cover around two hundred square feet?' That will usually stop them all dead and they will look at you with surprise… Such knowledge is rare!

The reason the small intestine is like this is to present as large an area as possible for the nutrients to be absorbed as the mix passes by.

On the walls of the small intestine are little grabbing finger-like things called 'Villi'. These are like the rare traffic cop who realises his job is to keep the traffic moving, they help to propel the mix you have introduced along to its final destination.

To further help move the stuff along, your small intestine uses muscular contractions. It squeezes the stuff along. Much like if you had some stuff in a plastic tube and you closed your hand around it and forced the stuff through the tube.

I tell you what, Nature is a lot smarter than we give Her credit for. We can't invent anything like that.

Having ground, sloshed, mixed together all the stuff that came in from the stomach it is now in a fit state to be received by the tiny blood vessels located in the wall of this miracle mile. They in turn send it to your liver where it gets even more treatment. Then whatever nutrition there was in what you ate goes out to the cells to build you up, to give your body cells good nutrition. At least, that was Nature's original plan!

Your body will always do the best it can with what we provide… Makes you think, doesn't it? It does its best, bless it, but I reckon we could all give it a bit more help!

We humans never give a thought to what is going on down there until we hit trouble. Ask people where the duodenum is and they will give you a glassy stare.

'Duo… What?' They will go.

But ask those same people have they ever heard of a Duodenal Ulcer… and then they know what you are talking about. There's PAIN involved. It is remarkable how well informed we become once we get pain.

The duodenum is the beginning of your small intestine… and a common place for an ulcer to develop.

Here is another party question for you to amaze your friends…

'How can you tell whether you have a peptic ulcer or a duodenal ulcer?'

And the snappy answer is… 'Most people can't tell the difference'.

But here is where you show your intellectual superiority… A duodenal ulcer tends to hurt most of the time. The pain is somewhere around your belly button. A peptic, or stomach ulcer as it is more commonly called, tends to give pain about half an hour after you have eaten.

In the old, unenlightened days, doctors would tell their patients to go on a milk diet for ulcers.

And do you know what?

This is just about the worst thing you could do!

Why? Because milk contains proteins and as you know protein causes your stomach to release acid! And more acid is something your ulcer definitely does not need.

I tell you, my friend, by the time we have finished talking to each other you will be able to dominate conversations. You will be the best-informed person in your group. I guarantee it!

Here is yet another thought for you to grab hold of…

From the time the wheel was invented and chariots and carts were invented, and horses, oxen and other animals tamed and trained to pull them… nothing changed for thousands of years.

Mankind used carts of one kind or another for all their transportation needs. Nothing changed. We plodded along contentedly. Life moving at a steady pace.

But in the past hundred years we made more use of the wheel than in the previous 40 centuries. We developed steam engines, machinery and motor vehicles.

And then life changed. We speeded everything up. But the point is, nothing had changed in all those centuries.

And it is the same with our diet.

Since time immemorial, way back into the dim mists of Time,

our diets hardly changed at all. The majority of people ate a simple, nutritious and healthy natural diet.

But in the past two hundred years out of the thousands we have been around, things changed dramatically…

We are smart! So we introduced fertilizers from chemicals. Much faster than cow manure. We no longer let our fields rest, we worked the soil to death. And this meant that pests flourished. But every cloud has a silver lining, as they say, and this spawned a whole new industry. Herbicides and pesticides became an essential part of farming. The farmers may not make much profit, but the chemical companies sure did!

Shows how inventive we are. Never mind that lots of people who had no concern with these chemicals got sprayed at the same time… It is all in a good cause!

But the sad fact is that farm people have a much higher rate of cancer than the rest of us. What happened to the idyllic world of pastoral peace? The thatched cottages with roses round the door? The quiet woodland scene with the still pool reflecting the sun's warming rays?

This was replaced by acres and acres and acres of one single crop. Kept going by massive injections of chemicals. Gone were the groups of shade-giving trees, gone was the quiet pool… replaced by a brown, sluggish cesspool of chemical waste.

And the farmer was working with chemicals all day. Chemicals to fertilise the soil gasping for good nutrition. Chemicals to kill the weeds that grew where no weed had grown before, certainly not in that quantity. Chemicals to keep his animals free of parasites. Chemicals to kill the billions of insects that now invaded his fields and devoured his crops. Insects that once were food for billions of other insects long since killed off.

And these chemicals got into the water supply… and are doing incredible damage today to all of us.

Small wonder that in this chemical environment the poor

farmer is exposed to contamination every day. In factories they have signs warning people about dangerous substances that are being used.

Perhaps every farm should have a big sign near the entrance gate… 'Danger… Hazardous Chemicals Sprayed Around Here!'

And our stomachs, our small intestines, our bowel, our livers have to deal with all this stuff… We have made a lot of progress in the past two hundred years, haven't we?

Never mind, we can do something to protect ourselves.

Let us press on with our tour of the underworld… next floor is Bowel country.

Here is where there is a lot of inaction. Some pessimist once remarked that Death starts in the bowel!

Only problem is, pessimist he may have been, but he was dead right.

Death does indeed start in the bowels… so does a lot of other misery.

But as I am an optimistic whose glass is always half full, I will show you how to make your bowel the fountain of youth! Now, you would like that, wouldn't you? To be shown the fountain of youth.

I have had people tell me they wouldn't like to live to be over a hundred… but that is because they associate age with disease.

But imagine this scenario… You are a hundred… and still playing golf, still enjoying a jolly sex life. Not as often, to be sure, but often enough! You are not bent double, crippled with arthritis. You do not have a dessert of medical drugs to keep you alive.

You are radiantly healthy, self-sufficient and enjoying every minute of your fulfilling life.

If you would like this, and especially if you don't believe it is possible, then read on. As my story unfolds all will be revealed to you.

Down where the sun don't shine!

If there is one area in your body that is going to cause you trouble it is down there where the sun don't shine… your bowel!

But hold on, just where IS your bowel?

As I said earlier, a lot of people complain of stomach ache and point to their bowel area and not their stomach. People tell me their stomach bloats… and point to the bowel. People tell me they are 'sick to their stomach', yeah, you got it, they point to their bowel!

So it is obvious that we are not too sure where our bowel actually is.

And very few people know what it DOES…

Even more sinister, my friend, very few people realise how much and how many of their health problems come to them from their bowel…

It has been said, and it is true, that death begins in our bowel.

You can safely say old age begins in the bowel…

Joy, happiness, serenity, all begin in the

bowel. I know people who have spent thousands of dollars on tape programmes that promised to change their lives. These good folk spend hours listening to these tapes… but for some reason their health obstinately refuses to change. Their energy levels stay low and let me tell you this, if you want to succeed in your life you MUST have lots of energy.

People take pills by the ton to get energy. I reckon lack of energy is the biggest energy crisis we have. You can't move mountains if your energy level is low. In fact, it is a task just to tie your blooming shoelaces, never mind anything else.

So the tapes are not much good without a healthy bowel.

And it is impossible to have dynamic energy with a bowel that isn't doing a proper job for you…

So come on, exactly where is your bowel?

As I am not giving you ten out of ten for being correct nor am I giving you nought out of ten because, like most people, you have no real idea… I am going to tell you. Then you have yet another party piece to dazzle other people with.

Casually drop into the conversation… 'Hey, have you any idea at all where your bowel is?' Watch their jaws drop with astonishment. They will be amazed by your question… Honest, they will be!

Anyway, let me tell you where it is…

It starts down in the right side, where it comes from the small intestine, and continues up the right side to the lower rib. Did you get that? Put your finger down to the bottom right of your belly, just up from where your leg 'joins' your 'stomach area'. Of course, this is NOT your stomach area as we often believe, it is your BOWEL area, so there!

The bowel continues up to just below the right rib and does a smart turn to the left. They call this the 'Hepatic Flexure'. Think of Hepatitis… Liver, that gives you a clue. Your liver is around there too… And we all know what a 'flexure' is… just think of flexing a muscle. Gosh, just imagine the power of what I have just told you! See yourself at the local pub... You join a group of friends and casually say, 'Hey, guess what guys, my Hepatic Flexure feels great today!'

Just imagine the effect THAT would have on them. I bet there will be dead silence while they take that in. What a reputation you will build up...

OK, so back to the bowel... It now treks along under your ribs to the left side where it does another turn and heads down to you know where. They call this the 'splenic flexure'... Very imaginatively, the part of the colon coming up the right side is called the ascending colon. The bit under your ribs is called the transverse colon and the bit heading down to you know where is called the descending colon... That is probably because it goes up, across and down... makes it easy to remember!

It's not only size that makes the difference between the large and the small intestine...

I can tell you were really impressed by the statistics I gave you about your small intestine. You never imagined you had such a clever long tube inside you, did you? You remember how I likened this to a squirming snake, I told you it had these folds and little finger-like things we call 'villi'? Do you remember? Of course you do! Well, the large intestine doesn't have any and it doesn't squirm... it pulsates. Don't you just love the sound of that word, pulsate...

Your colon doesn't have villi either. But it does have something the small intestine doesn't have. It has a lining. This lining is what they call a 'mucus' lining.

And it is this mucus lining that causes so much trouble...

This is where we get inflammation... irritable colon disease. We push little pouches out of it into the outside of the colon and get Diverticulitis. We even damage it and get polyps, which are small growths. And if we are not careful, this is where bowel cancer starts.

So we had better start taking better care of it! What do you think?

As I said, a healthy colon pulsates. It has a flowing muscular movement that moves the debris on and on until we get rid of it… down the chute into the toilet.

That's the theory, at least.

But for lots and lots of people that flowing muscular grace is restricted and in some cases, doesn't pulsate or flow at all…

Bad news! If it don't flow the garbage don't go!

Your large intestine is the great undercover garbage treatment works. It gets all the leftovers from your small intestine and was designed to work on it and deliver it neatly to your toilet.

But all too often that doesn't happen. You want proof? Simple… Look at the tonnes and tonnes of laxatives sold to try to force a once willing organ to do what it is naturally trying to do.

Spare a moment for your bowel. Think of all the stuff you put in your mouth. The lot drops down the tube, through your stomach, through your small intestine, and ends up in your bowel.

All that stuff, the junk food, the fried food, the booze, the hamburgers, the hot dogs, the chips, the chocolate biscuits, the cokes… the lot… all down the tube!

You may be astonished to hear that not all of it gets processed. A lot of it gets through the treatment plants… the mouth, the stomach, the small intestine… without being touched. You have seen peanuts in your stool, just to prove the point. But there is a lot of stuff there you don't notice. But the fact we don't know it is there doesn't alter the facts. It is there alright.

And it can cause us big trouble!

THE GERM WARFARE GOING ON IN YOUR BOWEL...

There is a war going on in your bowel. In too many cases the enemy is winning! As much as thirty percent of your stool is bacteria!

Here is an intelligence report from the embattled troops fighting for your survival in your bowel... This report indicates which battles are being lost as the enemy overwhelms the good guys.

Take a moment to have a quick peek...

Do you have Constipation? (Millions and millions of people do, even a lot who think they don't.) Do you get frequent diarrhoea?

What about headaches that seem to have no obvious cause?

Do you have skin problems? Rashes... even worse, boils in all sorts of inconvenient places? Maybe some unpleasant body odour?

And gas, wind, flatulence... Judging by the quantity of 'remedies' that are sold in pharmacies this is a very common problem.

Do you get sick easily? A nose that is always blocked up? Going down with whatever is going around? Bet it never occurred to you the reason could be your bowel.

Do people cringe and crawl away when you speak to them because of bad breath?

And when you go to the toilet do they have to call in the de-contamination squad to get rid of the stink?

And here is a cruncher... do you have lower back pain?

Do you find you need a lot of sleep, but no matter how much you get, you feel that another half hour or so would be great?

Do you belong to the army of allergy sufferers? Maybe, just maybe, your bowel has something to do with the problem.

You may be overweight and having great problems

getting rid of the final six or seven pounds or kilos… could be your bowel.

All these are signs that the battle of the bowel is being lost.

HERE'S WHAT SHOULD BE HAPPENING DOWN THERE…

In a perfect world we would all have perfect bowels. However, as you know, the world is not perfect and neither are we. On that point, I had a very strict father and I was under the mistaken impression that being perfect was the perfect goal.

It isn't…

People can't stand other people who think they are perfect. And we dislike them even more if they are, or appear to be, perfect! I comfort myself with that thought, because despite all my efforts to be perfect in my father and mother's eyes, like so many others, I never made it.

And, boy, am I glad!

But let's pretend we are all perfect and operating just as we were intended to.

Our bowels would be powerhouses. We would be almost disease free… We would have energy like you wouldn't believe… Life would be a ball.

Our bowels would pulsate beautifully… Supple muscles rippling away.

Inside our bowels, the mucus lining would be pure and free of any sort of pollution… no lumps, bumps, missing tissue, growths… just lovely, clean and slippery.

The busy bees of the bowel, the bacteria, would be working away 24 hours a day, creating B vitamins, boosting our immune systems, breaking down the waste matter into lovely compost.

When we went to the toilet we would have the primitive satisfaction of a big dump every time. And let's be disgustingly honest, there is something deeply satisfying about a big dump into the toilet… It may hark back to the days when we were toddlers and our Mums pleaded with us to part with large amounts of faecal matter. It was a matter of pride to fill our pants or the potty… We prefer to forget those days, but when we go to the toilet and let go a massive amount, we are quietly proud of ourselves.

Well we are, aren't we? Well, some of us are!

Mind you, it could just be that our inner body heaves a big sigh of relief to feel us get rid of that pile. And we unconsciously sense that feeling of relief… and it makes us feel good.

In our perfect bowel we would have trillions of good bacteria. As we ate well there was no feeding or breeding ground for nasty, ill-tempered bacteria. Just good guys. The yeast, if it were there, was well under control and no-one ever got Candida.

The time it took our waste products to go from the stomach, to the small intestine to the large bowel and out was optimum. This is called 'transit time'. This varies from person to person but for most people, it takes far too long… And while it is in there it is causing mischief.

So let's get back to reality…

Reality is very different.

For most of us the bowel can be a chamber of horrors.

The bad guys have taken over. The bowel Mafia run the joint. The yeast is happily lodging itself on the bowel wall. Gearing itself up to invade our bodies…

For some of us, our transit time (the time food takes to go along the route) can be anything from a week to a month. In some cases, they have found impacted faeces in some bowels 18 months old! Think about that one… and imagine what it must have looked like.

Well, I am sure you can't imagine what it looked like. It would be just too terrible.

That beautiful, supple muscular pulsation has stalled. It is now sluggish in the extreme or even stopped altogether. People have to resort to artificial means to dig the stuff out!

No wonder we get sick…

Did you realise your bowel was so important?

But the great news is what we have wrecked we can repair…

We can take steps to make up for our mistakes. We can be the prodigals where the bowel is concerned. Once we start to do the right things, the bowel will forgive us and start doing all the right things for us…

And once we do that, the headaches, the tiredness, the need for more sleep, the gas, the constipation, the general feeling of not being well, would all disappear as if by magic. We will enjoy a level of health and vitality we have only dreamed about…

Your whole life could change…

Now you will be able to tear through life like a tornado. Nothing will be impossible, because now you have energy. You are not being sapped by energy-sucking illnesses, headaches and the like… you will feel cheerful and full of joy.

Hard to believe that just putting your bowel right could do all these. But when you think about it, is it really so surprising?

What do you think happens when all this rotting stuff builds up in your bowel?

It is not harmless waste. It doesn't just SIT there doing its knitting…

IT GETS AT YOU!

Every single cell in your body is affected. Yes even to the cells in your brain…

They are all slowly poisoned from your bowel. You are told to wash your hands when you have been to the toilet. Well, you know why that is… but your cells cannot wash their hands of the waste building up inside them. Poor little things have to try to do their job regardless…

And while they do their level best it is not always good enough!

Oh, what we humans do to ourselves!

WHO'S ON A DIET ROUND HERE?

The answer to that question is... EVERYBODY!

Wanna argue? When we talk about diet we seem to have only one thought in our head... and that is losing weight. So if you are not on a weight-loss diet you think you are not on a diet... How wrong can anyone be?

There are a lot of diets... I see people on 'get fat' diets. I see them on 'arthritis' diets, that is a diet to get arthritis not to get rid of it. I see people on 'heart attack' diets. I also see them on 'high cholesterol' diets... I see them on 'ageing' diets and 'body breakdown' diets. As I just said, there are lots of different diets.

The trouble is so much bad food tastes so darn good

Basically, there are two kinds of diets. The best one is the 'building up' diet and the worst, and most common, is the 'breaking down' diet.

Breaking Down diets are full of sugar, white flour, grease, fat, low fibre... you know, the kind of foods or mock foods in so many cases... that we love. Hamburgers by the million, killing the planet and killing us... Sugar with everything and I mean everything! Excessive salt, great for arthritis and high blood pressure. Salt is essential but not in the quantities so many people shove in. We love lots of coffee, tea, alcohol, chocolates, biscuits, cakes, fried foods... and quite unfairly, it seems, sooner or later we get the bill.

It is this break-your-body-down diet that makes so many people overweight. Obesity is at crisis level in the Western world... and we pay a high price for it. I will be having a chat with you about weight loss in a later chapter... so enough said for now!

Contrast this with the build-you-up diet… By the way, if I haven't said this already, a diet is simply what you eat. So that gets rid of any mystery about diets.

Your digestion loves things it finds easy to digest. It is not happy with things you shove down there that takes lots of energy to break down. And let's be honest, none of us really likes things that take a lot of effort. And our inner body is no different.

So a good diet is easy to digest. The best result at the lowest energy cost. Your body is not stupid, you know! So away with lots of hard-to-digest meat with its complement of hormones, fat and so on… away with lots of fried, greasy foods that make your liver cringe in fear. Lots of lovely fresh filtered water… that's what your body often craves for.

It is surprising how many people are dehydrated. When you feel thirsty you have already gone past the stage when your body first craved water. You see these brave marathon runners and other athletes staggering into a stadium. The crowd roars its encouragement to this brave soul determined to finish the race at all costs. Their hero staggers, stumbles and finally collapses in a heap. What you are looking at is a classical case of dehydration. If that bloke had been able to keep his body flushed with water he would have galloped home.

So it is important to drink lots of water. But not from the tap… Tap water is not the best water. That innocent glass of water sparkling on your table is a chemical mix. I know it doesn't look like it. I also know the authorities want us to believe the water is as pure as pure can be. But the smell alone tells you something. Chlorine! And chlorine, as you know, is a bleach. But there are lots of unwanted outlaws in your water you can neither smell nor see… Fluoride (a by-product of the Aluminium industry), fertilizers, herbicides, pesticides. They would like us to believe these things are not in our water… but all the evidence confirms that the water table is contaminated with these residues.

I mean, think about it for just a second, you can't convince me that when people pour thousands of tons of chemicals on the land none of it gets into the water supply. That's asking too much from me... and you too!

But there are also parasites in the water. Oh, they will tell you they have been there for years with no recorded damage... But that would have to be nonsense. How can parasites in our water be harmless? Rubbish.

There is a lot of informed opinion that says some very serious diseases come from having parasites in the body. Just look at your dog when it has worms... not the best sight in the world, is it? But what about worms you don't even know you have! Lodgers who don't pay any rent and wreck the joint. Squatters who specialise in destroying the place... Every landlord's nightmare... and your body is the landlord for these unwanted freeloaders.

More about this in a later chapter...

But back briefly to the build-you-up diet... Lots of lovely fresh fruit, if you can find any. Lots of delicious vegetables. On this point, please don't boil vegetables. When you do this, as many people still do, all the water-soluble vitamins go down your sink. You will have the healthiest sink in town, but it is you I want to be healthy, not your sink!

Keep fried food to a minimum. Use Olive Oil to fry with, not blended oil from the supermarket. You deserve good stuff, my friend... I sincerely want you to have only the best.

We don't often think much about the nutritional quality of what we eat. We eat because that's what we were brought up to eat. Or because the advertisements tell us that is what all the 'in' people are eating. Or mostly, simply because we like the taste.

And the food technology industry is fully aware of this human frailty. They devote a lot of energy and money into researching new flavours, new taste sensations... all to get you to buy the product. Good nutrition may happen accidentally but not usually by design. Taste is everything! And it is also... nothing. Often worse than nothing because the taste sensation covers up the total lack of nutrition in the product.

People are astonished to discover that some brands of beautiful golden corn flakes are fakes. Just like a suntan out of a tube, the golden colour is dye. They look so much better all one uniform golden colour than if they were different shades of yellow.

And there are very few processed foods you buy that don't have sugar in them. I once picked up a packet of 'Natural' muesli... and counted at least four different sugars. There was sucrose, there was maltose, there was honey and there was syrup... definitely not a natural product at all. The manufacturer says it is natural because all these sugars are natural... that is debatable... But the label is misleading. This kind of stuff is not a health-giving, build-you-up food. Any more than a tan out of a tube is a natural sun tan.

It will pay you to learn to read labels, as I have remarked before. If you are serious about living longer, happily and full of energy then learning to understand what you are putting into your body is a must. A big must!

Because, getting back to your bowel, your bowel is the final destination of all this stuff.

I would like to chat with you in a later chapter more specifically about the various health problems we incur from neglect of this most important organ... the bowel.

But right now, at least you have more idea of what is going on down there than you may have before you read this chapter.

Here is something for you to chew on... It is my opinion that there are lots and lots of people on anti-depressant drugs who should not be.

Let us go into the next chapter to find out more.

5

Dear Doctor...
Why do I feel so
depressed?

You can bet your doctor hears that question hundreds of times. Sometimes it seems that the whole world is depressed. Just look at people walking down the street. How many do you see with head held high, eyes sparkling with enthusiasm, stepping out briskly? Most people shuffle along with head down, pictures of misery... well maybe not that bad, but not exactly shining lights.

When people ask me how I am my reply is... 'I feel FANTASTIC!'

The reaction is instant.

Fantastic? A disbelieving smile... How could anyone feel fantastic, for heaven's sake? It's not natural. Well, it's certainly not usual, that's for sure.

Most people say 'Not so bad!'

And, of course, not so bad means not so good either.

And I guess that about sums it up. Most people are not operating at optimum capacity. They operate like a motor vehicle that gets you there, but with poor acceleration, heavy fuel consumption and wonky steering.

What it boils down to is this. Let's be frank and honest with each other.

For most of us there is room for improvement in the health department.

How real is your depression?

Some researcher, in a vain attempt to cheer us all up, has predicted that something like fifty percent or more of us will be depressed by 2005. I find that statement depressing in itself. The thought of all those people chucking anti-depressant pills down their throats is disturbing. I really should take a positive view and go out and buy shares in whatever pharmaceutical company makes the most of these pills.

Can you imagine the scene in the sales office of some obscure pharmaceutical company. 'Hey, George' this to the Sales Manager... 'Have you read the good news?'

'No, what news?'

'Over fifty percent of the whole western world will be on anti-depressants by the year 2005!'

'Gosh, Fred, you just made my day. We must share this with manufacturing.'

Well, if I were in the business of making pills for depression I would think it wonderful news. I would see myself very cheerful and not a bit depressed. I would be laughing all the way to the bank, as some people say.

But are people really depressed or is there something else?

People tell me they are depressed 'all the time'.

Have you ever thought how much energy it takes to be depressed ALL the time. That takes real focus. I am not being sarcastic or making fun of depression... but really, it is most rare to be depressed all the time... unless you are in some psychotic state.

For some reason, there seems to be more women depressed than men.

For some it may be because they have a husband and for others because they don't!

I am joking, at least, I hope I am... so to press on.

Seriously, more women seem to be diagnosed as depressed than men do.

So why, I wonder, is this the case?

Do you know what I do when a female patient presents telling me how depressed she is?

Well, first up I ask about her domestic situation. If she has a husband who spends more money on gambling and booze than he gives her for housekeeping, no wonder she is depressed. I'd be depressed under those circumstances, wouldn't you?

She doesn't need a pill she needs a reformed husband.

If the domestic scene is fine, as it is most of the time, I ask more questions...

And I look in her iris...

And I ask her a lot of questions...

What else do you suffer from apart from your depression?

What is the best time of day for you?

Which is the worst time of day?

What foods do you like?

What foods do you like that don't like you?

What form does your depression take?

Are you irritable? Tearful? No motivation? Given to fits of anger?

So on and so on... It takes me about an hour to draw up a decent history of the patient.

And guess what?

No, give up because you will never guess the answer.

In lots of cases the depression is a liver that is not doing its job properly.

Yes, that's what I said. The real culprit is often the LIVER... and not the mind at all.

Now folks, if that is not picked up and the patient is given anti-depressant pills, these add to the load of an already overloaded liver.

So that person has a hard row to hoe to get better.

The liver, the cause of the problem, is getting even more work to do. This is because it falls on your liver to degrade the chemicals in the drug.

YOUR LIVER IS PROBABLY THE MOST OVERWORKED ORGAN IN YOUR BODY

Not a lot of people know where their liver is situated, as I pointed out in an earlier chapter... Even fewer know what it does.

So let's find out, shall we?

I know you love my little ice-breakers to use when you meet new people, so here is another one you can use to start a conversation with a total stranger... 'Did you know your entire blood supply goes through your liver every twenty minutes?'

I can tell you that comment really stops people in their tracks.

'Every twenty minutes' they will say disbelievingly. 'Fancy that.'

BUT WHAT HAPPENS WHEN THE BLOOD GETS THERE?

Your liver is a wonderful organ. It filters the blood to take out any impurities that have got into it. It has to take out any chemicals, heavy metals, in fact anything injurious to your body... but only if it is working as it should.

The lymphatics, the drainage system of your body, empties into the liver and when your liver is in good shape it sends the contents on to your bowel for disposal. By the way, your lymphatic system is something else that gets clogged up and doesn't empty as it was designed to do.

When I look in people's irises I often see what we call the 'Lymphatic Rosary'. It is a ring of little white dots around the outside edge of the iris.

It tells me that the person needs help to get the drainage system in better shape… Just as the drains from your home can cause problems if blocked up, so can your body's drainage system cause problems if it is blocked up. Makes sense, doesn't it?

A very important job your liver does is to store nutrients from your blood. It stores glycogen, some B vitamins for example. It sends the nutrients around your body to wherever they are needed. Always assuming your blood has some nutrients to send around! I'm kidding, of course, if your blood had no nutrients to offer the liver, you would be a basket case… and you are not!

People often ask me if I can give them what they call a 'blood cleanser'. I sometimes wonder how a blood cleanser would work. I picture lots of little workers around the body at strategic points with filters, buckets to put the rubbish in, scrubbing the blood nice and clean.

But it doesn't really work like that, as you know.

It is your liver that cleans your blood. So what these people are really asking for is something to buck up their liver. They have boils, or a spotty skin, pimples, zits and so on. So they want something to clean the blood to get rid of these unsightly objects.

But very often they need to change their diet and take some herbs to give their liver a helping hand…

Some of the herbs that help your liver are Dandelion, Milk Thistle, Barberry, Bayberry, Blue Flag and Schizandra. There are two important amino acids to help the liver. These are methionine and taurine.

You will find most of these ingredients in one complex in your local health food store.

SIGNS OF A LIVER THAT IS NOT WORKING TOO WELL…

It is a good idea for you to recognise when your liver needs a friend.

When you notice your stool is very light, almost white or even white. This shows your liver is not sending bile to break down fat. It is bile that gives your stool its familiar brown colour.

Another pretty obvious sign is when the smell of cooking makes you feel sick. Your appetite has done a nosedive and you have that sickly feeling in your tum… One symptom that is not always recognised is a pain just below the right shoulder blade. This is a real danger signal of a liver or gallbladder that is crying out for help… Don't ignore it, get it the help it needs.

One sign that sends most people off to their doctor is when the whites of the eyes turn a pretty yellow. This is bile and could indicate jaundice… hepatitis…

Not so obvious are the mental symptoms.

Here is where we get into murky waters, folks…

This is why I have the feeling so many people are on anti-depressant drugs for what could be a liver problem.

Here are some of the symptoms, and you could have some or if you are unlucky, the lot! Depression, irritability, tearfulness, given to outbursts of rage, no motivation, lethargy (you know, tired all the time).

These seem to be mental symptoms but they are also signs of a liver that is doing you in. Now, unless this is picked up you will find yourself on anti-depressant drugs, and as I have remarked before, these could make your problem worse.

I sometimes wonder about drugs… I have met people who have been on the same drugs for years and years. I ask them if they are any better, has their blood pressure come down, are they no longer depressed and so on…

And the snappy answer is usually no they are not any better. If they go off the drugs the problem comes back in spades. So if they are not working, if they are not fixing the underlying problem, why are people still taking them?

A lot of people are living longer these days, and that is excellent, but a lot of them are on life-support systems just as if they were on a machine plugged into the wall. If you pull the plug on someone on a life support system, they die. If you take someone off all the medication they are on, they too could die…

When I am in a philosophical mood it occurs to me that it might be a better idea to find some way of fixing the underlying problem. The drug is holding the symptoms in check, and that's fine, but it is doing nothing about the cause of the problem. And that's a worry!

However, I do not recommend you to drop your medical drugs without first consulting your doctor. He or she had good reasons to put you on these drugs and must be informed of your intentions.

A very good reason for doing this is just stopping the intake of some drugs can have a very serious side effect. You could drop dead! This is especially true of Beta-blockers… so chat with your doctor first.

Pity your poor liver. It has to break down the drugs you may be taking. One more load to bear, another reason for your liver to complain it is tough for it to do its job properly.

DO YOU HAVE ANY OF THESE LIVER SIGNS?

If you want to be radiantly healthy, it is a good idea to be able to recognise the signs of a liver that is on a go-slow campaign.

I have mentioned some of the complaints we get from a poorly working digestion, bowel, liver… but it will be a good idea to refresh your memory.

Have a look and see how you go…

You are carrying too much weight and no matter what you do you can't get it off.

You are constantly tired. Life is one big effort! This seems to affect the whole world.

Here is a 'biggie', headaches. I sometimes think that Life is one big headache for so many people, no wonder headaches are so common.

Something even your best friends won't tell you about... bad breath!

Here is another epidemic problem, Irritable Bowel. Legions of people are shoving antacids and all sorts of things into themselves in an effort to beat Irritable Bowel.

Some people can tell you everything they ate for breakfast, because it keeps coming back up into their throat... reflux. It often brings burning acid with it to make the whole episode memorable.

Have you ever wondered why it is that you can have two people standing next to a dog or a cat and only one of them gets an allergy attack? The reason could simply be the liver doing a number on the one who gets the attack. The liver of the non-allergic person deals with the offending substance and the other poor soul's liver doesn't!

Here in Australia people are very conscious of their cholesterol levels. Ask almost anyone about their cholesterol and they can tell you the number just like that. It's also quite remarkable how many people are on cholesterol reducing drugs... where it could easily be a liver problem.

If your liver is not burning up fat as it should, don't be surprised to find that fat is depositing on your arteries... not the best news of the day! And if the fat is building up on your arteries you can bet your boots it is building up somewhere else as well... like in your liver itself, round your heart... on your hips!

Have you ever seen someone in the grip of a gallstone attack? I can tell you it is frightening. The pain is intense and agonising. But gallstones need not happen if you have a good liver function.

A major catastrophe for a teenager is a face full of acne, pimples and zits. Not a big turn-on at all. I reckon people with a bad skin go about things the wrong way. They look for something to dab on it. They approach their skin from the outside-in.

It should always be from the inside-out!

Look at people's diets these days. Hamburgers by the million… Fried chips with everything… Coffee by the gallon, litre or whatever… No wonder their skin doesn't radiate health. The liver, my friends, if you have a bad skin, start with your liver, your digestion, your bowel…

And don't forget the liver spots I told you about earlier, those brown spots you see on people's hands and arms. These are the most common sites for them. Young people very unkindly call them 'age spots'.

I have told you all this in an earlier chapter, but it does no harm to keep emphasising these things. Gets them into your memory until you want to do something about it all…

LOOK TERRIFIC, FEEL TERRIFIC, BE TERRIFIC!

Which would you rather be, tired all the time, oozing misery, with a grey face, puffy skin OR full of energy, radiating happiness with a lovely clear skin?

Well, unless you are really down you would want to be radiating energy and happiness, I am sure.

In that case, do something about giving your liver a helping hand.

To detox or not to detox that is the question… Should you think about detoxifying yourself?

Well, let's have a look at it and see what you feel about it.

Because of our generally poor lifestyle (I know you could be the exception, but bear with me), lots of people suffer from what is called 'auto-intoxication'. That doesn't mean they get drunk all the time. It means that the body has poisoned itself.

Now that doesn't seem a very smart thing to do, does it? But it happens all the time… to lots of very nice people.

This is because they have a bowel that is overloaded and one that is not clearing the waste out. Silently, without any warning signals, sneakily in fact, some of these poisons get back into our body.

The liver is not handling this overload very well and this makes sure these poisons will get into your body cells…

This is often the case when people go to their doctor and complain they don't feel very well, but have no obvious symptoms the doctor can stick a label on. And if the doctor can't label it he has a problem doing anything about it… So you could end up on anti-depressants!

So the answer is YES, a detox is a good idea!

It is a very good idea to have an internal 'spring clean' every six months or so. What do you think?

Let's get rid of all that accumulated junk and give our cells a chance to breathe.

Here is a simple routine for you… nothing complicated or difficult.

Take digestive enzymes before your meals. This makes sure that as we are doing our cleaning someone isn't tracking muddy foot marks all over our nice clean floor. In other words, let's breakdown our food properly so as not to add to the load we are working on.

Next, take liver supplements. You can usually get a liver complex from your health food store. This will have the herbs I mentioned earlier… you remember them… Dandelion, Milk Thistle, Berberis and the amino acid Taurine.

Very important is to take something to clean up the bowel and to deal with parasites. I will give you the horror story about parasites in a later chapter… enough to give anyone the heebie jeebies!

If auntie says she had a liver test and it didn't show there was a problem, tell her that these tests are not the most reliable in the world. They do not look for function, how well the liver is actually working… so tell her the test showed there may not have been any abnormality in the liver… but that doesn't mean it is working as it should. That should keep her in her place!

Green Barley is a good thing to take when you are on a detox programme. 'Green inside is clean inside', as Doctor Bernard Jensen used to tell us. Doctor Jensen is a world authority on internal matters. He was also the pioneer in Iris Diagnosis. He can tell you tales about people's insides that make your hair curl!

Here is yet another conversation starter for you… Drop this one into the conversation and watch the eyes pop… 'Did you know there is only one thing different between chlorophyll and blood?' 'Wow!' everyone will exclaim 'Please tell us what it is'.

Then you can air your new-found wisdom and say casually… 'Actually, the difference is simply that chlorophyll has magnesium as the main mineral and blood has iron'.

That should really make them respect you.

If it doesn't, get a different audience!

But that is one of the reasons taking Green Barley is such a good idea. It helps your liver… it is packed with nutrients like enzymes and all those good things.

Oh, and one very important thing… when you are on a detox programme is it ESSENTIAL to keep your bowel open. In a good detox kit you will find it includes herbs to keep your bowel active.

It is no use draining all this build up out of your cells and letting it add to the load in your bowel… so that it all comes back in again!

So as you can see, your liver is VERY important when it comes to health. If you have a liver that has aged prematurely, you will age prematurely. And who the heck wants that?

If you are depressed, lack energy, have weight problems, have bad breath because a real friend told you about it, have bad skin, clogged up arteries, gallstone problems… gosh, what a list, then check out your liver!

Would you like to see where you liver is in your iris?

OK… here is what you do.

Try with someone else at first. Look in their right eye, which is on the left facing you. Gaze into their eyes, but don't give them the impression you are fascinated by them, and pay attention to the iris.

Look at the iris about where the figure 8 would be on a clock…

Now move back on a line to the pupil. That is the liver area.

If the liver is not up to the mark you will see it is darker than the iris around it. It can even be black…

Look around the iris for the brown overlay. Often when you look in someone's eye you will see all this brown, often in the upper iris but it can be anywhere. This brown stuff is… well, it's not polite to mention it in so many words or even in one word, but you know what it looks like…

This is also a sign of a liver not doing its stuff.

Now, please, whatever you do, do NOT tell the person whose iris you are gazing at what you see.

I have had patients come to me and say with utter despair 'My liver is shot!'

It seems some amateur iridologist looked into their iris, saw the liver signs and got some kind of black pleasure out of telling them their liver was 'shot'. Which is rubbish… If your liver was really shot you would be dead!

Now look at your own eye in your mirror… and what do you see?

A beautiful clear iris? Well, maybe… I hope so.

That ends our tour of your inside workings, your stomach, bowel and liver… so now, we need to look at specific problems.

Let us have a look at parasites that can cause you enormous problems and yet are seldom picked up. Let's find some natural ways to ease Irritable Bowel, Diverticulitis, Constipation and some health problems that seem totally unrelated to the bowel or digestion.

What we want to do is to get you full of boundless energy. So much energy that people will stand in awe at your capacity for getting things done.

We want to have your friends stand open-mouthed at your youth, at your beautiful skin, your suppleness…

In short, we want you to radiate health!

So let's get on with it… you and me on what, I hope, is a fascinating journey.

The incredible walking blood bank… YOU!

Did you realise you could be the unwitting host to a myriad of unwelcome, non-paying guests in your body?

These little Draculas are sucking away, getting into the best of your food before you do. You can find them anywhere, in your bowel, in your tissues, in your small intestine, your lungs… even your heart.

And these blighters are not your friends. They are blood sucking, nutrition-sucking, poisoning little no-goods… and most people have heaps of them tucked away in their body.

These are parasites and it has been suggested that parasites are the biggest undiagnosed cause of ill-health in the whole world. But when we think about parasites we think of starving unfortunates in Africa or other underprivileged areas. How wrong could you be!

Wrong, wrong, wrong… (I hate telling you that you are wrong, even if it does make me feel superior for two seconds or so). Parasites are not choosy. They are totally non-racial, they are not worried about how important you are in the world or anything else.

If they can get in baby, believe me, they get in!

Their total focus is survival of the species. And they are very good at it indeed.

CHECK THIS LIST OUT… YOU COULD BE IN FOR A SHOCK!

Now if you are like most of us, you innocently believe that it is impossible for you to have any disgusting parasites feeding off your body. OK. That's what most people think but they are still mistaken.

Just go through this list of possible symptoms of infestation… you just may need the pest inspector!

Do you have itchy ears? An itchy nose, perhaps? Or that most common and unconscious of actions… an itchy bum?

Hey guys! Do you do real well in bed most of the time or do you miss out more than you care to admit?

Do you have to have a list with you all the time because without one you forget what you went in for? 'What's your name again?'

How fast do you react? Do you feel your reflexes could do with a tune up?

Talking about that, do you sometimes feel your brain could do with a good old Spring clean to get the fog out?

Be honest, do you bloat? Do you have gas?

Do you find that food has lost its appeal, but your passion for sweet things (not members of the opposite sex) is getting out of hand?

Look in the mirror! Has your skin a yellowish look about it?

Does your heart tend to beat fast even though there is little in your life to get excited about?

Do you get pains around the heart?

Do you get pains around the area of your belly button?

And do you find you eat like a horse but still feel hungry?

What about your vision… Do you find it is sometime blurry or it changes through the day?

Here's a very common symptom, pain in the back, thighs or shoulders? Gosh, don't tell me that pain could be darned parasites having a go at me!

Tired all the time. Would like to join the Anti-Apathy Club but are too tired to go to the meetings?

Do you sometimes find you have numb hands?

Here is another common problem… do you sometimes have a burning sensation in your stomach?

I have met women who think that having problems with their periods is normal… it isn't… are you one of them? You could have parasites! Not a nice thought, is it?

Here is one we associate with old men… drooling when sleeping! And all the time we thought it was just Uncle Arthur's age and we now find it could be parasites…

Do you find your lips are damp at night but dry through the day? I bet you always wondered about that!

And here's one that you have always wondered about… does anyone you know grind their teeth at night?

To end on a low note, do you or anyone you know have a problem wetting the bed?

Now, my dear friend, you do not need to have all these symptoms, nor do they all necessarily indicate parasite infection. Let me explain a bit better. It is possible that you have some of these symptoms and they are caused by something other than parasites… but check parasites first before thinking you have some serious disease.

By serious disease I mean one that can have a label attached to it. Like high blood pressure, hardening of the arteries and so on…

The problem with parasite infections is they are great mimics. You can think you have a heart problem but it is a worm or other parasite giving you the symptoms. You may think your digestion is up to maggots, but it is maggot-like creatures feeding away that is upsetting your digestion.

Listen to this example. A young bloke came to see me complaining he was losing weight. He was a body-builder and ate huge meals, drank protein drinks, took tablets and heaven knows what else. He trained like mad but was finding he got tired more easily and training was not the fun it used to be.

This young man had spent many tortured nights thinking he must have a cancer... But his problem was simple. He had worms. Once he was de-wormed his weight returned to normal and his pleasure in pushing weights was happily restored.

Interestingly, this had not been picked up by anyone else. That is what I mean about parasites being such clever mimics. It is often hard to recognise what is before our eyes.

How normal is normal?

Have you ever thought you were going insane? People I have met sometimes tell me they think they are going crazy. Well here's some good news. If you think you are going crazy it is most unlikely you are.

And here is why it is most unlikely. Because crazy people don't know they are crazy. They think they are normal and YOU are crazy.

Someone who thinks he is Napoleon cannot for the life of him understand why you don't recognise him. So even people with mental disorders think they are normal.

So what is normal?

Let me tell you a true story (all my stories are true you can tell that because I usually call them 'case histories'). To move on... When I have a female patient I always ask about her periods as this is an important health indicator in women. This one lovely lady told me her periods were 'normal'. So I asked her if she had any pain or discomfort.

'Pain? Pain?' she said 'I have to go to bed I have so much pain!'

'But I thought you said your periods were normal?'

'Isn't that normal?' was her reply.

And that's the problem. We think our level of health is normal. We take our symptoms for granted. We have lived with them so long we think they are part of everyone's life. We take ourselves as the yardstick and judge the rest of humanity accordingly.

But our health is not normal. We may not have outright obvious disease but that does NOT mean we are healthy.

Why I labour this point is simply you could have signs of parasite infestation and not recognise them. A bit like someone who has a house full of white ants and doesn't notice it until the door falls off the pantry!

HERE'S A GRISLY THOUGHT… PARASITES EAT HUMAN BODIES!

And what's more they do it without us realising it. Even worse, as they eat they also release their wastes into our bodies… and these can be TOXIC! Parasites are very clever at being invisible. They are also very clever at surviving and reproducing themselves.

Do you know why they are so clever at hiding? Because we seldom recognise the signals of parasite invasion. We take being tired for granted, unexplained skin rashes are brushed off as 'heat rash' or something, constipation is a way of life for lots of people… we do not recognise these as perhaps symptoms of parasites in our body.

The awful truth is that there is no part of our body that does not play host to some kind of parasite at some time or another.

It is a bit of a worry too when you discover that medical tests only reveal something like 20% of the parasites. Even more worrying is that it is estimated there are something like 1,000 or more parasites that could be doing their number on you and there are tests for only about 50 or 60 different types.

That leaves a heck of a lot of creatures making a meal of us that are never detected by the doctor's friend, the test...

WHAT'S FOR DINNER TODAY?

For parasites that can vary... some love sugar, others will gobble up the vitamins before you do. If you want a real scare think of this, some of them actually attach to your cells and suck the goodness out of them! The parasites do very nicely, thank you, but you are being starved of good nutrition... and being poisoned at the same time.

To add to your misery, these parasites can live off you for twenty or thirty years. And you thought having your brother-in-law living with you was bad!

In your intestines it can be like Jurassic Park with worms up to twenty feet long living there! I am not kidding, twenty feet long... Gosh, no wonder we don't feel like tennis!

A good thing is you can usually spot worms. These spend most of their time in your intestines. The most common are pinworms, threadworms and tapeworms.

Pinworms are crafty. They creep out of our intestines at night, lay eggs around the anus... and they itch! So guess what, we scratch! And in this way transfer the eggs back into our body. Or we get them under our fingernails and transfer them into someone else's body. The pinworm isn't fussy about whose body it gets into. As long as it gets into one!

When we scratch we can dislodge the eggs onto the bedding or clothing and thus give them a free ride to their destination. Someone's body, mine, yours, anybody's!

These minute eggs can be waiting to be picked up in almost every room in the house. Talk about freeloaders!

Roundworms are no better. Some of these creatures inject digestive enzyme fluid into the wall of the colon so they can suck out the food they crave. I tell you what, doesn't reading this make you feel like rushing for the worm tablets?

If you have these creatures sucking away at you there is no doubt you will be suffering from some sort of nutritional deficiency. It is estimated there are hundreds of millions of people infected with roundworms of one kind or another all round the world. And this includes the Western world… we are not immune! I know we would like to think we are, but the truth is we are not.

And there is the tapeworm. This worm can grow to horrendous lengths, twenty, thirty feet! These are really clever and very hard to dislodge. They hook themselves into the wall of the intestines and then grow and grow by segments. Now get this… each one of these segments can become another tapeworm.

Tapeworms do not have a digestive system of their own, so guess what they use… ours! They suck in food we have digested!

You can do your best to get rid of these pests, but if you leave the head intact it can grow again… all twenty feet of it!

If you want to strike terror into someone's heart, show them a picture of a hookworm. This beast is a huge mouth and what look like teeth. It makes a big white shark look like a goldfish! Where you would expect to see a head all you see is this mouth waiting to get a hold of some part of you!

These beasts usually live in semi-tropical parts of the world… so if the global warming continues, we can expect them to become more common. Hookworm larvae get into our bodies by burrowing through the skin. So going barefoot in the areas where these creatures live is not the best of ideas. Once they get into your body they hitch a ride with your blood stream and get into the lungs.

Then they trek from there into the throat and you swallow them and get what for them is 'home', the small intestine. But their journey through your body is not uneventful. On the way they cause various respiratory problems, including bronchitis. They can cause weight loss, anaemia and nausea.

These too can outstay their welcome by staying in a body for as long as 12 to 15 years.

THE ULTIMATE PARASITE HORROR STORY!

Here is a story to send shivers down your spine. A story to make your hair stand on end. A story that will probably turn your guts to ice!

Wow! Gotta be quite a story, eh?

Well, imagine this scenario, my friend. Inside you could be a parasite that can be the trigger for cancer! Not only cancer, it could be for ALL diseases that plague humanity.

You are going about your daily business totally innocent of the fact that there could be lurking inside you a parasite waiting to do you in.

'Not me!' you say?

Well, maybe, but listen to this... Hulda Clark is a Naturopath whose research would indicate that inside most of us is a parasite called a Liver Fluke. And this Liver Fluke is the one bad cookie that threatens us every day of our lives.

OK, I can hear you mutter 'Who is this crazy anyway?'

Let me destroy that idea straight off. Doctor Hulda Clark is a Naturopath but she is also much more. She studied Biology at the University of Saskatchewan in Canada and received her Bachelor of Arts Degree cum Laude. And that means with the highest praise!

She then went on and obtained her Masters Degree with High Honours... not your everyday student, eh? Now as if that wasn't enough she went on to the University of Minnesota and earned her Doctorate in Physiology in 1958.

She worked in Government funded research until 1979 when she left the Government stuff and went into private research. Doctor Clark along the way developed a technique for scanning the human body. She is the author of two world best selling books: *The Cure For All Cancers* and her latest book, *The Cure For All Diseases*.

I give you this background on Doctor Clark to assure you that this is not some crackpot telling us about the liver fluke and its deadly association with killer disease, but a highly respected scientist.

So it may be a good idea to have a look at what Doctor Clark has discovered. Hulda Clark says that the various cancers are all caused by Flukes. Smoking may be a contributory factor in lung cancer, as an example, but it is not THE cause of lung cancer. Same with every other cancer... the true cause is the parasitic fluke.

There are a number of the Fluke Family, none of which would you voluntarily invite home to tea (but they come anyway!). These are the intestinal fluke, the sheep liver fluke, the cattle fluke and the human fluke.

It would seem these sit in your body until they are activated by solvents. And the bad news is there are lots of these solvents as residues in our food, toothpaste, mouthwashes, lotions and potions... So it will pay you to read labels. These are common in shampoos and the like. Here are some for you to watch out for... isopropyl alcohol, benzene, methanol, xylene, toluene... any of these ring any bells? They do with me, I can tell you.

The flukes tend to go to the organs that accumulate different solvents. The liver tends to accumulate isopropyl alcohol... so the liver fluke take up residence in the liver... just loves isopropyl alcohol, baby!

And this starts the cancer cycle in that organ!

Don't scoff. These claims are backed up by clinical research. I urge you to go out and get your hands on both of Doctor Clark's excellent books.

Here's a piece of advice you lovers of rare meat should think about. Undercooked meat is a wonderful place for parasites of all kinds to hang out. They just love this sort of environment. And you, you poor innocent, order your steak rare or even 'blue', almost straight from the poor animal.

You love your raw fish... OK, so you soak it in vinegar. Wonderful, except a lot of parasites love vinegar as much as you do!

You love your dogs, and so do I. So they show their affection by licking you anywhere they can... and could easily be depositing parasite eggs on your skin.

We live in a cruel world, my friend, all is not as innocent as it may seem to us trusting mortals... We have to be on our guard and most of all, be informed. We need to KNOW far more than we do right now!

Doctor Clark's research tells us that one hundred percent of cancer patients, and that's a growing army of people let me tell you, have both liver fluke and isopropyl alcohol in their livers. It doesn't matter where the cancer is... the initiator is comfortably embedded in the liver being sustained by the isopropyl alcohol.

This should make anyone with cancer jump out of their armchair shouting 'Eureka!' I was told, when at school, that a guy called Archimedes made the word popular in ancient Greece. He found out by filling his bath to the top with water and then jumping in that a lot of water went on the floor. Now I am sure you have noticed that yourself. But old Archimedes figured out that the amount of water is equal to the weight of the person jumping into the bath.

This is now called the 'Archimedes Principle' for reason that don't need a genius to explain to anyone… I just thought I would throw that in to show my attendance at school was not a total waste of time. And also, to give you yet another conversation starter.

Just watch their faces when you say something like 'Hey, when you jumped in the bath last night and all that water went on the tiles, guess what? The water equalled your weight!' Ignore the person who points to his or her overweight partner and remarks 'That can't be right, or Herbert (or Doris) would have flooded the whole darn house'. These people are among those who do not understand how smart you really are…

Let's get back to the life wreckers… the fluke family.

These cannot get a hold on us unless we have the isopropyl as well.

When this is present we get a story that makes Frankenstein seem like something from a Ladies Journal. Imagine this one… the flukes reproduce at a rate that would make rabbits look almost celibate! Now the plot thickens, as they say, enter the Growth Factor…

This element introduces true horror into the story… this stuff is called Ortho-phospho-tyrosine… and it is deadly. This Growth Factor makes cells divide… can you guess what is coming?

And this damned Growth Factor makes your CELLS divide… and that means only one thing. You have cancer!

So you have to set all the Alarm Bells ringing. Get your body into Action Stations, order defence forces to search and destroy this Growth Factor wherever it may be…

In my book, *How to Fight Prostate Cancer and Win* I talk about the humble Clover and how it contains something called Genisteine. This Genisteine is a must in your battle to prevent and cure cancer… Genisteine is a Growth Factor inhibitor… it slows it down!

Make taking Red Clover a part of your battle-plan against getting or getting rid of cancer!

DOCTOR CLARK'S MAGIC HERB FORMULA…

You must get hold of Doctor Clark's two books to get the full story. If you don't you will go off half-cocked, as they say… Now come on Auntie Maude, 'half-cocked' is not a rude expression so take that disgusted look off your face. It is an expression that has come from the days when men got their entertainment from shooting at each other with pistols. You know, take ten paces, turn and then try to blast each other into eternity. Well, my friend, unless your pistol was fully cocked when you turned and pulled the trigger you were likely to be dead unlucky. If it was only half-cocked and you pulled the trigger nothing happened to the other fellow… if he was a good shot you dropped dead!

So what does Auntie Maude think about that? Keep this one in your party conversation starter kit, too…

Hulda Clark's research has proven that three herbs are necessary: Black walnut Hull, Wormwood and Cloves. But read the books, get the full story… And then rush to your health food store and see if they can get these herbs for you.

Scan every label on everything to make sure you are not including the deadly Growth Factor, isopropyl alcohol, in your daily diet.

If you value your health, if you value your life, then you must do something to prevent parasites in your body. No-one is immune, not even you and me wonderful though we are.

HERE'S WHAT I DO… EVERY DAY!

I was told I had incurable cancer of the prostate gland. Enjoy what you can as long as you can… But I believe that a doctor's prognosis is often an opinion. And that's it… an opinion. So I set out to research everything possible to do with cancer. Not only prostate cancer, but all cancers.

Parasite killing was high on my list of priorities…

I became a small game hunter…

I have followed Doctor Clark's recommendations… indeed, every six months I go through the programme with the Black Walnut, Wormwood and Cloves treatment… and I sincerely urge you to do the same.

But I also discovered a couple of other things you need to know about…

The first is Colloidal Silver.

Now here is a bold statement for you… 'No disease-causing organism can live in the presence of even minute traces of the element of simple metallic silver'.

If that is not enough for you then listen to this… As an antibiotic Silver kills over 650 disease-causing organisms and note this carefully, resistant strains of bacteria fail to develop. Silver is absolutely non-toxic.

Talk about being one of the good guys in the big white hats. Silver is the best all-round germ fighter we have. Doctors are reporting that, taken internally, it works against syphilis, cholera, malaria, diabetes and severe burns. This quote comes from Science Digest.

I must confess I put the bit about the big white hats because in the cowboy movies the good guys always wore big white hats… I bet you noticed, didn't you. The bad guys all wear even bigger black hats!

Do you have Candida? You know, Thrush! If so you will be fascinated to learn that Silver kills fungi in six minutes. If that isn't a lightning strike, I don't know what is! Candida is a yeast in the bowel but a fungus in the body. So Silver is the way to go…

Got pimples? No, I am sure you don't, but I bet you know someone who does. Get the person to take the Colloidal Silver in water and to use it as a face wipe… they will love you for that because their pimples will disappear. What a wonderful thing to do for someone, especially a teenager.

Colloidal Silver is great for sore throats, just spray some down there. Put some up your nose for an infected nose. This stuff helps get rid of cold sores, stinking feet (not the feet, the smell)… it even works for bad breath!

Take some just in case your best friend won't tell you there is a problem. I am kidding, I am sure your breath smells of roses… but not everyone's does, I assure you.

But the most important action of Colloidal Silver from our point of view is this… it can cure and prevent ALL parasitic infections.

By the way, Colloidal Silver is safe for people of all ages. Little babies to their doting grandparents and all ages in between.

What was that you said? What the heck does 'colloidal' mean?

Let me ask you something, when you put too much sugar in your coffee you may have noticed a lot of it sits at the bottom of the cup. Right?

Well, with colloidal that doesn't happen. It stays in suspension but the particles are so small you can't see them even with your new spectacles.

This is because each tiny particle is charged with electricity and by a process too complicated for a simple bloke like me to explain, it never hangs about for five minutes and then falls gracefully to the bottom of the bottle. It floats there in suspension, even though you can't see it, all the time.

What this means is that it gets into your cells, where it is supposed to go, rather than slipping down to the bottom of the barrel, where it is not supposed to go. If you understood all that, give yourself ten marks and sit by the radiator.

Coining a phrase, the bottom line is the Colloidal Silver gets right into your body easily and quickly… and kills the nasties! So put a bottle on your shopping list. By the way, I put some in our dogs' drinking water… just to make sure the little darlings in their enthusiasm don't leave parasite eggs all over the place… a word to the wise?

A NEW WAY WITH OLIVES

When we talk about olives we think of olives perched on the end of a little stick in a martini, or gracing a salad… but what about olive leaves.

Not many people have heard of olive leaf extract, but they should. The olive leaf can halt the growth and spread of bacteria, fungi and viruses.

It stops the bad stuff in your cholesterol from having a go at you, and very important, it stimulates neutrophil activity in your body.

Now, unless you are exceptionally well-informed that last bit is incomprehensible. Neutrophils are the little bits of protoplasm (looks like bits of jelly) that float about in your body looking for something to eat. And what they love to eat are foreign bodies, bacteria, parasites… So having a lot of these little savages on your side is great. And olive leaf extract really gets them going!

Olive extract is great for detoxifying your body. So much so, that when you first start taking it you might find you get a mild headache or a bit of tummy rumbling. You can avoid this by taking a whack of Vitamin C with the Olive Leaf extract.

Gosh, there goes Auntie Maude again 'Be careful of taking too much Vitamin C, you'll get kidney stones'. Can you hear me groan?

This is what I call a medical myth. Doctors love to trot this out. Ask them who told them Vitamin C causes stones… I bet they don't know. They don't know because there is not one recorded case of anyone ever getting kidney stones from Vitamin C. Not one!

The amazing truth is Vitamin C STOPS you from getting

kidney stones. How about that? Being acidic, Vitamin C keeps oxalic acid in suspension so it can't form stones. And most stones are formed from oxalic acid, ask your doctor!

Doctor Michael Colgan, who is one of the world's top nutritional scientists, and who has perhaps the world's largest computer records, searched the computer files. Do you know how many cases he found reported in the medical literature? NONE. That's right, not one single case.

The medical literature, by the way, is all the published papers from all 3,000 medical journals published all round the world.

So I repeat, Vitamin C does not cause kidney stones, it prevents them.

Gosh, how wrong could any one be?

So there you go. I take around twenty grams a day, and have done since I was diagnosed with prostate cancer... no stones... no cancer!

This has to be my one favourite supplement...

If there is one supplement you should take, if you can only afford one, it has to be Lactoferrin.

This is numero uno in protecting yourself from evil. The list of qualities Lactoferrin has is more then just impressive... it is majestic! The king and queen of supplements.

Another bold statement from Uncle Ron... but give me a few moments just to list what Lactoferrin can do...

- Reduces tumours and stops them from jumping somewhere else.
- Boosts killer cell activity like you wouldn't believe!
- Promotes phagocytes to become more numerous and more aggressive in engulfing and eating foreign bodies in your body.
- Gives your bowel a boost... helps to create a lovely environment where good guys flourish and bad guys miss out.

- Works on viruses… antibiotics don't, so don't take them for the flu or so-called in case of secondary infection.
- Reduces inflammation.
- Kills Candida and other fungi.
- Is bad news for parasites.
- Switches on the genes that launch your immune system into action.
- Great to combat Herpes… one of the most common of disease causes, and one of the least recognised… With genital herpes on the march in our modern world this is good news indeed.

Can you see why I get so enthusiastic about Lactoferrin? I take it every single day… If you have read my book, *How to Fight Prostate Cancer and Win*, you will find out more reasons why I take it… and I urge you to.

Even if you think you have nothing wrong with you, take it.

When I wrote *How to Fight Prostate Cancer and Win*, Lactoferrin was not available in Australia. I am delighted to tell you that it is now available under the name 'LACTOMAX'.

It is my humble opinion that anyone should take this who wants to stay well…

So keep in mind your duty to keep sentries everywhere in your body to keep out parasites and to get them if they are lurking in the hidden recesses in your body.

As a matter of routine, every six months, follow Hulda Clark's regime for attacking and cleaning out parasites. Take Olive Leaf Extract and also Lactoferrin as part of your daily preventative routine.

I take QuickCleanse 'Bowel Clear' and recommend it to my patients. This has in it Wormwood, Cascara Sagrada, Rhubarb, Black Walnut, Elcampene, Golden Seal and Sage. These are all well-known herbs to combat and prevent worms and other parasites in the bowel. This formula also helps to cleanse your bowel of unwanted waste and helps to relieve constipation.

I can't emphasise enough the importance of being alert to the dangers posed by worms and other parasites in the body. It has been estimated conservatively that SIXTY PERCENT of ALL disease stems from parasites... So put anti-parasite action high on your list of immediate action... don't put it off... while you are thinking about it these monsters are breeding at a rate that is scary!

Come on, my friend, I want to be invited to the dance you will be having on your 100th birthday.

Let's now get down to specifics...

Let's have a chat about Constipation, Diverticulitis, Crohn's Disease, and all those other jolly subjects that spoil our quality of life... so let's move on to the next chapter. I hope you are enjoying the ride!

7

The big C...
and what it means
to you!

We often hear of the 'Big C' usually applied to cancer or perhaps even computers.

But the Big C that causes more people more problems than almost any other day-to-day problem is not cancer... not computers... but...
CONSTIPATION!

I can tell you sales of laxatives adds up to BIG business... I would love a dollar from every laxative sold. I would be as rich as Bill Gates of Microsoft!

Now here is something I bet will come as a surprise to you... did you know you can go to the toilet regularly and yet still be constipated? Yes, it's true. This is because only part of the bowel contents is being emptied. Imagine a core coming out but the walls of the bowel still encrusted with faecal matter... sometimes years old! Gruesome thought, isn't it!

And matter from this encrustation seeps back into your blood supply and slowly poisons you. You will not be healthy but you won't be sick in the sense you have something your doctor can pin a label on. You will just feel under par most of the time.

The fact is, it is difficult for your doctor to help you if he cannot put a label on your symptoms. He is trained to look for symptoms, group them together and then look up a drug to get rid of them.

So I would imagine that people who cannot be diagnosed are not people the doctor really feels good about treating. Not surprising, really.

How often should you empty your bowel?

This is something that experts argue about.

I know folk who empty their bowels regularly. Or so they tell me. How often is regularly? In their case, once a week. But they do it every week, so it is regular!

According to Doctor Bernard Jensen, who was a voice in nutrition long before it was a popular subject, reckons that regular is after every meal.

The reasoning behind this is simple. When you have eaten, a signal goes to where you store your waste while it is waiting to do a bunk (this place is called the Caecum).

This then sends a message to your brain and you think to yourself, 'Oops, I had better go to the toilet'. Because you just got the message from your brain… 'Time to go, kid!'

Now then, let me make a point here. If you want a dead certain way to get yourself constipated you only have to do one thing…

Ignore the signal. Don't go. Put it off to when you are not so busy. Miss the chance for a read of the newspaper or do a bit of meditating… your only chance to get away from the kids all day… and you blew it! Guess what happens now?

You stop getting the message!

And whacko! Soon you are really bunged up. Nothing moves. You have a super inside traffic jam in your bowel.

And when you do go… you clutch the seat in agony. Passing stool is tough for you. So that makes you even less inclined to go.

This is what they call a 'vicious circle'.

But listen to this one, enough to make you rush to the toilet and sit and sit until something happens. Doctor Jensen when giving patients colonic cleansing dug out stuff that had been sitting there for… wait for it… twenty years! Twenty blooming years! Can you even begin to imagine what it looked like? I won't spoil your lunch by describing it in lurid detail… enough to say it wasn't the best view of the day.

Doctor Jensen also pointed out something so obvious we would never have thought of it ourselves. If you eat twenty pounds, kilos, of food in a day, how much should you pass out? Most of it!

And if you don't pass it out, then where is it?

Sitting there in your bowel. And guess what it is doing? Going rotten.

Depositing slime on your bowel wall. Irritating your bowel. Breeding awful bacteria that make your breath smell, give you body odour, allow you to have Candida… and if you are horribly unlucky, could be the place cancer starts.

Modern man (I include females here, of course) is very conservative when it comes to releasing bowel contents. Primitive people have huge dumps. They pass heaps more than we so-called civilised people do.

I know people who are like a miser parting with gold. They hold on to their wastes as though it were precious metal. They let it out piece by piece as though parting with pieces of eight. Anyone would think they were parting with gold coins!

I bet you know people like that, don't you? Not you and me,

of course, it is always other people, isn't it? Well, it is if you are like me!

In fact, there are people who go so far as to say that constipation can be a bodily expression of a mental state. Now I don't want angry hordes of females demanding my head on a plate but someone suggested that frigid women are also constipated... What do you think about that?

Could you picture this bloke who has just been refused sex stomping off muttering 'Yeah, and I bet you're bloody constipated too!'

Never having met a frigid woman, how would I know? But that is what some psychologist was quoted as saying. I tell you what, and think about this you He-Men out there, it has been suggested that there is no such thing as a frigid female, only clumsy inexpert men! Don't send me any death threats boys, get out and read a good book on sexual technique!

It may have been the same guy who remarked that people who hold on to things are also quite often constipated. By that he meant people who nurse their hurts and their grievances and won't let go.

Wow, I have strayed off the beaten track again... sorry... back to what is constipation...

THE OFFICIAL DEFINITION OF CONSTIPATION!

The official definition of constipation is 'difficulty in passing stool'. Now slow Uncle Fred down. He is the one who just remarked that passing a stool would be painful regardless of the state of the bowel.

When they say 'stool' they don't mean a stool, like one with three legs. They mean the stuff you dump down the toilet. Politely called waste... but you know what we call it on the golf course or in the pub. (My wife just told me not to say it out loud... but you can say it!)

Anyway, getting back to the definition of constipation... and I bet you thought I'd forgotten all about that, didn't you!

As I said, the experts say constipation is painful passing of stool... but for most other people who are not experts they call constipation when you don't go to the toilet for ages. I have people who come to me complaining of having a headache. Quite often they tell me they have not had a motion for a week, sometimes even longer...

I don't care what they call it, if you don't go to the toilet for ages and ages, then believe me, whether you are constipated or not, you have a problem.

There are people who will tell you that no matter what they do, they cannot lose that last seven kilos or so of extra weight. They have been on every diet you can imagine. They have spent a fortune... but still no luck. The reason is probably that they are carrying around seven kilos of constipated concrete in their bowel that it will take dynamite to get rid of!

You think I'm kidding? No way, it's often a fact, man!

When someone is in this situation they will have to go in for colonic irrigation. The faeces will have to be softened and then washed off the bowel wall... And the practitioner will have to have a wheelbarrow handy to cart the stuff away. It is amazing how much comes out. You would wonder how people function with all that stuff stuck in the bowel.

Of course, the truth is they don't function. They are so used to a low level of existence they think that is normal. They don't realise there is a better way, that they could feel a million dollars.

But once all that stuff is out and the bowel can function properly, the change is fantastic. The person feels like a hot air balloon that has just dumped its ballast. Up, up and away...

Our bodies are like a grand piano. They need to be well tuned to play magnificent music... Go on, how well are you tuned?

You go every day but it is still tough?

Constipation creeps up on you.

You don't realise it is happening. You go to the toilet every day but it is tough going. Your stool is getting harder and sometimes you think there must be sticks in it. Sharp, pointed sticks!

And at times you think you will have to have straining bars fitted in your toilet. These are handles you clutch as you try to force some action down there. So you strain, your face goes red, your stomach looks like it belongs to Charles Atlas… and… and you get haemorrhoids. I told you Life ain't fair. It's bad enough having constipation without getting what we used to call piles!

Can I break in here with a story?

As you know, I am a Homeopath, and one day this delightful elderly lady came back to me and complained thus 'I can't use them drops what you give me for me piles'.

'Oh, and why not?' I asked.

'Well', she said 'Me 'usband can't come 'ome three times a day to 'elp me wiv 'em'.

'What!' I exclaimed 'They go in your mouth!'

'Oh my God, they don't, do they?' she cried.

What a test of true love… Imagine coming home to try to aim drops onto your dear wife's haemorrhoids. It taught me a lesson about being more precise with directions on how to take Homeopathic medicines.

If you think getting haemorrhoids is bad then look at this, quite a few people have a heart attack! They push so hard, they strain until they go from red to blue in the face… and then, bingo!

Lots of reasons not to get constipated, eh?

Constipation causes problems in other parts of your body

When we think of problems with the bowel we think of irritable bowel, we think of Diverticulitis, we think of Crohn's

Disease… our attention is focussed on the bowel. That is natural enough.

We seldom realise that headaches, backaches, uterus problems, skin problems, liver problems, to mention just a few, come from the bowel.

Straining not only causes haemorrhoids it can also cause Hiatus Hernia, called Hiatal Hernia in some parts…

This condition is when part of the stomach is forced up into the chest cavity. It is not pleasant… one of the first signs is discomfort when you bend down. Other symptoms can be reflux… when stuff comes up that should have stayed down.

If you have a Hiatus here is a little tip for you… First thing in the morning drink a glass of lukewarm water. This is on an empty stomach, of course. Now here is the part that sets the family off into hysterics.

Jump up and down, flat-footed, with your weight on your heels.

Go on, try it, never mind those who-know-no-better making snide remarks… What this does is drag the stomach back down to where it ought to be. A bit like a goatskin wine bag being whacked down, or better, being dragged down by the liquid contents.

It takes courage to do this but it does work. You have to do it every day though, without fail.

THE INCREDIBLE LEAKY BOWEL SYNDROME…

If you don't believe your bowel can cause you BIG problems in other parts of your body, listen to the 'leaky bowel' story…

Often I see patients with problems such as eczema, asthma and arthritis… now who would connect these three with each other?

See what you think of this little plot. How often have you known a baby born with eczema? This little mite is treated with cortisone creams... and whoopee, by the time the child is about four the eczema is gone. A triumph for cortisone creams? Well, not really...

What has happened is the eczema has been suppressed...

And guess what happens now... the child develops asthma.

You must have noticed this strange thing, haven't you. The curious thing is the asthma is seen as a totally new problem. We have fixed the eczema, now the child has developed asthma... very inconsiderately, I may add.

But the asthma is the eczema in a new disguise.

Ask someone whose child has baby eczema if there is any asthma in the family history. All too often there is.

The cause of the asthma, the eczema and often arthritis is what is called a leaky bowel.

This doesn't mean your bowel is leaking goo all over the place. No, what is happening is the bowel is letting things into the body it shouldn't. The problem starts with poor digestion. You will find these kids often had colic as babies... and still do have problems.

Gather round, you will be the expert in no time at all. You will be the life and soul of the party with your unusual knowledge... to continue... The digestive system does not break down all the protein properly. That would not be such a problem if it all passed out of the system.

But with these people it doesn't.

Some of it goes through this leaky bowel wall into the bloodstream. Now guess what your body does when this happens?

You give up? OK. I will tell you.

It shoots out inflammatories.

This is because your body recognises the protein particles as viruses, because that is what they are made from. Your body tries to deal with viruses by incinerating them. The big burn. That is why you get fever when you are sick...

But here is a problem. I know you have spotted it.

There are no viruses to burn up. The fires are all going mad, but no victims to burn. So what does your body do with all these inflammatories floating about? It sends them up, out and away through the skin…

In the form of eczema.

Now let's get right into this, folks. You are an intelligent person or you wouldn't be my friend and be reading this book… when you daub cortisone cream on the inflamed skin what are you doing for the cause of the problem?

You hit it in one. Yes, you are right…

Absolutely nothing!

And that's the real problem. That is why the child gets asthma and is sentenced to puffers and all that jazz for the rest of its life.

So what is really needed is not cortisone cream but to have the cause of the problem fixed… and you are about to learn how to do just that.

OK, first up let's look at digestion.

This is a problem because proteins are not being broken down properly and we need to do something about it. So the first thing to do is to give the child help in this department. That is done by giving a digestive enzyme. The best is a vegetable enzyme because this works in all kinds of stomachs. It is also usually in a capsule which can be opened and the contents sprinkled on the coco-pops or whatever the child has for breakfast.

So now we have got the protein broken down properly, so what's next.

Well, now we deal with the bowel wall. As I said, this child's bowel wall is letting things in it shouldn't. This means we have to strengthen it.

Makes sense? Of course!

And we can do that with Vitamin A. Vitamin A helps to strengthen all the mucous membranes in the body. Mucous membranes are linings… your bowel wall, your throat, stomach… anywhere and everywhere. Vitamin A is also top for helping overcome infection.

But wait a cotton-pickin' minute… Vitamin A is poisonous, isn't it? It causes problems for unborn babies and heaven knows what else, doesn't it?

In a word, NO.

It can cause problems in large amounts given over a long period of time. For generations the standard amount in one tablet was 10,000 i.u. Over all those years there was never any reports of anyone being hurt by these amounts. And let me tell you, there were lots of people taking two and three capsules or tablets every day.

Then there was a reported case of a mother having a baby that was malformed and this was put down to the fact the mother had been taking Vitamin A. Shock, horror, gasp! Let's ban it. This seems to always be the first thought that comes into the bureaucratic mind.

However, common sense and expert opinion prevailed. As one lady doctor pointed out, far more babies are born with birth defects from lack of Vitamin A than were ever born with birth defects because of it. Cleft palate has been associated with a lack of Vitamin A in the mother… And rickets in the slums of London were widespread because of lack of Vitamin A in those poor children.

So you can safely give the child Vitamin A in the standard dose, which is 5,000 i.u. or 2,000 i.u. With a small child it is probably best to give Vitamin A in Micel form. This is liquid and is much easier to give to a child who has a problem swallowing capsules or tablets.

To digress, which is most unusual for me, this business of bureaucratic banning of substances. It amazes me how the authorities, especially the medical lobby, demand double blind, cross over, random, research costing millions to approve anything. The fact that two million people report good effect from a herb is not good enough.

However (and here is something for you to think about), it takes only one episode of something going wrong for them to want to ban the whole box and dice. These are the people who say with a perfectly straight face that only complicated tests, the so-called scientific method, is good enough. This is only to prove it is effective. Any story is good enough for them to want to ban something.

Always for the public good, of course!

Mind you, all that testing didn't stop Thalidomide, did it? And other drugs that caused death and destruction. If you have a look at the Physician's Desk book on medical drugs you will be surprised to find that quite often the benefits of the drug take up the least space. Most of the space is taken up with contraindications and warnings of the side-effects.

Oh, enough of that.

Back to the leaky bowel.

Here is something you need to know. You may wonder why some people have a leaky bowel in the first place. Well, the antibiotics that have been given can be a cause of the leaky bowel. This is because they actually encourage the overpopulation of the bowel with harmful bacteria. They do this because antibiotics are like gangsters spraying everything in sight with bullets. They kill the good as well as the bad. When the slaughter is over and you stop the antibiotics, the bad bacteria tend to come back in droves.

These create lots of poisonous wastes… think about it!

We do anything to relieve pain, and no wonder. However, like everything else, there is a price to pay. A lot of the non-steroid anti-inflammatory drugs also cause the bowel to become permeable. That is, it now lets things through that it didn't do before.

No, you don't have to live in a monastery or retire to a cave in Tibet. Read on and all will be revealed...

We have done something about the digestion, we have done something to strengthen the bowel wall... now we must buck up the bowel itself. We do this by giving the child a good quality good–guy bacterial mix to make sure the bowel is crowded with bacteria that are working for the child and not against it. You can get specially formulated acidophilus compounds for kids.

This is particularly true if the poor child has been loaded up with antibiotics in a futile bid to prevent 'infection' from the eczema.

Now our next job is to attack the inflammatories that are cruising around looking for the non-existent viruses. The best way to do this is to give Evening Primrose Oil. If the child is small then you can get this in Micel form too... Give it in the fruit juice.

Zinc is essential for helping healing. And that is what we are about, healing the lesions of eczema. Take note that on most bottles of zinc the directions are completely wrong. That's what I said, wrong!

They often say 'take one tablet three times a day with food'.

Problem here is that zinc binds with certain elements common in food and that makes it unavailable to the body. So you have been wasting your money all this time. Tell that to Auntie Maude, get one in!

The best time to take zinc is one tablet just before bed or first thing in the morning, on an empty stomach.

To relieve the misery of the itching, and the sad sight of a small child scratching away, use a herbal cream. I am torn apart when I see small children with their hands all bandaged up and tied to the bed so they cannot scratch. This is a form of torture worthy of the Spanish Inquisition.

A good Homeopath can make up a mixture to relieve the

itching for you as well as recommending a gentle, but effective, herbal ointment.

It is important to make sure the child has a healthy bowel movement every day. Do not use a laxative… give the child a good diet.

On this point, I am often astonished when a mother tells me her child will not eat a good diet. Here is a two-year-old child dictating to her mother what she will and won't eat.

I ask the mother 'Who is in charge of the child?' Does she honestly believe that a child of two years of age can make sensible decisions about what is good for it. Surely it is her responsibility to take charge here.

With my own three children, if they refused to eat something or refused to eat at all out of awkwardness, I went along with it. I just didn't worry whether they ate it or not. Because healthy children will eventually eat what is put in front of them. Hunger is a great appetite stimulator.

I tell the young Mum to put the food in front of the child. Ignore the tantrums and wait. Eventually the child will eat. If you have a very difficult child you may have to enlist the services of a health professional to help you.

Whichever way it goes, a healthy child depends on a healthy diet and it is the parents' responsibility and not the child's. OK, so there will be some of you ready to throw the dish of food at me… I understand that.

But no matter what, a little child is not capable of making decisions that affect its quality of life… and diet does affect that child's quality of life. Believe me, I am not being critical or nasty. Think about it!

GETTING BACK TO CONSTIPATION…

Guess what has to be one of the most common of human complaints?

Got to be headaches. People have headaches all the time, some most of the time, some now and again… but always it is headaches.

They have migraine headaches, sick headaches, throbbing headaches, dull headaches, headaches at the back of the head, at the front, at the sides, all over… headaches, headaches, headaches!

Headaches come from tension, they come from too much caffeine, from too little caffeine (in some forms of migraine), from constriction of the blood vessels, from a liver that is complaining bitterly and from constipation.

Constipation causes quite a lot of headaches. The vague, 'I don't feel well but I don't know what's wrong' kind of headaches.

And no blooming wonder.

All that waste matter clogging everything up. Waste getting back into the bloodstream and trekking all over the place. No wonder people get headaches and don't feel well. There used to be an advertisement years ago and the headline was great. It went 'Do you feel one degree under?' And it hit a button with most people, because so many people feel at least one degree under par.

Another reason for doing something about your bowel…

Your bowel needs oxygen…

Go on, it doesn't breathe so why would it need oxygen?

Here is something for you to chew on. As you know, humans are bulldozing the rain forests at an alarming rate. But what do not seem to occur to anyone is these are the lungs of the planet Earth. And we are destroying them willy-nilly.

And for what?

To provide very poor grazing land for cattle. And where are the cattle destined to end up? In hamburgers. They are needed to feed our insatiable appetite for hamburgers.

Is that a fair swap? Oxygen for dead meat? Life for death?

Because that is what we are doing.

Trees convert our waste, carbon dioxide, into life-giving oxygen. Less trees equals less oxygen. Less oxygen less energy. Less oxygen more cancer. Cancer cells don't like oxygen. No wonder cancer is on the march in our world today.

Your cells need oxygen for energy, to burn up wastes… reduced oxygen spells big problems down the line for humanity.

This world of ours is not going to end in a spectacular way with flames, noise, hurricanes of fire… The four horsemen will creep into town, as I have said before. Quietly they will encourage us to keep on doing what we are doing… and we will choke ourselves to death. First we choke the rivers, we empty the seas, we degrade the soil, we poison the air… and one day we wake up and are faced with world-wide famine, world-wide epidemic diseases that no antibiotic can stem…

It is interesting to note that all previous civilisations thought they were immortal. The Sumerians, the Assyrians, the Babylonians, the Greeks, the Romans, the Mayans… all those that have gone before and have disappeared.

And we are going the same way.

Our much vaunted technological wonderland cannot survive our destruction of the planet. We are not that smart.

You can make a difference.

You can make a difference by what you buy in the supermarket. No more meat, no more dairy… demand soy products that are not hybrids bred to resist pesticides… do not contribute to the wastage of our resources.

And start by becoming amazingly healthy… and health starts in your bowel.

Because of the decreasing oxygen supply I supplement with oxygen every day. And girls, here is some exciting news…

Oxygen could be one way to reduce weight. It has been suggested that lack of oxygen can cause an increase of fluid round the cell. So taking oxygen as a supplement can reduce this fluid, increase energy and help you to get rid of unwanted kilos.

Tell you what, looking after your bowel has never been so vital for good health as it is today.

MUCOUS THE GLUE THAT KILLS!

Mucous under control is necessary for the linings of your body. It is also used as a defensive weapon to flush away things irritating the linings in your body.

Just as oil is necessary for the quiet, smooth running of your car. But just imagine how your car feels when the cylinders are clogged up with old oil. This causes incredible drag on the cylinders making it hard for them to push up and down. Your car struggles to get up any speed and you can forget about going up hills!

It is the same with your body.

Excess mucous slows everything down. Makes you spend a lot more energy just to perform every day actions.

Once I was talking to a pathologist who spent most of his day cutting up dead bodies doing autopsies. He told me he was astounded at the amount of mucous in most of these corpses. It was everywhere! In the pelvic cavity, around the organs, clogging up the systems…

'How people operated under these conditions beats me' was his opinion. A bit like the heart surgeon who complained that when he was doing by-pass surgery and cut an artery, all he could smell was rancidity.

That should tell you something.

What it tells you, for those of you who are like me and have to have things explained to them, is that your diet needs attention.

Now one of the big problems with diet is we work very hard to get enough money to afford a lousy diet. A lot of poor people have lousy diets, but theirs tends to be lots of rubbish snacks, huge amounts of cordials and cola drinks, chips and stuff like that.

Wealthier people have a lousy diet of big steaks, rich sauces with lots of cream. They can afford delicious pastries and handmade chocolate biscuits... The sort of diet we poorer people do our best to copy!

And boy, does it do us in!

I told you earlier how they used to make wallpaper paste from white flour and water... how it makes mucous like glue that sticks on your bowel wall. And meat, dairy products, white flour pasta, cakes and biscuits all do the same. You could call these gummie foods. They gum up the works with mucous.

Bad bacteria love mucous. To them it is the promised land. They dig in and make themselves at home. They also invite all the friends and relatives in too... and they have billions of them (and you complain about your relatives!). They burrow in there and set up house. One of their guests is a creature you would rather not know. Cancer! Cancer of the bowel starts with excessive mucous coating the bowel wall and providing a free lodging for all sorts of undesirables.

Excessive mucous also causes the bowel to clog up and constipation is only one of the many problems we are now faced with. Mucous was designed by Nature to be an occasional thing. It was to help keep things moving along... but excessive mucous does just the opposite. It goes off!

When it goes off it breeds germs. It becomes toxic, and that means poisonous. And all because we find it so hard to change our eating habits.

So out with meat, out with dairy, out with sugary things... In with plenty of vegetables, in with foods like chickpeas, beans, lentils. In with plenty of salads and in with more recipe books featuring food to be eaten in its natural state.

It is not a joke or an over-simplification to say that what you eat today walks and talks tomorrow. When you look in your mirror you are looking at the result of all the choices you have made over your lifetime.

If you have chosen unwisely then you may not like what you are looking at or what you are feeling like either!

If you would like to see a bright, happy, healthy face looking at you… then you gotta change what you have been doing. If you keep on doing what you have always been doing you will get what you have always got. This is so obvious none of us even suspect it! We keep on keeping on and wonder why happiness is so elusive.

Get hold of this little thought. I suspect that many relationships fail because of diet! Yes, that's what I said, diet.

Not because the couple argue about what to have for tea or not to have. Oh no, it goes deeper… bad food makes for bad manners.

What I really mean is if the diet is wrong, if a person's body is clogged up with mucous, if they are constipated, then how on earth can they be a joy to live with?

The truth is they are not! And there's the rub as Will Shakespeare once remarked. Someone who is constipated is seldom the life and soul of the party. Someone who has a liver doing a number on them is an irritable, bad tempered, fly-off-the-handle at anything sort of person… Definitely not a source of joy and laughter.

A woman who is constipated could have a bowel pressing on her uterus… with disastrous results on happiness. She could have permanent headaches (bang goes sex… I mean non-bang goes sex). How can a relationship survive?

I bet very few marriage counsellors ask about diet…

If things aren't going too well… it might be a good idea to have a look at what you are having for a meal tonight. It just could be what you eat is destroying not only your health but love and happiness too.

So next time you are visiting some people and they play the game of shooting each other down, sniping away, telling secrets to everyone… do a little investigating. Watch what they put in their mouths… it could be a clue to what is coming out!

Constipation is very important but there are other things too!

Let me tell you a little story. It is quite true and makes a point. It won't take long and I bet you may even recognise the characters.

I used to know a couple who lived in a nice house, in a nice suburb… but behind that nice front door was a nice suburban hell on earth. These little boxes of devilry are more common than we would like to think. It is really quite strange how two people in a house can spend most of their waking hours trying their best to do the other one in.

When you visit these people you can often feel the tension in the air… Anyway, getting back to this particular couple… They were both professional people but the wife held a higher position and earned more money than the man… I tell you this to give you a bit of background information.

I was there for the first time and went to the bathroom (not being at all constipated). I opened the door and stood there amazed. The floor was full of old toothpaste boxes, soap wrappers and empty tampon boxes… an absolutely unbelievable mess. It was almost like visiting the local garbage dump.

They asked me if I would like a cup of green tea and I followed the wife into the kitchen. I declined the kind offer when I saw the pile of dirty dishes, stale food encrusted pans, and plates half full of ancient meals. It was a real shock to the system.

To sit down you had to clear piles of old newspapers, magazines, chocolate wrappers… and heaven knows what else before you could clear a place to park your bum.

Here we had two well-educated professional people living in what could only be described as a garbage dump.

So what was going on?

Well, my friend, the answer will probably not surprise you as you must have seen human pride, stubbornness and unreason in full bore before...

The problem was the husband was into job demarcation. He believed that everything that came under the heading of 'housework' was a woman's job and he wanted no part of it. He was the 'provider'.

His wife pointed out that she was a working wife with a more responsible job than his and as far as 'providing' was concerned, she earned more than he did. So why should she do anything under the label 'housework' simply because she was a woman.

So neither of them would do anything under the heading of housework... and the house-that-was-a-garbage-dump was the result.

I heard they eventually got divorced, which was not surprising. The Department of Health had been notified of the cockroaches, mice and so on that invaded the place and they raised a stink too.

Now let me ask you a question. Do you think that simply emptying their garbage bin would have done anything to clear up the mess in the house?

Well, of course not.

And it is the same with your bowel. Cleaning out the waste in the bowel is very important... But equally important is making sure that all the garbage in your cells, tissues, organs also clean out their accumulated garbage.

When you think about it, there are a lot of people just like that house. On the outside it seemed fine. A neat garden, nicely painted... but inside it was a tip. The outside of the house was deceiving. It gave no clues to the chaos inside. But imagine how many people there are who look fine on the outside. You would never guess looking at them the problems going on inside their bodies. Their tissues, organs and cells are like the inside of that house. Clogged up with garbage. And even going to the toilet every day is not enough. It is like emptying the garbage bin at that house.

Emptying the house garbage bin was not enough. It did nothing for the rubbish built up inside. Same with us, going to the toilet is not enough. We must do something about the hidden garbage piled up inside.

This is why you must seriously consider going on a detoxification programme. Oh, why there! A detox what programme?

Sounds difficult, doesn't it? When we think of detox we think of men in plastic suits with perspex helmets and gas masks… all very serious stuff.

However, to detox your body is not difficult. In fact it is quite simple, easy and anyone can do it…

The trick is to get yourself a programme already made up. I like programmes that are already made up for me because that means someone else has done the thinking instead of me having to do it.

Like most people I find making lots of decisions very painful. In fact, it gives me a headache and a feeling of desperation in my stomach!

In Australia I recommend the QuickCleanse programme to all my patients, friends and anyone else who can put up with me when I get on my bandwagon of health.

This is a great programme that covers all the bases. It has been well thought out and best of all it works.

I AM GREAT AND THE LAST THING I NEED IS DETOXIFYING!

Wow! Meet superman or superwoman…

Anyone who seriously believes they are as pure as driven snow is in a happy, but dangerous state of delusion. Consider the facts my friend. We live in a world that has become a toxic jungle.

You get emissions from carpets, from chemicals in your kitchen and laundry cupboard, from the water out of the tap. You get them from car exhausts, from factory emissions (yes, they still do send out toxic wastes), from pesticides, herbicides, fungicides, fertilizers, industrial solvents, heavy metals… the list is a chemical horror story, believe me.

Now if you are one of Life's innocents and have not heard the news then listen to this little gem. It has been discovered that DDT (banned in some countries but not all) sprayed in Africa is finally found… and get this, in the fat of Polar Bears in the snowy wastes of Antarctica.

So what makes anyone believe it doesn't get into their body? And what would convince any thinking person that all the other stuff doesn't end up inside us?

I AM FINE… I DRINK TANK WATER AND GROW MY OWN VEGETABLES

Congratulations. Full marks for effort. I admire you and applaud what you are trying to do… but… but… consider this…

In this modern world, especially in Australia, when we build a house we spray the area where the house is going to be built. Spray is not always the correct word. Deluge with chemicals, may be a better description. This is to deter, wipe out, do-in the white ant menace.

After soaking the site in chemicals we lay a plastic sheet on it and pour the concrete. And kid ourselves that none of that chemical warfare can affect us. After all, it is the white ants we are after, isn't it?

But as time goes by these chemicals can leach into the garden… and into our vegetable plot. So our lovely, home-grown, organic vegetables can be absorbing toxic chemicals.

I told you it was a cruel world and you didn't want to believe me…

Drinking rainwater from a tank sounds innocent and pure. It does, doesn't it? People tell me with a virtuous air that they only drink tank water.

Oh, I hate to do this to you, but here is some more bad news. Gosh, how I hate to be a party-pooper, but someone has to do it…

Consider this about rainwater. At one time it was the loveliest, softest, most gentle of waters. Recommended for washing one's hair, a beautiful complexion and almost anything else you can think of.

Nowadays rain water kills trees. It causes curtains to rot in the wash.

The rain brings down the chemicals we have sent up there. These land on the roof of our house and join the bird droppings, the lead from the petrol fumes, chemicals from your local friendly factories and so on…

And this all goes into your rainwater tank. And in that tank there is bound to be rotting debris from your house gutters.

Sorry to disillusion you, but even people who drink their water from a water tank would be well advised to join all the other wise people who only drink water that has been through a filter.

Now do you believe me when I say everyone should complete a detox programme at least every six months?

It is just like cleaning the rooms up in that awful house I told you about and getting the garbage out there into the garbage bin.

This way the garbage from the house goes into the bin. The bin gets emptied regularly and the house stays nice and clean… same with your body. Keep the rubbish coming out of the cells and into the 'garbage bin' of the bowel and lymphatics and good health is the result.

So let us now chat about the various problems people have because of a bad bowel, constipation and a body sludging up with unwanted elements that would be better out than in.

Let us go hand in hand into the next chapter…

8

I feel awful today… just like I did yesterday!

When I was a child we used to describe some people's lives as 'Come Day, Go Day, God Send Sunday'… a monotonous daily round relieved only by doing nothing on Sunday.

For far too many people even Sunday brings little relief from their bowel problems. Wind, gas, bloating, indigestion, Irritable Bowel, colitis, Diverticulitis, Crohn's Disease… the list makes you realise how fragile our grasp on Life really is. When Billy Shakespeare wrote about all the ills that flesh is heir to, he knew a thing or two back then!

So let's see what we can do to relieve these problems.

What alternatives are there to an endless roundabout of antacids, stomach calming drugs, laxatives and so on and so on. Despite all these patent over-the-counter or prescribed medications, little seems to change. Sending Sunday is not working…

FIRST, LET US TALK ABOUT GAS, WIND, BLOATING…

Now you may think these are not big problems… but I hate to say this to a nice person like I know you are, but you are wrong.

These can be big problems.

I have heard of people who after a meal have to clutch the seat of their chair with both hands. They hold on grimly because they know if they let go they will whizz round the room like a newly released balloon.

Why, my friend, there are people who when showing friends their prize roses will not bend down to smell them. This in case they blow their friends away!

What kind of life is that?

People are rushed to the doctor with all the symptoms of a heart attack. Pains in the chest, a pain going down the left arm… and all caused by a colon distended by gas.

The answer to too much gas is better digestion… and improving the state of your bowel. Bad bacteria in your bowel release histamine… and guess what histamine does… it causes allergies. And it causes gas!

Another often unrecognised cause of gas is the ever-present Candida Albicans… this is a yeast overgrowth in the bowel. If you are suffering from Candida and have tried 'everything' here's a couple I bet you have never tried. In fact, most people have never heard of them. The first is Lactoferrin, a potent destroyer of Candida. You get this in Australia as LactoMax. In other countries check with your local Health Food store.

The other thing to use as well as the LactoMax (Lactoferrin) is Colloidal Silver. These two will do a tremendous job for you and you will feel the best you have felt for years!

If you are socially unacceptable because you are sounding sulphurous trumpet calls with your gas then you really must take a course of lactoacidophillus, Bulgaricas and Bifida. Only get a good brand and take it, do it on a regular basis. Like good guys everywhere, your bowel good-guys bacteria are constantly being shoved around by the bad ones.

And remember, the bad bacteria produce Hydrogen Sulphide that smells just like a truckload of rotten eggs. That's not what you want in your bowel, do you? Of course not!

Been reducing fluid lately?

Have you been on a diet and been taking fluid tablets? Lots of people pop these like lollies in an attempt to get rid of excess fluid. One problem with this is that with the fluid you can also flush-out sodium and potassium and upset the whole cellular balance. Low sodium can also cause flatulence… a posh word for gas.

Taking antacid tablets, and some people chew these as though they were Lifesavers, can cause gas. This is because these upset the natural balance of your digestion. If you do not digest protein properly you will get gas, among other things.

Here comes the guy with the shattering bad news again…

Lots of people take calcium as a supplement. And for most people this can be a good idea. But it depends on which one.

Elderly people come and ask for dolomite. This is because it is the cheapest. They get a bit taken aback when I ask them if it is for their DOG.

Because I reckon only dogs with their high acid stomachs can digest the stuff. Dolomite gets its name from the Dolomite Mountains in Italy.

And that is what dolomite is, ground up calcium carbonate… better known to us all as chalk. The stuff teachers used to use before white boards and computers. And chalk this up, this kind of calcium can cause gas!

It really is not fair… is it?

And to really rub it in, the chlorine in your drinking water and in your local swimming pool can also cause you to get gas. Now that really is not fair. I mean, drinking water and swimming pools. What will they find out next?

Wind, gas (call it what you will) is an embarrassment. It is no fun if you are known as the 'wind maker'. So it is important to know the foods that cause a lot of people to take off like a rocket.

Cabbages are well known as gas producers, as are Brussels sprouts and any other member of the sulphur-rich cabbage family. As any child will tell you, one of the reasons they hate broccoli is because it is a potent gas producer. Some say with the right technology we could run our cars on broccoli! For some people cauliflower can be a problem. And you people keen to keep vampires at bay by eating loads of cloves of garlic… that's why you are keeping the vampires away, it's the gas you are putting out!

Beans are legendary stuff when it comes to gas. Most of the world's champions at farting eat buckets of beans. One reason for the bean being such a powerful gas builder is people don't soak them overnight before cooking them. The trick is to soak them overnight, drain off the water and then cook them in fresh water. This reduces their gas producing ability quite a lot.

Have you heard of food combining?

There is a lot of evidence to suggest that combining certain food groups will give you mucho gasso. Take a look at one of the world's favourite foods, the hamburger.

Now if ever a food was designed to do us all in, it is the hamburger. Listen for just a moment, I know you probably love them… but this is science talking.

Combining protein with carbohydrates is a dead certain way to get a bucket load of gas. And what do we have in a hamburger? Meat, which is protein, neatly packaged in a bun, which is carbohydrate.

It gets worse!

Fat and fried foods are guaranteed gas producers. And your friendly hamburger is a concentrated fat bomb.

Talk about food combining! Combine the meat, the bread and the fat and what do you have? A gas time bomb! Waiting to give you gas, indigestion and irritation to your bowel. Would you consider a hamburger a health food? Not unless you were selling them!

Can you grasp how important your bowel digestion and elimination are to your total health?

They are VITAL!

You may need to take digestive enzymes for a while to help your digestive organs break down food more effectively. Watch what you eat. As we age, foods we could once digest, now give us problems. Meat, fried foods, dairy… these are a few to think about.

Lack of fibre causes a lot of problems.

Not only gas, but Irritable Bowel, colitis, Diverticulitis…

But please, don't rush out and buy a kilo of unprocessed wheat bran. This is often far too rough for people with bowel problems. And there is the other thought, quite a lot of people are allergic to wheat! You could be one of them.

The best fibres are substances such as oat bran, linseed, psyllium husks and slippery elm bark. In Australia, as I have already remarked, you can get all these in one formula from your health food shop. The brand I take every day is called QuickFibre Plus. I recommend this to my patients and I can confidently tell you I have had only good reports about the results.

LET US TALK ABOUT IRRITABLE BOWEL…

Irritable Bowel must be one of the most fashionable health problems in the western world. So many people suffer from this condition.

Irritable Bowel has been known as 'Mucous Colitis' or as a 'Spastic Bowel'. With the modern day love of acronyms it is often called IBS. Don't you just hate acronyms? I do. I try to read something and because I am not 'in the know' I do not recognise these letters. Even Kentucky Fried Chicken call themselves KFC. I bet Colonel Sanders turned rapidly in his grave when he got that message!

Enough of my petty dislikes, back to Irritable Bowel.

What causes it, anyway?

Wheat allergy is a common and often undetected cause. It is a good idea to keep a diet diary. Enter down everything, and I mean everything, that you put in your mouth.

It is easy to miss things when doing this. I had a friend with a problem… he had a gut like the prow of a sailing ship. Well, not like the ship exactly, more like the sail when full of wind. He did a diet diary… but missed out the six packs of beers he drank every night. So be sure to write down every single thing.

Also, record when you have attacks of Irritable Bowel. If you are unlucky enough to have it all the time, record the times when it is more troublesome than usual. See if you can see a connection between what you are eating or drinking with the onset of pain.

Look, I don't want to drive you mad by harping on about bowel bacteria… but… the good bacteria keep you warm by heating up the body… they provide Vitamin K so your blood can clot. I could go on for hours about these wonderful little critters. Thankfully, I won't! But just to let you know that what they call 'dysbiosis' or bowel bacteria out of whack can be a cause of Irritable Bowel Syndrome. So there!

Not only has the indiscriminate handing out of antibiotics been responsible for breeding a new race of SuperBugs, it has also caused a lot of people to get Irritable Bowel. I don't have to tell you of all people, that this is because antibiotics kill the good as well as the bad.

By the way, here is something else to drop in at a cocktail party when the conversation flags a bit. Did you realise that the word antibiotic means 'anti life'? Something to think about, eh?

INTOLERANCE! THE CURSE OF THE MODERN WORLD!

Whenever you pick up the newspaper or switch on the news on the television… most of the murders, gang wars, national and international bloodshed are caused by intolerance.

Certain religious groups think that God gave them a monopoly and so are intolerant of the other groups who also think God gave them the monopoly. And the other groups hate them with the same enthusiasm.

Racial hatred is alive and well and a lot of people are just the opposite because of it… dead and definitely not well. One of the most disgusting expressions I have ever heard is 'Ethnic Cleansing', a phrase that simply means murderous genocide. Slaughtering people for no other reason than they do not belong to the same ethnic group.

I am surprised that Hitler and the Nazis did not coin this one… I bet Hitler is kicking himself wherever he may be. What a nice clean way to describe something so dreadful!

But back to you, my friend, and your Irritable Bowel.

Your bowel is a very intolerant place.

Intolerance has been described as when a sinner turns into a saint. Like the guy who stops smoking and is incredibly intolerant of smokers. Or like someone I once knew who cheated on his wife almost from the first day they were married. He became a born-again married saint when he was too old and ugly to keep on keeping on… and became very vocal about men who cheated on their wives.

Our bowels are even more intolerant. They are just about the most intolerant place on this planet.

Just take a look at some of the things bowels take an instant and abiding dislike to… Wheat, as I just remarked. The problem here is that wheat is part of the deal in almost everything you buy in a packet.

Too much fructose. This is fruit sugar but now it comes neatly packaged from corn. Corn syrup is in lots of ice-creams, syrups, cakes, lollies or candy as some folk say, and in lots of places where sugar, sucrose, was used. This is because corn syrup is sweeter than honey, as the song says, and a lot cheaper to produce. Powerful reasons to use corn syrup!

But this can cause your bowel to become intolerant of fructose.

And take note of this, sucrose or cane sugar, breaks down to glucose… and… and fructose in your body. So you can see how some people can easily become intolerant of fructose. Not everybody, mind, just some people.

A very common cause of Irritable Bowel is lactose. This is milk sugar. You are going to hate me for this… but dairy is not good for you.

What? Are you crazy? Dairy not good for me!

This is like throwing bricks at someone's mother. I mean, how can anyone say that dairy is bad for anyone. I mean to say guys, don't you listen to the ads?

You have to hand it to the people who promote dairy. In times gone by I am sure I would have been burned at the stake for saying dairy is bad for anyone. When I go out to talk to community groups I am always attacked in question time by the dairy people in the audience. I don't blame them at all. Making comments about dairy is threatening to their livelihood. When I tell a patient to get off dairy they always cry 'But where will I get my calcium?'

We have been well brainwashed to believe that we need cow's milk to get enough calcium. Otherwise we will end up a puddle on the floor with no bones at all. We see pictures of people hobbling about because of Osteoporosis… And we don't want that to happen to us, no way!

But let us give a little unemotional thought to this, eh? Why not? Remember, it is difficult to think clearly or to discriminate when the emotions are running away like an avalanche down a mountain. So let's not get emotional about milk. Promise?

Humans are the only species to drink milk after being weaned. And the only species dumb enough to drink the milk of a totally difference species from their own. Milk designed to nurture and help grow a creature the size of a cow, for heavens sake. Compare a human being to a cow!

Nature never ever intended cow's milk for humans. A lot of people look at me in astonishment when I tell them Nature intended cow's milk for cows! Advertising is what myths and legends are made from.

Getting back to the cry 'Where will I get my calcium from?'

My reply is brutal. Simple. To the point.

'Ask the elephant. His bones are a damn sight stronger than yours. Or ask the tiger, the lion, the wild beast or any other of nature's animal kingdom.' It is true, isn't it? We are the only animal labouring under the belief that we need the milk of another species to survive. You have to wonder how the millions of people on this planet who never see milk survive… but they do…

But Nature gets her own back. Play now, pay later was known to Mother Nature long before the discount stores used it in their advertising. Heaps of people are intolerant of milk and milk products. In fact, there are loads of people wandering around complaining about their sinuses… but what they are really showing is milk intolerance.

Your tremendously intolerant bowel responds by becoming irritated, very irritated indeed. And we call it Irritable Bowel.

I am different from everybody else.

Well of course you are. And in more ways than you probably realise.

People's bowels develop their own particular and peculiar intolerances. One person will find they cannot tolerate wheat bran, another will discover that chocolate brings on an attack. One man informed me that lettuce in salad gave him a problem… and I believe him!

Watch out in your own case. You may find that something out of the ordinary is the cause of your problem. However, I must say that in most cases I find that by asking people one question I can often spot the cause of the problem.

This question is 'What do you like eating most of all?' Bread lovers often have an intolerance to wheat and other grains. Milk lovers often have lactose intolerance. So just have a look at what you love to eat and check out if there is a connection.

A very common cause of Irritable Bowel is a shortage of digestive enyzmes. I mentioned this before to you. OK, so why tell you again and again. The reason is we forget. We need reminding all the time. Just like we need reminding to pick up the dry cleaning after work… No-one is perfect, so don't worry about it.

Do you remember how I went on about Vitamin C NOT causing kidney stones? Of course you do, this was exploding a medical myth. You may be surprised to learn that one of the major causes of kidney stones is an Irritable Bowel.

That seems rather strange. How can something going on in your bowel affect your kidneys? Well, of course it can. I told you how a poorly functioning colon could cause all sorts of health problems from period pain in women to backache in anybody. You remember?

What happens is that because of excessive acidity the calcium is not absorbed so well in the bowel. Here is another little gem for you to drop in at your local meeting… Only ten percent of minerals you take in are actually absorbed. So if you gobble down a calcium supplement of 1,000 milligram you will be lucky to get 100 mg from it.

Ah, but if you have an Irritable Bowel you get even more punishment. The calcium tends to stay in solution so more calcium now has to be eliminated by the kidneys… more calcium in the kidneys, more chance of stones. No wonder my Dad told me Life was not fair. He was dead right!

But there is a bright side to all this.

You are probably cursing that you need calcium to prevent osteoporosis and here am I telling you that an Irritable Bowel could cause you to get them.

Here is something to surprise you. Taking calcium supplements will stop you getting kidney stones.

How can that be? You ask and quite rightly.

The reason is when you take a calcium supplement, the large amount neutralises the acid and improves absorption. It is a mixed-up old world, ain't it? More means less.

Talking about calcium supplements to keep your bones good and strong… look out for the most absorbable kinds of calcium. Calcium citrate is a very absorbable kind of calcium. Calcium carbonate, chalk, is not.

In the old days they used to say that the ratio of calcium to magnesium was two to one. Two of calcium to one of magnesium. However, these days experts are suggesting that we have underrated magnesium. The ratio should be at least one to one. There is a lot of evidence to suggest that magnesium is the major factor in bone regeneration… Just thought I'd throw that in for you.

I reckon one of the major concerns with Irritable Bowel Syndrome is the sufferer can have poor food absorption. This means they suffer from malnutrition, and often don't even realise it. The bowel doesn't do its job. It can't do its job. So even the best food is not absorbed.

The food is not broken down properly and so goes into the bowel in a less than perfect state to be absorbed. Even worse, it sits there. And it doesn't sit there quietly. It ferments. And fermentation produces gas, among other things. Other things? Like what?

Like more bad bacteria. Like more irritation for the bowel wall. Like making the problem even worse. Talk about a vicious circle. This is really vicious.

Any arthritis in your family?

You remember how I told you that a leaky gut could be a cause of arthritis, eczema and asthma? Well here is something interesting for you to think about. There appears to be a link between Irritable Bowel and arthritis, as you would expect given the leaky bowel connection. I wouldn't be surprised to find that people with Irritable Bowel also have some connections with eczema and or asthma too.

But what is encouraging is that if you improve the Irritable Bowel, you are bound to make it less leaky and this must improve the other conditions. So you could find that by taking steps to ease your Irritable Bowel Syndrome you could be easing the pain of your arthritis, if you have any, at the same time.

Perhaps Life is a little fairer than we thought! If you are on medical drugs of any kind it might be an idea to have a chat with your doctor in case there is anything in any of them which influences bowel health. It may be one of them could have something in it that irritates your bowel. I remarked how intolerant bowels are and how easily irritated… a bit like Uncle Fred!

So what are we going to do about it? Well, we have been all through Irritable Bowel. It is more complicated than we realised at first, isn't it? But no matter what has caused us to have the problem what we want to know now is what can be done about it.

The sooner we get a programme going to ease the problem and eventually solve it, the better. What do you say?

OK. Then the first place to start in my opinion is two-fold. Diet and digestion. D and D.

You need gentle fibre. Notice I said 'gentle' fibre. You don't need the rough stuff that you can get from unprocessed wheat bran. Get psyllium husks, slippery elm bark, linseed, oat bran. You can buy all these separately and mix up your own. However, here in Australia I prefer to use a product called QuickFibre Plus that has them all in and is flavoured too.

I recommend people add fibre to their diets whether they have an Irritable Bowel or not. Prevention is definitely the wise person's choice. Six dangerous words are 'Maybe It Won't Happen To Me'. The odds are that it will!

And a low-fibre diet can cause a lot of other bowel problems. One of the most common being Diverticulitis. No point in getting a problem if you know how NOT to get it, is there?

So avoid the gas producing foods we discussed: cabbage, cauliflower, broccoli and the like. Watch out for spices too. These can cause a lot of problems for people.

Check the foods or other stuff you are in the habit of putting in your mouth to make sure they are not causing you problems.

Take a good quality digestive enzyme to make sure you are breaking your food down properly in your stomach.

ALOE VERA JUICE EXCELLENT FOR IRRITABLE BOWEL SYNDROME

I have found giving patients Aloe Vera juice is wonderful for soothing an Irritable Bowel. It is soothing. It is calming. It is healing.

Aloe Vera helps to ease constipation by cleansing the colon, so it is a great daily part of my health routine. But for Irritable Bowel it is excellent because it reduces inflammation. It is such a soother it is great for easing peptic ulcers.

As you can see, Aloe Vera could be part of everyone's daily healthy routine, not just mine, with good effects. Oh, and if you are one of those poor souls who suffers from heartburn, then Aloe Vera is just for you. It eases heartburn wonderfully.

I have had excellent results giving Aloe Vera juice as part of a total therapy for Crohn's Disease. Crohn's is ulceration and is not a nice thing to have at all… but good old Aloe comes galloping to the rescue every time!

As a matter of interest, Aloe Vera is a mine of good things. It has 18 amino acids, five different carbohydrates. It is packed with trace minerals. These are nutrients only needed in very small amounts, but if you don't have these tiny amounts, you could be in big trouble.

I like the fact it has Germanium in it. Germanium is a potent anti-cancer element. Aloe Vera has the vitamins B1, B2, B3, B6 and Choline. It even has Vitamin C in it. So as you can see, this is something that can only do good. All you need is about an eggcup full each day.

Not hard, not expensive but GOOD FOR YOU!

As a bonus, it is a mild and gentle laxative… what more could anyone ask for?

CAN DIET HAVE ANYTHING TO DO WITH IRRITABLE BOWEL?

When you look in the mirror tonight before you go to bed, have a good look at yourself. What you are looking at is the result of all the choices you have made in your whole life.

As I have said before, what you eat today walks and talks tomorrow. And what you have been eating over the years, walks and talks, staggers and limps for some people, today. We cannot escape the fact that we are what we have eaten. We will become what we eat.

These are all choices.

We are not helpless flotsam floating on the sea of Life. We are not blown hither and thither by the winds of fortune. We choose our destiny. Sadly, no-one ever told us that when we were growing up. We didn't realise we were making choices, did we? We just did things… and now we are paying for it.

Yes, diet does make a difference for people with Irritable Bowels. And so does thinking. As a man thinketh so is he. True

2,000 years ago and true today. It will be true tomorrow too and as long as we are on this planet.

No man has a greater love than that of sugar. We love sugar. We sing songs about our 'sugar baby'. We call each other 'honey'. We say 'Isn't she sweet.' We just love our sugar… pure, white and deadly.

Sugar is not your friend if you have an Irritable Bowel. So you are going to give it up, aren't you? Yes you are! Not when you've finished the packet in the cupboard, but now, today, this minute…

You have a choice, of course you do.

You can keep eating sugar and sugary things and keep your Irritable Bowel. Or you can choose to give up on sugar and at the same time give up having an Irritable Bowel. But you can't do both!

So it is up to you.

No dairy either. Dairy can cause an Irritable Bowel. Never mind what you saw on the telly about dairy. Like a lot of products, the advertising is often much better than the product. I have spent a fortune believing ads about golf clubs… and I still slice with clubs that are unsliceable, according to the advertisements.

You need fibre in your diet. Oh how often have you heard that chant? You need more fibre, you need more roughage, you have to pack your bowel. I know people who have gone out and done just that. They have packed their stomach with fibre of all kinds. Funny enough, they often felt worse, not better.

As you know, there is fibre and there is fibre. Not all fibre are the same. With an Irritable Bowel the last thing you need is roughage. Your bowel is tender… it is sore, it goes into spasm, it doesn't feel well. And roughage can make everything so much worse.

What your bowel craves for is gentle fibre. Fibre that soothes, fibre that does not irritate, fibre that caresses the bowel wall. It loves slippery elm bark, it loves psyllium (pronounces silly-um), it loves linseed. If you are going to have bran remember, I have said it before, your bowel hates unprocessed wheat bran. Horses love wheat bran but a lot of humans can't stand it.

Eat good simple food. No white bread, remember the wallpaper paste I told you about? Complex carbohydrates are the best ones.

Play the cards you were dealt, baby!

In Life we get dealt cards we don't always like. I drew prostate cancer so I decided to beat it and wrote a book about it. This is known as being given a lemon and turning it into lemonade. Gets back to choices!

But there is one card you have to play if you are of African or Mediterranean descent. You probably don't have the enzyme to digest dairy products. And if you eat them, drink them, lap them up, there is a very good chance you will end up with Irritable Bowel Syndrome… as well as other seemingly unrelated problems.

A problem that is of mounting importance is the adoption by the rest of the world of the lousy Western diet. Now come on, shout at me if you like, but honestly, the average person's diet in this country is terrible. If it weren't, everyone would be jumping out their skins, singing away, happy as anything. But as I have pointed out before, and you have remarked when walking down your street, everyone looks bloody miserable. Well, they do! They all shuffle along, head down, looking as though they have just lost a fifty dollar note and are looking for it.

And the rest of the world, labouring under the illusion that west is best, is working hard to afford our pathetic food habits.

In their own culture, eating traditional foods, they enjoy good health. They come over here, start eating out at hamburger joints, drinking milk for which they have no enzymes, and lo and behold a change takes place.

They start getting Irritable Bowels, gas, bloating, Diverticulitis… and that arch enemy, cancer. And all because they stopped chomping on brown rice, soy products, stir-fried vegetables and started filling up with corn flakes, hamburgers and other 'goodies'.

Yes, diet is important. Diet is vital if you want to get better.

And your mental diet is important. Very important indeed.

Harbouring resentments, brooding anger, simmering rage, green jealousy, envy, self pity, hatred… the whole nest of mental vipers will poison you. Let sunshine into your life if you would let go of Irritable Bowels.

Negative emotions are powerful and destructive forces raging inside you. They silently tear you apart. These negative emotions can cause Cancer, Irritable Bowel and a whole host of disease states. When someone is in the iron grip of any negative emotion it depresses their immune system. A major health problem today is so many people have an immune system like a kitten when they really need one like a tiger.

Remember Lactoferrin (LactoMax in Australia and New Zealand) is a very potent immune system booster.

YOU ARE NOT JUST AN IRRITABLE BOWEL!

When people have a problem of any kind, that problem tends to become the total focus. This is natural. It is like visiting someone in hospital. The only topic of conversation tends to be sickness. If it isn't the problem of the person you are visiting, you can be sure each person in the same ward will become an engrossing topic.

'Yes, and that lady over there is Myrtle, her husband left her three years ago… she's just had her appendix out, poor dear.' You know the kind of conversation you've been through it.

But you are more than your Irritable Bowel. You are a total person. And this applies to any problem you have in your life.

You and the problem are not the same. The problem will go and you will remain.

You will recall how I told you the colon can cause problems in other seemingly unrelated parts of the body. This is because you are not in watertight compartments. You cannot separate your bowel and keep it sealed off from the rest of your body.

So when treating your Irritable Bowel you have to take a total approach. Sure, drink your Aloe Vera to soothe the angry bowel, but take the long view.

The mistake most people make is they concentrate only where the problem seems to be. So people with an Irritable Bowel will focus almost entirely on high fibre. Someone told them lack of fibre is the problem so to fix it they eat more fibre.

But the problem does not go away.

We will not chat anymore about the right kind of fibre, we have been through that already. What I want to emphasise is this, to beat the problem we have to attend to digestion, the liver, bowel efficiency as well as the actual problem… the Irritable Bowel.

We have to get the whole box and dice, the whole works ticking along harmoniously. Smooth as silk, your whole system giving a polished performance worthy of an Oscar. That's what we want.

Remember the couple with the disorderly house? Emptying the garbage bin would not be enough? Well, the same with the Irritable Bowel. If we don't attend to the whole system the best we can expect is temporary relief… and if that is all we want we may as well just take a soother pill!

So my advice is to go on a seven-day detoxifying programme. Here in Australia your local health food shop can show you several. My own preference is for the QuickCleanse programme because this is a total internal cleansing programme. It helps the stomach, it helps the liver, it helps the bowel and it helps to restore the intestines to smooth efficiency.

And once you get all this working, you will feel tremendous.

But you have to keep working at it. We don't want the problem to come back. So keep up the good diet, every six months do a detox, keep up with the Aloe Vera. Get checked out to make sure you don't have Candida.

Should you be compelled to have a course of antibiotics, make absolutely sure you have a course of Acidophilus, Bulgarica and Bifida once you have finished the antibiotic course. This is a MUST...

As an extra, if you have any children who have been on antibiotics, make sure they too have a course of bowel bacteria. If they don't you can almost guarantee they will get everything that is going around. And we don't want that, do we?

So now let us move on and have a chat about that other modern-day curse, Diverticulitis.

9

So you've got bags, and they're not full of money!

You've got Diverticulitis and you are not very happy. Well, I am not surprised you are not happy, neither would I be with that problem.

First up, let's chat about Diverticulitis. What the heck is it? How do we get it and how can it be fixed?

There are actually two conditions, one is Diverticulosis and the follow-on condition is Diverticulitis.

It has been estimated that half the American population has Diverticulosis. I would bet the same figures apply here in Australia and in most of the world that has embraced the western-type diet with such enthusiasm.

SO WHAT IS DIVERTICULOSIS?

What has happened is because of inadequate diet (I am being tactful here), the pressure in the colon has caused little pouches to form. These have been pushed out into the abdomen.

Trouble starts when the Diverticulosis becomes Diverticulitis. I think I may have given you this little bit of wisdom before… but I will tell you again no matter what my wife says about me telling the same stories again and again! (Does your wife/husband do that too?)

The suffix 'itis' means inflammation. So when you see that at the end of a word you know it means pain… Tonsillitis (inflamed tonsils), Bronchitis (inflamed bronchial tubes), Diverticulitis (inflamed diverticulae). You can airily drop this one in conversations with almost anyone. They will be genuinely amazed. I find when I drop these little gems into my conversations the listener's eyes glaze over with admiration… At least I think it is with admiration!

So Diverticulitis means that the little pouches in the colon are inflamed. And that is because they are infected. If you want to feel really sorry for yourself, you can also have Irritable Bowel Syndrome at the same time. That is really wearing a hair shirt and being lashed with misfortune, isn't it?

How can you tell if you have Diverticulitis?

Tell-tale symptoms are pain in the lower left of your abdomen. You will no doubt know that pain in the lower right side often indicates your appendix is inflamed. So look to the left side for Diverticulitis.

You will also have bloating, pain and all those lousy symptoms we associate with problems in the bowel. You could also find you suffer from constipation followed by diarrhoea. People with Diverticulitis are not usually happy little pilgrims… and no wonder! I mean, would you be happy?

WHAT HAVE WE DONE TO DESERVE DIVERTICULITIS?

That is a particularly cruel little subheadline. What have you done to deserve Diverticulitis? It seems unfair that getting Diverticulitis can be all our own fault. I would much rather be able to blame someone else.

But sadly, in this case, we have to own up to it. We did it to ourselves… with our SAD diet. For SAD read Standard Australian (or American) Diet.

People tell me they eat a 'good' diet. When I ask them what they have it goes something like this… (If I have told you this before, let it be a lesson to you. We only learn by repetition, so read it again!)

Breakfast is usually corn flakes or sugar pops or similar with milk, and a couple of slices of white toast and a cup of coffee. If in a hurry leave out the cereal and just have the toast and coffee. If in a real hurry, leave out the toast as well and just have black coffee and a cigarette!

Do you honestly consider this a good breakfast? Be honest.

In the middle of the morning it is not unusual to have a cup of coffee with biscuits or cake. For lunch 'whatever is going'. This can be a salad roll. The salad is usually very tired having been made some hours before from lettuce and stuff bought a few days before. The roll is usually white flour… and we now know what that does to the bowel! Of course, we have a coffee afterwards… sometimes even a piece of cake if time and the budget can afford it.

Tea, dinner, supper (whatever they call the evening meal at your place) is usually meat, potatoes and vegetables. The meat and potatoes occupy most of the plate. When the meal is over, the meat has gone but a token bit of potato is left as we do not want to put on weight. And if anything is left it will be the vegetables.

The proportions are usually wrong way round. The vegetables should fill most of the plate. The potatoes and meat should be minimal.

To follow this splendid meal they tell me they often have ice-cream. Most ice-cream has ice but very little else. In fact, I once read an analysis of some popular ice-creams and the ingredients were similar to those used in paint remover. I am sure that the one you buy is as pure as can be, but check the ingredients just in case!

Now we relax in front of the telly with coffee and cake... or beer and pretzels.

A lot of people don't even have that splendid example of modern meal-making. They buy ready-made television dinners in foil packs from the supermarket... ready-to-cook pizzas and the like... and even worse, munch them after warming them up in the microwave while watching television. Why, you may find this hard to believe, but a lot of people are so engrossed in the drama on their TV set, they could not tell you what they just ate.

If the TV show is sufficiently stimulating it will affect the ability to digest the stuff you just ate. Emotions affect digestive enzymes. If you are really angry, for example, or frightened, digestion stops altogether. The stomach goes on 'hold' until the imagined emergency is over.

So watching TV while you eat is not only death to conversation, it can be death to your digestive system... and ultimately do you no good at all.

Meals are best eaten in a relaxed atmosphere. That's why dinner parties can be so good for us all. Good food, a drop of wine and excellent conversation are all good for digestion.

DIVERTICULITIS ON THE INCREASE

Like so many other modern diseases, Diverticulitis is on the increase. This problem was very rare 50 years ago... but since the appearance of so much processed, devitalised stuff we comically call 'food', a lot of diseases have become very common.

And Diverticulitis is just one of them.

If you are a sufferer of this malady then the first thing you have to consider is a change of diet.

Now I realise that suggesting people change their diet is a bit like suggesting they change their religion but you won't get better if you don't.

I remember someone told me the following story which I pass on to you for you to think about… or not to think about, whatever you choose!

This chap was watching this young married lady making bread. She came from an old-fashioned family who still made their own bread. She mixed up the dough, kneaded it into shape and then did something quite strange. At least this man thought it strange, she chopped the ends off the dough before popping it into the pan or whatever people call the receptacle for the dough…

Curious, he asked 'Why do you cut the ends off the dough before putting it into the pan?'

'Because it is part of the bread-making process, that's why.'

'Really? And who told you that?'

'My mother taught me, that's who.'

Normally when told that mother said this is the way one does it, we accept it without question. But our man was even more curious… so he persisted…

'Does your mother live round here?'

'Yes. She lives round the corner.'

So our friend went round to see the mother, a most charming lady as mothers so often are…

'If it is not a rude question, could you tell me why you cut the ends off the dough before you put the loaf into the pan?'

'Because it is part of the bread-making process, that's why.'

'And who taught you to do that?'

'My mother, that's who.'

'Oh really, and is your mother still around?'

'She most certainly is. She has the granny flat behind the garage.'

So our friend went and met Grandma.

'I am really consumed with curiosity. Could you please tell me why you cut the ends off the dough before you put it into the pan?'

'Certainly. It was because otherwise it wouldn't fit into the pan!'

I tell you that tale to illustrate how we take in matters of diet, eating habits and so on almost with our mother's milk. We rarely question them as we rarely question the other values we have been programmed with over the years.

So asking people to change their diets can cause quite a lot of internal resistance. We don't feel too happy about it. And that is understandable. It goes against the grain to be told that the roast dinner is not the best thing in the world. That eating pizzas, hamburgers, TV dinners and so on is bad news when someone thought it was the best news they had heard all year.

But whether we like it or not, the simple truth is if we don't want bowel problems like Irritable Bowel and Diverticulitis we must take steps to eat a high fibre diet. As I have pointed out already, this is not your usual diet with unprocessed wheat bran sprinkled over it!

And if you are unlucky enough to be suffering from Diverticulitis, you will not get better unless you change your ways!

Change is a problem for most of us.

I remember once someone said to me 'You learn something new every day'.

My response was 'Yes, but only if you are not careful'.

The fact is we do our very best not to learn anything new if we can help it. Learning something new means change, and we don't welcome change. We prefer that something new should be done for the first time somewhere else... We cling to our beliefs as though they are fastened to us with superglue!

Oh I know you could be the exception, but I am talking about everyone else of course, not you and me!

So you will change your diet to rid yourself of your problem. Good, that is very sensible of you.

Recognise that Diverticulitis seems to be caused by what they term a 'low residue' diet. That is a diet low in vegetables, fruit, grains and so on. It is a diet high in meat, white flour (the glue-maker), white sugar, sweets, cakes, packaged foods… you know the things I am talking about. I think they often call them 'family favourites'.

Diverticulitis is on the increase, especially in people who have reached the magic age of 30 years. It is sad how we enjoy our lousy diets when we are young but not as we age. Of course, you have to remember that when you were younger you had the digestion of a billy goat. They are reputed to be able to eat anything, even barbed wire!

Ah, but when we get older we eat the same food but with a different result. We get Irritable Bowel, Diverticulitis, Indigestion, Constipation, Wind/Gas, enough to light up a city. Our digestive system is simply telling us that enough is enough. Time for a change.

In one of those irritating 'holier than though' moods I can assure you that in what we call 'primitive' societies, those who don't share our views of civilisation, don't have the problem. And something else to drop into conversations is that when they expel the waste out of their bowels they pass HUGE amounts. Often making the elephant droppings look like fly specks.

Compare that to the stuff so many of us put out. Hard little balls like rabbit dung, black shiny balls covered in mucous, long thin tubes, turds like burnt offerings… and often in amounts so small you would wonder why it took so much effort to get them out.

We are a funny lot is some ways, don't you think?

I ask my patients what their stool looks like. It can tell me a lot about them. You would be surprised how many looked at me with amazement.

'Look at my stool when I have been to the toilet?' This in a voice filled with incredulity. 'I never look at it, I just flush the toilet.'

I imagine these good folks, after doing what is necessary, looking away as they feel for the lever to flush the toilet. Perhaps they get up and quickly slam the lid of the toilet down so they cannot see the result of their labours.

I remember once when one of the African potentates was building a new palace he wanted toilets that flushed away the debris continuously. He had seven toilets flown in from overseas, in different colours, to try them out. This exercise cost thousands of dollars, by the way, in a very poor country.

He wanted a continuous flush toilet so he would not be reminded of this earthiness. He wanted to be a god, and presumably, gods don't empty their bowels.

Now you may laugh at that but why is it so many people have no idea of the colour, the consistency or anything else about what goes down the toilet?

So make a habit of looking at it.

Transit time is important. Transit time is not how long it takes you to drive along the freeway. It is how long it takes for something you eat to pass through your system. The longer it takes, the worse it is. It can go through too quickly, of course.

To measure your transit time you can do a number of things. One is eat some nuts and look for them in your stool. If the thought of inspecting your stool so closely fills you with horror then do as I do. I drink a big helping of green barley. This is very good for someone with Diverticulitis, by the way. As the good Doctor Bernard Jensen is fond of saying 'Green inside is clean inside'. You will pass green coloured stool. You can't miss it.

Or eat a load of beetroot. In this case, if you eat enough, you will not only find your stool looks as though you have a bleeding problem, but your urine will also scare the pants off you when you see that red stream!

Bulking up is not just for body builders

When we think of bulk, some of us think of body builders. But in this little chat we are talking about bulk in the bowel. When you eat the favourite low residue diet your bowel has a problem expelling it. And I have warned you often enough of what happens when we don't spring clean our bowel every day.

For a healthy, Diverticulitis-free colon, we need bulk. BULK, baby, bulk!

Your bowel wall is really punished when there is not enough bulk. The muscles in the wall of the bowel have to contract with extreme force. Not just ordinary force, but extreme force. Contrast this with the efforts of those who eat a high residue diet. Very little contractual effort is needed. The bowel wall muscles have an easy time of it. And note that it is the extreme force that causes the little pouches to form. This is because of the extreme pressure resulting from the contractions.

Another point for you to consider is that this pressure can strip the lining off the bowel wall. Yes it can! And that can cause enormous problems for a person. Even to eventually getting bowel cancer… which sadly is also on the increase in our modern wonder world.

Can diet really perform miracles?

You would think, reading some magazines, that it is true that diet can perform miracles. Well, as we Scots say, 'I hae me doots'. I have my doubts.

Mind you, when you add linseed, psyllium husks, slippery elm bark, oat bran and oat meal to your diet, it can seem like a miracle. Just listen to the complaints that have been relieved by this simple change of diet… Constipation, Colic, Irritable Bowel, Gas, Heartburn, Nausea, Diverticulitis, Bloating, Abdominal Pain, Tender Backside. I guess in some ways it is almost like a miracle.

It is hard to believe that just by adding bulk to one's diet that so many modern-day problems can get relief.

Mind you, it is important to change to a high residue diet. Eat a lot less meat, no white flour, no sugar. Eat lots more vegetables, salads, fruit, legumes. Legumes are things like lentils, chick peas, beans and so on.

People are often told to eat raw vegetables. This is something to do gradually. A digestion used to modern-day pap will find it hard to digest raw vegetables. Rushing in and gobbling up raw vegetables has caused quite a few people to feel awful. There they were, trying to feel wonderful and ended up feeling dreadful. Introduce raw vegetables gradually. Grate them up. Puree them. Make them easy to digest. They will still provide bulk for your colon.

You have heard the word 'roughage' used when describing a necessary change in diet. The word roughage conjures up a picture of this harsh, irritating stuff powering through the bowel… And doubts creep in!

How can something rough help a bowel tortured with inflammation?

The fact is roughage changes once in the bowel. It becomes soft, bulky, absorbent. Just what you want… It mops up. It absorbs. It gives your bowel walls something to work on. If you are using QuickFibre Plus or its equivalent, it is also soothing. Just what you want!

DID YOU KNOW DIVERTICULITIS CAN CAUSE ANAEMIA?

This is surprising isn't it? Diverticulitis can often be a hidden cause of anaemia. So if you have the pain and also feel washed out most of the time, get a blood count done. The theory is that the bacteria that have made those little bowel pouches home, chew up all the Folic Acid preventing it from getting into the blood stream.

But here is the good news item. By eating lots of good bacteria culture, you destroy the bacteria and restore the absorption of the Folic Acid. That is always assuming your diet has Folic Acid in it.

It is obvious, I hope, that one cannot absorb what ain't there.

This is a hidden problem with some of the vegetables and fruit we get in the supermarket. A vegetable can only be rich in minerals if the soil in which it is grown is rich in minerals.

Read that again. If the soil has been robbed of its value by over fertilising with chemicals, if it has been over-worked and never been allowed to rest and recuperate, there is a good chance it is deficient in minerals.

And if that is the case, then the fresh green vegetables will also be deficient in minerals. Just as you should never judge a book by its cover, never assume that because the vegetables and fruit look nice and fresh, that they are full of nutrition.

It is not only the lack of nutrients in the soil. It is the time from the vegetables being harvested to the time they actually get into your home. When you consider that a lettuce loses half of its Vitamin C within hours after being plucked from its bed… you have to wonder how much is left by the time it gets to the supermarket and from there to your plate.

The other factor is cooking.

It is quite surprising how many people still boil their vegetables. I remarked earlier this may give you the healthiest kitchen sink in your neighbourhood, but is does nixies for you.

WHAT ABOUT COLONIC IRRIGATION?

I am often asked what I think about colonic irrigation.

I have met people who are hooked on them. They seem to trot off every month and have a wash out. I wonder it they get some sort of season ticket or what.

In quite a lot of cases, a colonic irrigation is necessary.

Laxatives do not clean out the impacted faeces concreting the bowel wall. Even an enema will not do that. So stronger measures are needed.

A skilled operator is a 'must'. Warm water is forced into the rectum in varying amounts and with varying pressures. The operator decides on the flow after assessing each patient.

And I have heard reports where impacted faecal matter has been removed which was over twenty years old. As I remarked earlier, not a pretty sight. But very necessary to get out if the bowel is to have any hope of working as it was intended to.

May I make an observation here? If you are having colonic irrigation, do not forget even this form of therapy needs help. You still need to take bulk foods… you still can take herbs with benefit. It is a good idea to take a course of QuickCleanse 'Bowel Clear' whilst having the colonic programme. This will loosen up the impacted faeces, dislodge parasites and prepare the colon for the irrigation.

I am quite sure you will get much more effective results by combining a programme like QuickCleanse or its equivalent with the colonic irrigation.

Doctor Norman Walker was a great advocate for health. I have long been one of his admirers. He radiated health and really did 'walk the talk'. He was one of the pioneers in healthy living. He told his followers to have colonic irrigations if they were looking for a fountain of youth.

When I talk to people who have had colonic irrigations but who didn't feel they got any benefit from it, I find that is all they did. They just had the irrigation and nothing else. A colonic irrigation is not a tool for miracles.

As well as the colonic, it is vital to eat the correct diet, take the supplements to loosen up the faeces… give yourself all the help you can.

So if you have Diverticulitis, read this chapter again and make notes.

Set a date, like tomorrow at the latest, for changing your diet, getting 'QuickCleanse', Aloe Vera juice and doing the things I suggest.

You will not only heal your Diverticulitis, you will feel incredibly healthlier. You will be a lot more cheery. Life will indeed become a bowl of cherries.

CROHN'S DISEASE, A MODERN DISASTER!

Crohn's Disease is something you wouldn't wish on your worst enemy. But wait, when I describe it to you there is bound to be someone who would wish it on his or her worst enemy.

Crohn's is described as ulceration of the small intestine. However, for the really unlucky it can mean ulceration of the whole tract. This is a very difficult condition and one that causes people untold misery and pain.

I have known people who have been laid up for years because of the weakening effects of Crohn's Disease.

The patients I have had who suffer from this disease look really ill. A lot of them look like characters out of a Charles Dickens novel about nineteenth century London. Pale, underweight, dark shadows under their eyes and a look of dejected misery clouding their face.

And no wonder.

I have had very good results using Aloe Vera. I have explained at length to you the extraordinary result achieved with this almost magical plant.

The next thing I have found very helpful is Slippery Elm Bark powder. You mix this up in water and it makes a drink with all the appeal of a glass of mud. Never mind what it looks or tastes like, it can do wonders for inflamed tissues. It soothes and lays a protective coating over the poor damaged tissue, giving it a chance to heal.

Any form of bowel disease tells me there is an imbalance in the bowel bacteria. Because of this I urge patients to take a course of acidophilus. Tell Auntie Maude that taking yoghurt will not do the trick. She has to take a course of acidophilus, so there!

I would recommend anyone with Crohn's to take Vitamin A. Vitamin A is excellent for healing and strengthening mucous membranes. It follows that it would be helpful to healing the ulcerative tissues in the bowel.

It has been found that people with Crohn's are often deficient in zinc. So adding zinc to the list is a good idea. Don't forget to take zinc on an empty stomach.

It is amazing how Folic Acid features so much in bowel disorders. You may remember I mentioned how important Folic Acid is in Diverticulitis? It is equally important in helping Crohn's Disease. So make sure you add Folic Acid to your shopping list.

The world's favourite breakfast drink is bad news for sufferers of Crohn's. Yes, I am referring to that well-loved health drink, orange juice. This is something that is not healthy for anyone with Crohn's.

Because of the high incidence of inflammatory prostaglandins on the bowel wall it is essential to counteract them. You do this by taking Omega 3 oil... this is Fish Oil. I would recommend taking Evening Primrose Oil too. These two oils contain other prostaglandins that counteract the inflammatory kind doing the damage. I can imagine you thinking 'prosta what?'. Prostaglandins are a kind of hormone that sits about and causes inflammation. To make them easy for the scientists to remember they have titles like E1, E2 and so on. Some cause inflammation and some prevent it.

The ones in Omega 3 and Primrose Oil prevent inflammation so are good to take.

I would recommend taking a good quality mineral supplement.

One of the problems for people with Crohn's is malnutrition. Because a meal can often result in diarrhoea and pain, they are inclined not to eat very much. This creates a shortage of minerals, especially zinc and magnesium, Vitamin A and D and also minerals. That is why I recommend taking a good supplement.

As in most health problems, diet is very important. Do not neglect this part of your healing process. The diet for Irritable Bowel is also helpful for Crohn's Disease patients.

In the next chapter, I want to have a word with you about your liver... gallstones and the other problems.

So let us go forward once more...

10

An excremental liver can be a pain…

You have had glimpses of liver problems as you have read this far. I told you how your entire blood supply goes through your liver every twenty minutes… and how blood cleansers are not little elves with brooms brushing away at your blood corpuscles.

But as the liver is such an important organ I thought it might be a good idea to spend just a short time chatting about it.

We hear a lot about Hepatitis C these days and how it ruins so many people's lives… but there are a lot of other liver problems that do a good job of messing things up for us!

You may have heard the expression 'getting up with excrement on the liver'. I have cleaned that up a bit in respect of your sensibilities. What we freely say we do not always welcome in print.

But when we describe someone as having got up with excrement on his liver we mean he has woken up in one giant foul mood. So we have enshrined a basic principle in our popular sayings. If your bowel is out of order, some of the contents will get onto the liver, with dire results.

It is interesting how valuable information gets lost in popular sayings. While people say so and so got up with excrement on his liver they are saying something important. It is of little use going on a liver cleansing diet unless you first make sure you have a clean and working colon. So the saying is quite literal, although while people say it, they don't really think about the meaning of it.

So before you embark on a sensible course to detoxify and fortify your liver, make sure you are not constipated, have Irritable Bowel, colitis or Diverticulitis. All these problems of the bowel must be fixed first! The liver is the great mood maker…

I have to be careful here. I am getting on my bandwagon again!

But I do think a lot of people are on anti-depressant drugs who should be on a liver cleansing programme. Set the scene. Someone, usually female, goes to the doctor and is very depressed. She is anxious, nervous, down in the mouth, not coping. Now the doctor acts in accordance with his training and I understand that. But what he will tend to do is look at the symptoms.

And what are the symptoms?

They are all mental ones. So it is obvious the patient needs some form of anti-depressant. If she is really bad and doesn't respond to the drugs she will get either a stronger drug or a referral to a psychiatrist!

The liver has to break down the drug and this will throw an extra burden on it, making it even less able to do its job properly. What is being treated are the symptoms of a poorly performing liver and not the liver itself. I must hurry to put in here that naturally all mental problems do not stem from the liver. But quite a lot do!

There are other symptoms that can give you a clue. Feeling slightly sickly can be common. You find cooking food puts you off. You find your appetite is not as good as it was. You find that greasy, fatty foods do not agree with you.

Another interesting liver sign is where your eyesight varies through the day. One part of the day you see fine, but a little later things are not as clear. This is a common liver sign. The eyes and the liver have a close connection.

Another real give away is a pain under the right shoulder blade. This can signal either a liver in trouble or a gall bladder in trouble.

If you get 'sick' headaches as well as feeling down and out, then it is almost certain you have a liver in trouble.

Liver cancer seems to be more common these days. This is not really surprising. Do you think your liver was programmed to deal with car exhaust fumes, acid rain, pesticides, herbicides, fungicides, chemical fertilisers, artificial colouring in foods, preservatives, emulsifiers, thickening agents, irradiated foods, genetically altered foods that no-one has ever seen in Nature?

And your liver has to deal with polluted air, polluted water... the list of chemicals seems endless. We pay a very high price for our self-praised society. We think we are the bees knees as societies go... but as I have remarked earlier, unless the planet goes through a great healing we will go the same way as all the societies before us. Down the tube!

I am glad to say I am optimistic that despite the daily news I feel there is change in the air. Governments are becoming more aware of the place traditional medicine has in healing... more people are becoming aware. People like yourself, for instance, reading my book. More and more people are buying this book in a search for alternative ways to enjoy health. I believe this is all part of a global awareness that things are not right. It shows people are searching for the truth and are not prepared to take all the adman's persuasive chat any more. And this will be good for the planet!

Can one person change the planet?

That is a question I am often asked. My answer is simple, direct and to the point. 'Yes, you most certainly can.' If you want to save the rainforests in Brazil and elsewhere, just stop eating meat in any form. They are destroying the forests to provide third rate grazing for hamburger cattle… the more people who don't eat meat, the less cattle will be needed.

If you have the will, you can do it… and you will be a darn sight healthier too!

Oh dear, there I go again, let's get back to your liver…

Tell you what will do your liver in quickly. Good old-fashioned stress.

Anxiety, worry, stress, frustration, anger (especially anger) will really do a number on your liver. And don't forget fear. Fear really creates bad juices.

Fear can kill people. Fear stops digestion. It shuts everything down… stomach, intestines, bowel, digestion. It is bad news. Learn to go with the flow.

Here is a little thought for you. I bet if I asked you to write down all your fears on a piece of paper for me. Then tucked the paper into an envelope and put it away for three weeks or so. After three weeks I will take the envelope and ask you to tell me what you wrote on the paper. Guess what? It is almost certain you won't be able to remember most of them. And those you did remember probably didn't happen.

Worrying is a waste of time and energy. It is needless suffering. The answer to worry is to do something. If you can do something about the problem, do it. If you can't do anything about it, then why crucify yourself by worrying yourself. People have been heard to say 'I'm worried to death about (whatever it is that is worrying them)'. Did you notice the affirmation there? I am worried (telling yourself to keep on worrying) and then the real kicker, 'to death'. And people do programme themselves for a permanent early retirement and it becomes a self-fulfilling prophecy.

If it wants to rain, I always let it! No use wasting time and energy worrying about things you cannot possibly do anything about.

HOBNAILED LIVERS ON THE MARCH!

Hobnailed livers on the march... I will translate that for you. I was being smart. A damaged liver especially one damaged with cirrhosis is called a 'hobnailed liver'. Guess why? Because that is what it looks like... an old hobnailed boot. And I say 'on the march', because damaged livers are increasing in our modern world.

I am not sure if everyone in these more affluent times remember hobnailed boots. When I was a kid we had these boots with nails in the soles to make them wear for a long time. We loved them because you could slide so well with hobnails on the soles of your boots. Hobnails were the trademark of the working-class people. I wore mine with great pride. A better way of feeling 'grown up' than smoking cigarettes or dope!

But hobnails should be on the soles of boots, not on livers. I have remarked before, and I will say it again until it really sinks in, alcohol and fried foods damage your liver. They don't just throw an extra burden on an already overworked organ, they damage it.

THE GREAT CHOLESTEROL HOAX

Cholesterol. The word strikes terror in many a heart. Cholesterol, the arch enemy, clogging up our arteries, killing people all over the place.

Actually, that's not quite true. It has been shown that high cholesterol can be related to heart disease, but it has not been conclusively proven.

However, I think it is better to have a reasonable cholesterol level rather than one too high. But to explain this a little further, it is not all the cholesterol that causes problems. It is the LDL part, not the HDL part, that causes problems. LDL is the 'bad' cholesterol. I remember it by associating LDL with lousy. Lousy, darned Lousy, is how I remember… it is LDL that is the bad guy in this scenario.

Did you know that you need cholesterol? Yep, without it your sex life would be non-existent. It may not be the best right now, but if you had no cholesterol you wouldn't even have a glimmer of lust… That's because cholesterol is needed for the sex glands, and lots of other processes in your body.

THE MYTH OF THE LOW CHOLESTEROL DIET

Your cholesterol has gone through the roof. So you are told to go on a low cholesterol diet. Hey and guess what happens? Rage, frustration, bitter words… your cholesterol goes up even higher!

Now how can that be? Where is the justice here, for goodness sake? Here you are, doing all the right things and being punished for it. I take your cholesterol going up instead of down as a punishment when you expected a reward. So what the heck is going on here?

Well, my friend, the fact is it is your LIVER that produces most of your cholesterol and not your diet. Your liver produces as much as 85% of your cholesterol and your diet only 15%. Did that surprise you? It surprised me when I first found that out.

What is more, your liver is aware of the level of cholesterol coming into your blood from your diet. Your liver knows everything… it analyses your blood as it is filtered through it. Very clever, don't you think.

So what your liver does is manufacture more cholesterol. It only knows the good things about cholesterol. No-one has told it about the bad effects of cholesterol, so it pumps more out.

Now here is the interesting bit. I have brought cholesterol down from 10 to below 4 in three months simply by giving the liver some help. I have found in lots of cases that high cholesterol is a liver problem. Give the liver help in the form of herbs and vitamins and lo and behold, down goes the cholesterol.

Now that really is something interesting to drop in when conversation flags at the next barbecue you go to. Gosh, how people will respect you, be careful though, once people see you as an expert they expect you to give them free advice!

BILE JUICE IS GOOD FOR YOU!

I am kidding. Wait a minute... don't go rushing out asking for bile juice at your local health food shop or pharmacy.

But you do need bile, otherwise you would have big problems. Lack of bile makes it difficult for you to absorb fat. Your digestive system uses bile to break down and absorb fat. If you have too little bile this is what happens. The fat combines with calcium and forms a kind of soap. Yes, that's what I said, soap!

This stuff is indigestible and is one of the causes of gallstones.

Now wait a minute. Just where is your gallbladder?

You will be delighted to find out it is a pear-shaped sack hanging down between the lobes of the liver. It is where the bile is stored by your liver. The liver makes it, sends it down to the gallbladder, where it is held until it is needed by your body. There is a little canal (called a duct) from the gallbladder to the small intestine, which as you remember is really the long intestine.

In your body is a complex and very clever communication system that relies on hormones, chemicals and even electricity to kick start things. So it is with your gallbladder. When you eat food with fat in it, hormones send a message to the gallbladder, 'Hey, watch out, here comes de fat, baby!'. And the gallbladder contracts and squeezes out bile.

If that's not a minor miracle, I don't know what is.

Don't you marvel at the smartness of our bodies? While you are sitting there reading this, a million things are going on in your body. And, like the rest of us, you are usually totally unaware of all this activity.

Bile breaks fat down into little droplets so it can be absorbed into the body. It is not only fat that needs bile, but Vitamins A, E, D and K all have to be broken down by bile before we can use them.

To make enough bile you need enough protein. Not lashings of protein like body builders take. The problem is most people have too much sugar in their daily intake. They call them 'refined carbohydrates' and they are not your friends. If you have too many of these and not enough protein you get problems you don't want.

What happens is if there is too little bile or not enough in the gallbladder and it doesn't contract properly, the bit of bile that is in there stays there, then fat is not digested.

As I told you, this fat combines with calcium and iron and forms soap. Imagine that, soap! These soaps interfere with digestion and cause constipation. If you don't do something about it then more trouble comes along. It really is quite strange how the causes of many health problems are not where we actually have the problem. Lack of bile can cause osteoporosis, crumbling of the vertebrae in your spine, anaemia, fractures... and who wants this lot?

You can tell if there is a bile problem. It is bile that colours your stool. No! Auntie Maude, not the one in the kitchen, the stuff in the bowel, for heaven's sake! So if you have a gallbladder problem that is not giving you any pain, you can tell there is a problem because your stool will be light in colour. With advanced disease, the stool will be white... not a drop of bile.

With this lack of bile there will be a large mass of undigested food sitting in your bowel. This mass of food putrefies because it has become the breeding ground of millions of harmful bacteria.

Now here is something not many people realise, these bacteria release histamine! And you know what histamine does, don't you? Yep, it is the stuff that makes hay fever and allergies so unpleasant. Instead of anti-histamine drugs maybe the person needs attention to the liver, gallbladder and bowel!

But that's not all these bacteria cause. Not by a long chalk, body odour, bad breath, bloating... It really is unfair... but you remember what my Dad said about that!

To have a healthy gallbladder, eat protein. Not meat, but beans, chickpeas, soy products... these all supply protein. Oh, and in case you think going on a very low fat diet is helpful, it isn't. We all need fat. It is just that too many people have too much fat. Animal fat is the worst kind.

We have to have some fat to use Vitamins A, D, E and K and also carotenes are essential fatty acids. These are best known as Omega 3 and Evening Primrose Oil. Starflower Oil and Flaxseed are two other sources of essential fatty acids... But they all need some fat to be absorbed by your body.

It all sounds very complicated but leave it to your body, it is far smarter than we are. It sorts it all out if we give it the right tools for the job.

I am sure you are beginning to see why it is so important to work at getting a digestion that works properly, a bowel system that does a good job, a liver/gallbladder working well together. It has been said that death starts in the bowel and when you consider the multitude of diseases caused by poor digestion, constipation, liver misfunction... I believe that death does indeed start in the bowel. Oh, and so does old age.

A very important spring for the fountain of youth is the bowel and its supporters.

GALLBLADDER DISEASE… SHALL I HAVE IT OUT?

At one time medical people took everything out that could be taken out without killing the patient. As you know, quite a few did die, but that was accidentally and not on purpose. Thankfully, when you die from an operation, it is accidental so no-one is to blame. At least that is how we are conditioned to think!

Tonsillitis? Out with the tonsils. Colitis? Let's cut out some of the bowel! Uterus problems? The answer is straightforward, cut it out, cut it out… and the problem is solved. Back problem? No worries, we can remove the offending discs and even cement up your spine for you! Got a problem with your cartilage… no trouble at all, we can whip 'em out. Got really bad arthritis in your knees and hips? Your troubles are over, we can replace them all. Plastic hips, knees… even breasts… ain't science wonderful?

If you go to a surgeon, he is trained to think of solving your problem with surgery. It is not realistic to expect anything else, is it? This is not a criticism, I am making a point.

But Time marches on. We now know what Naturopaths and other health professionals have been saying for years, 'cutting things out is not always a wise option'. The tonsils are an important part of our immune system and cutting them out did not do the patient any favours. People have had their gallbladders removed and have not found the promised land. Hysterectomies have not been as blissful as some people expected.

So we are now realising there are other options. If you have your gallbladder out, your liver has to assume that function. You have to have bile and only your liver can deliver it. Before listening to the siren song of an operation, why not try herbs? Why not try nutrition?

If you have gallstone pain, try taking Homeopathic Belladonna. This is great for most cases of gallstone colic. And try Homeopathic Chelidonium for that pain under the right shoulder blade. Chelidonium can do wonders for lots of liver complaints. It can even help small stones by coating them and making it easier for them to be passed out.

CHECK OUT IF YOU HAVE ANY OF THESE LIVER SIGNS!

Your liver is important. If your liver is in any sort of trouble, so are you. People die of liver trouble. People's lives are made miserable because of liver problems. I don't want this to happen to you... go through this list and see if you have any of the problems listed. If you do, it would be wise to get a liver check-up from your health professional. OK, so here we go...

- Sudden bursts of irritability
- Depression for no apparent reason
- Lack of motivation
- Tiredness without any effort being expended
- Overweight, especially around the middle (unless you are drinking excessive amounts of alcohol)
- Headaches, especially 'sick' headaches
- You try but cannot lose weight, especially around your midriff
- Bad breath
- A yellow or brown-coated tongue
- A feeling of nausea and you can't stand the smell of food cooking (fat makes you feel sick)
- Digestive problems such as heartburn, reflux and bloating
- Irritable Bowel Syndrome or similar bowel problems
- High cholesterol (remember what I told you earlier)
- Gallbladder problems
- Pain under the right shoulder blade is a real give-away
- Some skin problems can be from the liver
- Allergies
- A weak immune system

- Sludged-up arteries
- Age spots, sometimes called 'liver spots'

You would not have all these signs unless you were very unlucky. But if you have some of them, it could very well be your liver. A pain under the right shoulder blade is almost always a liver or gallbladder problem. Constant feelings of nausea are also very often liver signs. Any yellowing of the whites of the eyes is an obvious liver sign.

Any of the mental signs if there is also nausea is almost certain to be a liver problem.

Drugs and your liver

In our modern world, drugs play a major part. We are a drug-dominated society. I am not talking about heroin and similar drugs which are a major problem around the world. I could go on about these for hours.

Hard drugs are something I never had to deal with when I was younger. I lived in a world where young people believed the world was their oyster. We knew that in those days hard work and loyalty were well rewarded. Unlike today, where companies fire people to make more profit regardless of length of service, loyalty or anything else.

As youngsters we had something so many young people today do not have. We had hope. Don't you sometimes think the older generation has let the younger one down? High-level corruption seems to be accepted as normal behaviour. What kind of example is being set for the young people today?

And equally important to any thinking person like you, is what kind of world are we leaving for our grandchildren? Indeed, when you see the way we waste the world's resources you can be forgiven for wondering if there will be anything left to sustain life in fifty years or so.

One answer is for us not to tolerate corruption in high places. We need to demand the resignation of politicians and others who take corruption as one of the perks of power. Corruption on high seeps right down through society. Corrupt police encourage crime. Corrupt morals encourage immoral behaviour at every level.

In the interests of a healthy society and a future for our young people we need to speak up... LOUDLY.

But back to medical drugs...

If you think these are harmless, think again.

Doctor Michael Colgan in his book, *The New Nutrition* says that in America 130,000, yes one hundred and thirty thousand people die every year from toxic drugs in hospitals. These are drugs that have been prescribed for patients. I know the figure is comparable in Australia and I am sure it will be the same in other medical drug-oriented countries.

I had a visitor to my home and he carried a plastic bag full of the drugs he had to take. Drugs for a heart condition, more drugs to combat the side effects of the main drugs and so on... more than one drug for the same condition. People who have to take all these medical drugs to prevent dropping dead are on life support systems the same as if they were plugged into the electricity. Pull the plug on the life support patient and death follows. Pull the plug on taking all the medically prescribed drugs and death can follow.

Your liver has to degrade all these drugs.

Your liver has to deal with these drugs. They throw yet another burden on an already overworked organ. No wonder we find so many people with signs of a liver under stress. And people take these drugs for years.

Have you ever wondered why it is that so many cancers seem to set up home in the liver? They jump from what they call primary to secondary and that is all too often the liver. The primary is where the cancer was first spotted, let us say in the colon. Colon cancer is on the increase along with Irritable Bowel, Diverticulitis, Crohn's Disease… Think about that.

And then wonder why it is that the colon cancer so often leaps into the liver. Cancer tends to strike our weakest organs. It goes where the immune system is least effective.

Could it be our livers are so over-stressed, so overworked, that they have been weakened to the point where they cannot fight cancer cells when they migrate?

Doesn't this make it even more important to work on strengthening your liver, your digestion, your bowel, assimilation, elimination? Doesn't it stress the importance of powering up your immune system?

Can I tell you a little story underlining the importance of this?

On a routine visit to my doctor when I had prostate cancer he noticed a small basal cell carcinoma just above my eye. Neatly in the corner it sat. I thought it was just a pimple or a bite and wondered why it wasn't going away. My doctor, who is a really top guy and very supportive of what I do, noticed it.

He organised for me to have it out. I had to go to hospital, have pre-med and post-med and all that jazz. A very competent plastic surgeon took it out and did a first-class job…

But here is the interesting part in all this. When I got back to the ward the nurses came round with their trolley full of little containers.

I asked them what they wanted and they told me they had come to give me my pain-killers as prescribed.

They were astounded when I told them I didn't want or need their pain-killing drugs because I had no pain. I had to do a real job of convincing them because they could not believe anyone could have an operation of this kind and not have any pain.

But I didn't have any pain. I put that down to all the

supplements I was taking to deal with my prostate cancer, which I had at that time. Mind you, I have a confession to make, I didn't tell anyone at the hospital I had prostate cancer... enough for them to know I had a basal carcinoma!

I always try to get a result using natural means. My liver can deal easily with vitamins and minerals, Lactoferrin, polysaccharides and so on, because they are natural substances it deals with all the time. It is not conditioned to deal in chemical drugs. These are manufactured and not usually found in Nature.

You have no doubt heard of cirrhosis of the liver. We may not be sure what it is exactly. We know it ain't the best thing to have. Usually, we think of cirrhosis as being a problem for alcoholics. But you can get it from taking drugs too. A liver overloaded with toxics from whatever source can develop cirrhosis. This means the liver is crippled.

HERE IS A LIST OF DISEASES YOU SHOULD KNOW ABOUT...

It is interesting when looking at the diseases that inflict us with so much misery. Our public 'health service' has little to do with health. It is really a disease service. It devotes an ever increasing amount of public money in trying to combat disease. Very little is spent promoting health.

It is worth noting how many diseases come from a toxic bloodstream, which means a liver that is unable to perform properly.

The most common and obvious is hepatitis. This is on the increase in today's toxic world. Less obvious is overweight. The world is searching for the perfect weight-loss programme. A good place to start looking is in the liver.

Migraine headaches can come from the liver. Eating foods that cause a reaction... are foods not broken down thoroughly? Some migraines are called 'bilious attacks'. 'Bilious' means from the liver. Migraine sufferers are often worriers. They are often extremely conscientious people who push themselves too much.

I have already pointed out that worry, fear, emotional highs all can cause your digestive system to pack it in. If your digestive system (and I include your liver, bowels, the whole works) closes down, you get problems all over the place. And one of the problems can be a migraine.

We are very much aware of the overweight person, but seldom worry about people who are underweight. But this is a problem for quite a lot of people. If appetite is lost because of a sickly feeling, suspect the liver as being involved.

Make no mistake, your health and longevity depends to a great extent on the health of your liver.

Not a bad idea to start a 'I love my liver' club.

At the end of this book I will pull it all together for you. I thought of telling you all about liver herbs in this chapter, but decided it would be easier for you to understand what to do if I dealt with it separately later.

I want to take each of the complaints we have discussed together and give you the remedies. This way you will be able to focus more effectively and can, should you need to, draw up your own plan to enjoy wonderful health.

As cancer is on the increase and striking terror in so many hearts, I would like to have a bit of chat with you about it in the next chapter.

11

Getting killer cancer under control

Why on earth would I be chatting about cancer in a book all about the bowel, digestion and the liver?

Well, for a number of reasons. One is having had cancer, I am all too familiar with the emotional impact. When you are told you have cancer, reason tends to go out of the window. You find yourself in a state of utter panic. The problem with this is even the most bizarre solutions are grabbed with all the fervour of a drowning man clutching at a straw!

The other reason is so many cancers start their life in the bowel and digestive system. This means that a large number of cancers are preventable.

The reason the bowel is such a breeding ground for cancer is the poor condition of so many bowels. If the bowel wall is covered in slime, this provides a wonderful breeding place for harmful bacteria. These damage the bowel wall and if the waste is not kept moving on and out, then cancer can develop. If the bowel is full of putrefying waste that is just sitting there it too breeds massive amounts of toxic-producing bacteria.

If the bowel wall is irritated, inflamed, this too provides a readily accessible home for toxic bacteria.

So as you would agree, a healthy bowel is a must in preventing (or helping to heal) not only bowel diseases, but cancer and other unwelcome visitors.

You don't have to have cancer. Oh I know we are told it can be genetic, and I am sure that is true in some cases. But far more cancers are caused by lifestyle. Poor diet, constipation, bad digestion, inability to process poisonous wastes from our environment.

The liberal use of chemicals in our society has a lot to answer for in my opinion. Pesticides, herbicides, fungicides, additives of all kinds, lead, heavy metals and solvents all have to be handled and detoxified by our body and the truth is, in many instances, we are not doing a very good job.

BUILDING A RIP-ROARING, TWO-FISTED IMMUNE SYSTEM…

There is no doubt in my mind that the first line of defence in preventing cancer is a rip-roaring, two-fisted, battle-ready immune system.

It is also the first thing I do when dealing with someone who has cancer. Build the immune system. All too often the person with cancer has a depressed immune system.

If your bowel is up to maggots, if your liver is under-performing, then ten to one your immune system is lagging behind.

Let us first talk about prevention.

The brutal fact is all types of cancer are on the increase. Prostate cancer now kills as many men as heart attacks. As many men die from prostate cancer as women do from breast cancer.

We hear a lot about prevention of breast cancer and nothing about preventing prostate cancer.

And so it is up to us to put this right!

To prevent cancer, as I remarked, we must first boost our immune system. And your bowel is part of that system, a very important part.

As I have had prostate cancer, I am particularly aware and take supplements every day. If you would like to find out more about prostate cancer in particular, then I heartily recommend you invest in a copy of my book, *How to Fight Prostate Cancer and Win*. This is now an international best seller and a book I honestly believe is saving the lives of thousands of good men. Fathers, brothers, sons, husbands… are now alive by following the guidelines in my book.

Getting your bowel in a healthy condition is vital. Take the herbals, make sure your bowel is heavily populated with the health-giving bacteria. Give yourself the valuable detox programme at least every six months. As I have remarked, I follow the QuickCleanse programme as this has been formulated to spring clean your whole digestive system and get it back on track. I take QuickFibre Plus every day because this keeps my bowel working beautifully. Big dumps are essential to good health.

I also take Lactoferrin in the form of LactoMax. This is a great formula. Lactoferrin is a big bertha in the war against disease. It can reduce tumours and stop them from jumping somewhere else. It promotes killer cell activity. You will remember how I said your bowel is an important part of your immune system, and Lactoferrin promotes the growth of the good bacteria in your bowel. As a bonus, it kills off Candida, a sure sign of a compromised bowel and immune system.

May I make the point that we need a boisterous immune system whether we have cancer or not. We need it to deal with the perils that surround and attack us every day. With air travel making it so easy for diseases to become world travellers, any sensible person takes steps to protect themselves and their loved ones.

Lactoferrin promotes what they call neutrophils. These are the little beauties that gobble up foreign matter in your body. They have to spot the offender, surround it, and then close in for the kill. So the more you have of these the better.

In what seems like the realm of science fiction, Lactoferrin talks to your DNA and gets it to release the killer cells to attack cancer cells.

So because I want an immune system that does not take rubbish from anything, I take Lactoferrin (LactoMax here in Australia and New Zealand).

Bovine Cartilage is another incredible anti-cancer agent. Bovine has a record that has to be seen to be believed when it comes to helping people battle cancer.

In fact, if you don't want killer diseases, if you want to really have a first line whack 'em on the head kind of immune system you need three supplements.

The first is Lactoferrin, the second is Bovine Cartilage and the third is one you may never have heard of, but you will. This is the miracle of glyconutrients.

WHY REALLY NICE PEOPLE GET SICK!

It used to puzzle me as a Naturopath how many people still got sick no matter how well they ate and looked after themselves. I used to wonder why it was that no matter what people did, they still got sick.

Why was it that people who did everything right got sick? It just didn't seem fair.

That was until I was introduced to the work of Doctor See.

Doctor See is a world-renowned scientist in the area of immunology. I am not sure there is such a word as 'immunology', but you know what I mean, don't you?

He discovered something very important. Something you need to know. Something that made sense when considering treatment of disease, be it cancer or anything else.

What Doctor See discovered was this... Our cells communicate with each other chemically and electrically.

Let me give you an example of how cells need to communicate. Let us take diabetes as our example. When the insulin with the glucose on its back arrives at the cell it knocks on a tiny door called a receptor. The receptor is supposed to answer the knock, open up and let the boys in. However, if the door does not open, the glucose stays in the blood causing high blood sugar levels.

Now my friend, why would the receptor be so darned awkward and not answer the knock? Well, it needs chromium to even hear the knock. If the person is low on chromium a lot of the receptors will not open. That is why it is a good idea for late-onset diabetics to make chromium part of their daily routine.

You see how important the marker, chromium, is, don't you? As a matter of fact all your cells have markers on them. Or they should have.

This is particularly true in the case of the bad-guy cells like cancer. They should have big sign shouting 'Hey, guys, over here, I am a CANCER cell'. Then in theory, your immune system goes into red alert and sends in combat troops to wipe them out.

But there can be a problem, as Doctor See discovered...

THE IMPORTANCE OF GLYCONUTRIENTS

What Doctor See discovered was we have to have eight glyconutrients for our immune system to do its stuff. These are called 'polysaccharides' and you need eight of them for all your cells to be correctly marked. What it amounts to is your cells cannot communicate with each other if the message is not there or only partly there.

Look at it this way, compare your iron-clad immune system to a top of the line SAS unit. These guys are incredibly well trained in the killing and survival arts. Now imagine a red alert signal goes off and these commando types are sent out to search and destroy.

Off they go in search of the enemy. But now picture this, they cannot identify the enemy. The enemy has no distinguishing marks. They have some device that prevents our crack unit from recognising them. The SAS cruise by their camp and do not recognise it is the enemy they are passing.

So now the enemy can penetrate our defences, attack us at will, bring in more like itself… and one day even kill us.

If you don't have all eight of these glyconutrients then it is difficult for your own internal SAS, your immune system, to recognise the enemies within.

But here is a different scene. Our gallant SAS have managed to bring with them a device that reveals the enemy. They have a device that causes the enemy to show up in his true colours. His cover is blown and the SAS moves in for the kill… They can now search successfully and destroy. Completing their mission!

Glyconutrients are the secret weapon.

The eight glyconutrients are the secret weapon that makes every cell able to communicate. And this means the good guys can spot the bad guys and do something about them.

It was because the nice people who had worked so hard to build up their immune system were still not getting the results they would have expected.

Doctor See identified these eight glyconutrients. He discovered that a lot of people only have two of them in the average diet. Sure, your body can manufacture the whole eight from the two, but not very well and not all the time. The end result is a top immune system, like our SAS unit, unable to correctly identify the enemy.

But Doctor See found that by supplementing with the glyconutrients, lots of good things happened. Not only were the immune cells attacking the enemy cells, the person had more energy, felt better in lots of quality of life ways.

I took these as part of my cancer-beating programme and take them every day as part of my ongoing health and longevity programme. Doctor See has now copyrighted his formula. It is a world first and I cannot recommend it enough to you. Any thinking person will want to get into these vital supplements. This discovery answers a lot of puzzling questions. I now tell all my patients to take them, and I urge you to do the same.

At the end of this book I will tell you how you can get hold of these very important nutrients.

There are lots of other supplements you can take to arm yourself against cancer and other diseases. You can find a complete run down on them in my book, *How to Fight Prostate Cancer and Win*. I urge anyone with cancer of any kind to get this book. I also urge people who don't want the problem to read it too. It could be a life saver!

YOU NEED MORE CHOICES… BUT YOU ARE NOT AWARE OF THEM!

The big problem when confronted with cancer is our minds go blank. In most cases terror takes centre stage. Cancer is seen by most people as a death sentence.

The mind runs around like a rat in a trap. Any outlet that promises escape is grabbed, no matter how bizarre. The only choices given, quite naturally, are medical ones.

But there are other options the cancer patient needs to know about.

The record of chemotherapy and radiation is not one of incredible success. I have spoken with men who have had both treatments for their prostate cancer. But still it went on inexorably dragging them to an early grave. I have met men who have consented to having their testicles cut off… a bid to halt the testosterone flow… and still got cancer of the bones that killed them.

I was alarmed when watching a documentary on television where doctors proclaimed that what they did to prostate cancer patients was what they had always done… and for no other reason. They claimed that these treatments had never been proven effective. This really scared the pants off me. How many men put their trust in these treatments, only to be disappointed?

I believe conventional medicine and traditional medicine would be better working together for the benefit of the most important person in this equation, the patient.

The grim fact is that at a time when the immune system needs to be reinforced it is weakened by chemo and radiation. And what is worse, to my mind, is some patients are warned not to take any supplements whilst on chemo. Did you know that large amounts of Vitamin C can reduce the side effects of chemotherapy? It can stop the loss of hair and the nausea associated with this treatment.

I ask myself this question… would it not make sense to give the chemotherapy all the help possible by fortifying the person's defences?

I really don't understand the reasoning behind telling patients on chemo not to take any supplements.

Never mind, as far as options are concerned the three most important, as I said before, are Lactoferrin, Bovine Tracheal Cartilage and the glyconutrients. In addition, taking every means possible to boost the body defences by means of diet, vitamin/mineral and herbal supplements.

The Lactoferrin and the Bovine work to stop the tumour from growing. They do this by what is called 'anti-angiogenesis'. Angiogenesis is the trick cancer cells have of setting up their own blood supply. Cancer cells are larger than normal cells and need more blood. Crafty blighters set up their own field kitchens for blood. But the Bovine puts the blockers on and works to close it down. This starves the cancer of blood and whacko, it has a job to survive. Bovine does something else too… it puts the brakes on the cancer's ability to reproduce. As you well know, cancer cells reproduce at an alarming rate so slowing this down is tremendous.

The Lactoferrin starves the cancer of iron, which they love and also curbs the growth. Equally important is its ability to stop the cancer from metatastising, that is jumping somewhere else.

And the glyconutrients make the cancer cells visible so they can be attacked. The great thing is all these three boost production of the killer cells.

There are several types of killer cells but these guys launch the lot!

Wouldn't you take all three if you had cancer? I most certainly did and I recommend other people to do the same.

Herbal immune boosters

I will briefly tell you some of the great herbals people should be taking to build an immune system like a nuclear bomb. Pinebark or Grape Seed is a very potent immune booster. Others are Pau D'Arco, Astralagus, Cat's Claw, Betacarotene (a lot of cancer sufferers have been shown to be low in betacarotene), Vitamin C, the B vitamins and essential fatty acids.

I am almost apologetic for reinforcing digestion, liver and bowel fortifications. But they are critical to good health. I cannot repeat this often enough.

If you would like to know more about preventing and fighting cancer then a good investment is to get my best selling book, *How to Fight Prostate Cancer and Win*.

Now folks, one of the big unsung problems of our age is Candida. Otherwise called 'Thrush'… and hey you guys, don't skip this chapter, men get it just as women do.

The difference is women show more visible signs of this widespread problem. As it is a problem that starts in the bowel and is made worse by wrong diets, I think I should tell you how to fix it.

So come on, let's keep going…

12

The plague of deadly spores... are you a victim?

How many people do you know who complain that they find Life hard going? They feel depressed when they really have little to be depressed about. How many people do you know who are always complaining about headaches? Probably nearly everyone you know!

And how many people do you know with skin problems? Rashes, pimples, itches, psoriasis, hives... you name it, they've seen it or got it! Then there all the things you and I have been chatting about... constipation, gas, bloating and all the other ills that plague us in that part of our world.

In a hushed voice, what about all those guys and girls who have a problem with sex? Not too much, but inability to get at whatever is available. No or low libido, a nice way of saying they seldom get the urge!

Millions of people will tell you all about their muscle aches and pains, their nervous troubles, circulation problems, muscle weakness... have you the time to listen to them?

Breathing problems, bronchitis, wheezing, getting out of breath picking up a tooth pick. Along with this, what about all the folk you meet with ear problems or hyperactive kids.

A HIDDEN CAUSE OF ILLNESS DOCTORS DON'T ALWAYS SPOT!

The people with all these troubles are not usually hypochondriacs. They are not imagining they have these problems, they are real!

The trouble is unless you have a very visible sign of disease you are not going to get much sympathy. You have to be limping down the street with your leg in plaster to get any real respect for your condition. Keep on complaining about all those aches and pains and you get the reputation of being a moaner. No-one suspects the life of secret or noisy misery you live!

Which is not fair at all.

LET'S GET BACK INTO THE BOWEL!

Here we go again, back into the bowel. I bet you have always taken your bowel for granted. Well, let this be a lesson for you. Never take it for granted. It is a vital part of your anatomy. Your health, vitality and general charm depend on it!

It is hard to be charming if your bowel is upset, especially if it is giving you bad breath and sex is painful. Add body odour to that and you are doomed to spend your life alone!

But read on, help is here!

You know by now your bowel is not some quiet dark retreat but a mighty metropolis with a population of billions. No matter how crowded the giant cities of the world may be, they can't hold a candle against your bowel.

Like all great area of population there are all kinds in there. As some people say, 'It takes all kinds to make a world'… this is especially true of your bowel. Talk about a mixed bag!

But again like the big city, not everyone gets on with everyone else. Your bowel is not an example of social harmony. There is constant, never-ending, vicious competition for survival. I bet you never thought of your bowel that way, did you?

You have one guest down there that is of no value to you at all… a complete freeloader, a bum, a clinger on, a parasite who takes all and gives nothing back. This mongrel is constantly trying to do you in even more by getting on the bowel wall. It is kept off by hordes of good bacteria who prevent it getting on by sheer weight of numbers.

But if you have antibiotics… watch out!

As you well know, antibiotics in, good bacteria out. We have talked about this earlier. When antibiotics are let loose they are like the gangsters in the days of the Great Depression. They make the Valentine Day massacre look like a children's picnic! The climb into everything in sight: good, bad and indifferent.

This creates a problem, because now there are not enough good guys on the bowel wall. So now our smartass sees the opportunity and whammo, gets right on there. This chancer is Yeast. Not the yeast you bake bread with, a different kind and this is not affected by antibiotics.

This yeast sits there biding its time. It is always waiting for an opportunity to get more space. It likes to invade other territory, especially your bowel wall.

After antibiotics, it seizes its opportunity. Whizz, bang, it is in there as fast as it can. It thinks it is its birthday and Christmas all rolled into one.

But now something sinister happens!

Once the yeast is on the bowel wall something sinister happens. It changes! Like some secret invader it changes and adopts a new form. So it can get into your bloodstream it changes into a fungus.

These spores filter through the wall of the bowel and hop

into your blood for a free ride right around your body. They get everywhere... in all your organs, tissues and cells. They are a miniature army of occupation.

This born-again yeast loves sugar. It thrives on it. It has a passion for the stuff in any shape or form.

But there is the down side to this. Anything that feeds also excretes. I have never heard of constipated fungi, have you? So after feeding on the sugar it has to get rid of the waste created. And it does...

This makes problems for you!

For women it creates special problems. It gets into the vagina and the woman get the vaginal symptoms we call 'Thrush'. This often follows a familiar pattern. The woman gets cystitis, she is given antibiotics for the cystitis, and bingo! She's got Thrush!

A word here in your ear. If you get cystitis, try Cranberry capsules from your health food shop or pharmacy. Another excellent herb is Corn Silk. These two herbs work wonders and saves you from needing antibiotics.

IT GETS BACK TO HAVING A TOP-GUN IMMUNE SYSTEM

It is strange, but no matter what health problem one investigates, the immune system always looms up. It is vitally important to do everything you can to maintain a strong immune system.

I know I keep going on about it, but I dearly want you and yours to be wonderfully well. So I keep harping on about it. I know you understand!

Antibiotics weaken your immune system.

To my mind, antibiotics are for dire emergencies. They are the United States Fifth Cavalry that comes galloping over the hill just in the nick of time to save everyone from certain death. Just like they do in the movies!

I have tolled the bell before about the superbugs now on the scene as a result of wildly giving antibiotics for almost everything. Like some people have chips with everything, or tomato ketchup on everything, some doctors hand out antibiotics with equal abandon.

You have noticed how kids who have been on lots of antibiotics never seem to get well. They are always at the doctors with snotty noses, dark shadows under their little eyes, whining and not at all happy. Anything going around and they will catch it… colds, flu, head lice, skin problems. You name it they get it! Poor little things.

Contrast this with the child who eats good food, never has antibiotics, has a strong immune system and is seldom at the doctors. Some cynic may say he doesn't get antibiotics because he never gets sick. Some other will say that he never gets sick because he doesn't go on antibiotics!

The point is, work on your immune system all the time.

BUT GETTING BACK TO OUR ENEMY, THE YEAST CONNECTION!

This waste gets into your blood and as your blood goes everywhere, so does the waste. This creates enormous problems.

A big problem is the symptoms of Candida Albicans, yeast, infection are very much like lots of other illnesses with no yeast connection.

Have a look at some of the symptoms. They could be for other causes, couldn't they?

- Fatigue, tired all the time, no energy.
- Feeling spaced out, drained, everything is an effort.
- The curse of modern life, poor short-term memory.
- Find it hard to say Yes or No, decision making is a problem.

- A common problem is numbness or tingling in hands or feet.
- Can't get to sleep? Toss about half the night?
- Muscle and joint aches and pains… swelling in joints.
- Pain in the abdomen? Gas, bloating, burping?
- Constipation or diarrhoea.
- Vaginal burning or itching.
- Prostatitis… and even impotence!
- No sexual desire or very little… the headache may be Candida!
- Some even connect Endometriosis to Candida
- Check out this one, your PMT could be due to Candida and not hormones!
- Are you tearful, cry easily, get upset over every little thing?

These are only some of the symptoms. When you read all the symptoms it is a bit like looking at one of those medical textbooks. You know how it is, you get to feel you have every one of the complaints you are reading about. Gosh! I've got that feeling, heavens, that describes how I see myself, I have heard about that, I wonder if that is what I've got!

Candida has been described as the great mimic. That is why your doctor has a difficult task to recognise when a symptom is really coming from Candida. I know when allergy testing comes up, it is amazing how often Candida comes up as the cause.

In some ways, it is like trying to decide if depression, anxiety, irritability is a mental problem or a liver crying out for help. In the case of the liver, there is nearly always other symptoms that point to the liver. For example, there is often a feeling of nausea accompanying the mental symptoms.

In the case of Candida, there is usually a craving for sugar or sweet things. In the female, of course, there is often Thrush, so it is easier to pick up.

So what can be done about Candida?

One of the things I have noticed about Candida from treating hundreds of women especially for it is this: It keeps coming back!

I tell patients not to treat Candida lightly. I am often asked how soon will it go away. We humans are an over-optimistic lot in some ways. We have a health problem for twenty years and expect some miracle worker to fix it in twenty minutes.

One lady was very insistent about me giving her a more precise time for getting her well. I am usually vague and try not to give a prognosis. In my opinion, a prognosis is only a guess. Sure, at times a well-educated guess, but a guess just the same. Think about it for a second. People are not mass-produced. We do not pop out of some pre-programmed machine like a plastic mould.

So the time it takes to get well hinges on a lot of different things. You know the kind of thing without me telling you… so I will tell you just the same. (That is something else that amuses me, beware the person who says 'I don't want to upset you… BUT'. You must know they are going to say something to really get you going. 'I don't want to be rude… BUT'. I especially chuckle when someone says 'With all due respects' because I know that usually means with no respect at all. I guess that is the amount of respect they think I am due, none!)

So even though I am saying I don't have to tell you, I must think I DO have to tell you… sort that out when you have time!

Getting back to this insistent lady. No matter how I told her about our biological differences, she persisted, she insisted, she would not desist.

So I told her this little story…

I said 'Look, I spoke to God about you only this morning. And this is what God told me to tell you. He said he is no longer into miracles. He tried that once and look what happened. He said he doesn't want it to happen to me, so you will have to let Nature take her course.'

So with that she was satisfied. I mean, who would dream of arguing with God?

But the truth is Candida can take up to two YEARS to get out of the system for some people. I remember one lady who had been symptom-free for months. She went to a friend's 40th birthday party and drank the toast in champagne. Next day she was in the grip of Thrush again. It was lying there just waiting for a hit of sugar to get the energy to launch another invasion.

HOW IMPORTANT IS DIET?

Diet and environmental hazards are critical to the success of any 'Let's Kill Candida Campaign'. Candida is crafty. It is also a tough opponent. Just look at it, it disguises itself as a hundred other complaints. It lies dormant, apparently on the ropes, but bounces back as though nothing had happened. It can grab the tiniest amount of sugar or sugar-derived stuff and prosper. With Candida you have to be on your guard all the time.

So diet is very important indeed. You have to change your ways, I am sorry to tell you. It is amusing how people twist and turn to get out of reforming their diet. I told you earlier, getting people to change their diet is about as difficult as getting them to change their religion. In some people, even harder!

But change you must. No sugar. No, no, no, not a drop, not a smell of it… none, nothing. I may be repeating myself, but perhaps not, but read the label and look for anything ending with 'ose'. Sucrose, fructose, lactose, maltose, dextrose and as I remarked in an earlier chapter, even honey.

Coffee and tea are out too, I am sad to tell you if you are addicted to either of them. The reason is caffeine causes the liver to release glycogen, which is stored sugar. This is seized by the Candida with glee. 'Whoopee, sugar baby, more sugar, I LOVE it!'

Don't forget, that includes honey. I feel bad telling someone with Candida not to eat honey. We are brought up to love honey. I used to dream of living in a land of milk and honey, even if I wasn't sure what it was. It sounded terrific! But sadly, not for Candida sufferers!

Alcohol is also sugar to the Candida. So you do not have to reduce your alcohol intake, you have to stop drinking any at all. Sorry, folks, not one drop must pass your virtuous lips. You have to get on the wagon and stay there until you get the all clear. I know you don't like that advice, but ignore it and you will make your yeast overgrowth very happy indeed.

What about dried fruit? Sorry, I feel like a real Sadist here, no dried fruit. The reason is dried fruit is concentrated fructose... as are fruit drinks. In a glass of pure orange juice, how many oranges are there? Would you sit down and eat six oranges in one go? One of the worst drinks anyone can have is cordial. In Australia these are made from water, sugar, colouring and flavouring. If you want a hyperactive child, give him or her lots of cordial.

According to all the books you must avoid bread, cookies or anything made with yeast. Yeast-free bread is hard to find I am told. I told you yeast is a toughie, it must be if it can survive the hot ovens bread is baked in. Imagine it surviving that heat!

If you like spicy food you are going to look for any sort of excuse to deny the truth of the next no-no. No condiments, this means sauces, vinegars, BBQ sauces and the whole range of these delicious sauces (I don't have Candida so I can gloat a little here). In the spicy goods file include smoked meats, pickled anything, hot dogs, pastrami, sausages...

If you are a true Scot you won't like this advice either, no re-hashed leftovers. Leftovers attract mould, not the best for anyone with Candida.

In the fruit department, no melons, watermelons, cantaloupes... especially no cantaloupe.

Mushrooms are out as are delicacies like truffles. Cheeses are a no-go area too, except for cottage cheese. The worst cheeses are Blue and Roquefort as these are mouldy cheeses. It is the mould that gives Blue the flavour and aroma of a library full of ancient books.

You will notice that most canned products have either syrup or some form of sugar in it. This is because quite often sugar or a sugar-derived product is used as a preservative. Something to look out for if you are addicted to peanut butter, make sure the peanuts are absolutely fresh. Stale peanuts, dated peanuts and even some fresh products can get mould on them.

Look round your home for mould. The shower is a favourite place for mould to lurk. Look all round the bathroom. Look in cupboards and check for damp. If there is damp it is likely there could be mould. Check the kitchen, especially under the sink. Same with the laundry area.

It is a very strict diet regime… but one you MUST stick with if you are serious about getting rid of Candida. You hear a lot of jokes about diet, which shows we take it seriously. My friend reckons you only have to give up two things to lose a lot of weight. What are they? A knife and fork!

Too many people are on an everything diet. On this they eat everything and stay fat! A bit like the see food diet, they see food and they eat it!

Enough of that idle chatter! The whole point is this… no course of anti-Candida will work permanently without a strict diet regime. You have been warned!

BUT WHAT CAN I EAT? YOU'VE BANNED ALL MY FAVOURITES!

When I have finished telling a patient all the things she can't eat, she will look at me with big sorrowful eyes and cry piteously,

'But what CAN I eat, you've taken away all my favourite foods!'

Life looks like a long dreary road without tea, coffee and alcohol. How is a person supposed to survive without sugar? Where will the energy come from?

On that particular point I have to tell you that it is a myth about sugar giving you dynamic energy. The real truth is sugar drains your energy. It makes it harder for you to remember things you used to remember. Your body has to rob itself to digest sugar because sugar brings only empty calories to the table. When you eat sugar insulin is released and down goes the energy level. Diabetes is one of our fastest growing diseases thanks to our love affair with sugar.

What a miserable existence it will be without spices… sugar and spice gone and we are left with nothing nice… Or so it seems.

I listen to this tale of woe totally without sympathy.

There are heaps of things the Candida sufferer can eat. Try lots of vegetables, great to prevent constipation. Try delicious salads. You can still eat some fruit. You can have apples, bananas, pears, berries, paw paw, grapes, all in moderation bear in mind

I am often delighted when someone says with an air of great wisdom, 'Everything in moderation'. I pause as though considering this weighty statement. 'All things in moderation? ALL things?' Well my dear, try cyanide in moderation, try arsenic. There are lots of things in this world that are not good for you whether in moderation or not.

I am also tickled when someone tells me with an equally grave air that it must be safe because it is natural (or herbal). Belladonna or Aconite are deadly herbal poisons. Oleander is natural, but eat the leaves at your peril!

'Our children's teeth' is clever slogan making. It assumes that if you are against fluoride you must be in favour of bad teeth for our kiddies. We all want what is best for our children but what is the evidence to support fluoride? Very little.

First up, have you ever considered that putting fluoride in drinking water is medication without permission? Not everyone is in favour of fluoride, believe me. I have seen children with the tell-tale white marks on their teeth showing an overdose of fluoride. This makes bones, and that includes teeth, brittle. But we are medicated whether we want it or not.

And what an inefficient way to medicate anyone. Who believes kids drink lots of water? Who can control how much they drink? What is a safe dose of fluoride? Is it safe for older people too? Has it done what it is supposed to do, reduce caries?

Research has revealed that there is little difference in tooth decay in children whether there is fluoride in the water or not. Remember, lots of toothpastes have fluoride in them. More kids are brushing their teeth these days, so they are getting enough fluoride that way. If some children are in danger it would be far more effective to take them to a dentist. This way the dentist could assess the teeth and if necessary use fluoride on them.

All these hazards help Candida. They insult our immune system, a compromised immune system can't do much to defend you. The yeast connection just loves a weak immune system.

WHAT IS THE BEST WAY TO DEAL WITH CANDIDA?

You have heard all the bad news, now it is time for the good news.

Candida can be beaten as long as you are prepared to pay the price. No matter what anyone desires from Life, there is always a price to pay.

Some people elect not to pay the price demanded, and that is fine too. We all have free choice and it is always our own decision.

The price is diet, the determination to stick with the diet. The determination to take the supplements without question. Let me tell you, once your ego gets into the act things can go quite badly for you.

We have a number of things we must do to get rid of the Candida once and for all. We have to overwhelm it in the bowel. We have to create conditions for vast numbers of good bacteria to flourish in our bowel. This way we can be sure they will climb onto the bowel wall and dislodge the yeast. It is a war down there and we need reinforcements by the million.

So the Candida person needs to take the best acidophilus products they can afford. Lots of different strains of bacteria are best.

Load up on these so your bowel is able to overwhelm the yeast and get it back where it belongs. If you have lots of good bacteria they will keep the yeast under control.

The next job is to kill the spores floating around in the blood and to kill those that have set up house in different parts of our body.

There are three deadly agents against Candida. If you want to free your body from Candida, I recommend you have a course of all three.

The first is something I have mentioned earlier, Lactoferrin. The more I investigate this the more amazed and bewondered I am (I made up bewondered). I am lost in wonder at the range of this natural substance.

When I was researching to deal with my prostate cancer, no-one had heard of Lactoferrin. Today it is becoming a household word…

Lactoferrin stops Candida in its tracks. When Candida notices Lactoferrin is on its way it runs for cover. But there is no hiding place. Lactoferrin is on a 'search and destroy mission'. Lactoferrin stimulates your body to produce millions of killer cells. It also stimulates the release of millions of neutrophils. These engulf the Candida and gobble it up.

But that is not all the Lactoferrin will do. It helps to restore the balance of the bowel. It creates the conditions for the good bacteria to multiply dramatically.

As an aside, can I tell you Lactoferrin has been shown to have powerful antiviral activity? So when the flu is sweeping the country get into the Lactoferrin. For myself, I shall be taking Lactoferrin rather than having flu shots.

In Australia, the Lactoferrin I endorse is LactoMax Pro by Ross Gardiner. This is about as pure as you can get it. I used this in my battle against cancer. My files and the files of Ross Gardiner bulge with letters from people ecstatic about the results they have got from LactoMax Pro.

Ross Gardiner was the first manufacturer to recognise the importance of Lactoferrin in Australia and has performed miracles to get it out so ordinary people could reap the enormous benefits from it.

The second product I can recommend to you is also not very well known and that is Colloidal Silver. I have mentioned it earlier to you. Colloidal Silver is remarkable too. It is a natural antibiotic and fungus killer. It kills fungus on contact. It is also excellent for ridding you of parasites. It is tasteless, has no odour and no bad side effects.

Silver has been used as a preservative for centuries. The ancient Greeks and Romans found that milk would stay fresh for longer if stored in silver containers. Obviously, only the rich made this discovery. The poor couldn't afford silver so their milk went sour (that is if they had any).

More down to earth, the American pioneers of the fabled West found that if they had a silver dollar to spare, if they put one in the water barrel the water stay fresher longer. They also found that a silver dollar in milk would keep it fresher longer. I would imagine as they rolled and bumped their way across the limitless prairies they would have nothing to spend their dollar on, so they may as well pop one in the milk! They hid their silverware from the Indians in the water barrel, that is how they found silver kept water tasting better. I am surprised they hid their silverware from Indians. I would have thought they were in greater danger from fellow travellers or roaming gangs of whites. Anyway, as you can see, silver has been known as a preservative or antibiotic for a long, long time.

What has been discovered is silver kills bacteria. Unlike antibiotics, silver does not breed superbugs. The astonishing fact is silver kills over 650 deadly disease-causing organisms. Yep, you heard me, 650!

In the colloidal form the silver is easily taken up and used by the body. It is fascinating to discover how colloidal silver works. It suffocates the fungus within six minutes of contact with it. This has been proven in tests at the University of California Medical Laboratories

Most importantly, Colloidal Silver has a formidable reputation in the battle against Candida. It is also effective against the different Herpes viruses. Herpes is more and more being uncovered as the cause of many disease conditions. Herpes was never suspected as a cause until recently.

The best way is to take a tablespoon of Colloidal Silver in pure water three times a day. I would also recommend that you make Colloidal Silver as part of your daily immune system boosting routine. I do this by taking at least one tablespoon a day. I also put it in our pets' drinking water to keep them clear of parasites. Remarkable stuff, Colloidal Silver.

The third remedy I recommend to you if you really want to be totally free of Candida is Olive Leaf Extract. This is another old remedy re-discovered. Olive Leaf has been known for at least 170 years but, like so many great natural remedies, lost favour when chemical drugs seemed to offer so much, so much faster.

Olive Leaf Extract was used as treatment for Malaria as long ago as 1827.

Olive Leaf Extract works by penetrating the infected cells in your body and shuts down the replication processes of the virus. From the anti-Candida point of view, it halts the growth and spread of the fungus. Just what we are looking for, isn't it.

I suggest it might be a good idea when influenza is on the prowl to take Olive Leaf Extract. It does viruses no good at all. Certainly just speaking for myself, I take it every day and if the flu virus raises its ugly head, I take more.

So as you can see, there is no need to suffer the outbreaks of Candida with all its unpleasant side effects. Get on the diet I told you about, get into the Lactoferrin (LactoMax Pro in Australia), the Colloidal Silver and the Olive Leaf Extract… and laugh at yeast overgrowth, Candida.

It may be, dear reader, you have never heard of Candida, much less suffered from it… but there is sure to be someone you know who has and does suffer from it. Tell them the good news, share the information in this chapter with them, they will love you for it. Better than sending them a dozen roses!

By the way, do not neglect water. When you feel thirsty you are already dehydrated. It is wise to drink plenty of filtered water… you cannot trust the water out of the tap in most cases. I advise drinking water that has been filtered or through a water purifier. And drink plenty! This is particularly true if you have bowel problems and are on a diet or supplementing with fibre.

It is surprising, perhaps even a shock to the system when you realise how many of our modern health problems are caused because we do not drink enough water.

But let us now go forward once more…

Here is something you may not realise… enzymes are often the missing key to abundant health and vitality, so let us explore the ways enzymes can help us in our search for exuberant health.

13

Without these workers you wouldn't be here!

The more I study the body the more astounded I am. It is too much for me to believe all this happened just by chance. I do not liken our bodies to a machine. That is too simplistic for me. Your body, my body, all bodies are miracles of co-ordination. There are mysteries not yet solved. Processes not understood or misunderstood.

Even as you read these words thousands of different activities are taking place, without your control and without your permission!

Not the least wonderful of these activities are the actions of enzymes. Most people have heard of enzymes. They're the things that digest food or are in meat tenderisers, aren't they? Let me tell you something startling, if all your enzymes went on strike you would be reduced to a puddle on the floor! Not a pretty thought.

You have thousands of different enzymes, all highly specialised. Each one has a specific job to do. Talk about job demarcation! These boys were into it before we thought of it.

YOU DO NOT HAVE UNLIMITED SUPPLIES!

Now you have to bear with me. You see, I really do want you to have a wonderful quality of life. When I used to go out talking about nutrition to Rotary and other groups, I often started my chat (I never gave speeches, only 'chats'), I would stand up there, look at all those people in the audience. Now bear in mind I had watched them devour their steak, potatoes and carrots. Noticed how they sprinkled even more salt on them regardless of how much had been lashed on in the kitchen.

I looked at the premature grey hair, the balding scalps, the sagging waistlines, the wrinkled faces... stop! You think I am being most judgmental and very unkind. Well not really! What I am really doing, apart from being critical, is comparing the biological age of everyone with an estimated chronological age. What that means, in English, I am comparing their body's age to their birthday age.

Most people I see are a lot older biologically than they ought to be. I am reminded all the time how 6 out of 10 of us die from nutrition induced disease. As I have said before and no doubt will say again, we dig our graves with our teeth.

But getting back to my opening remarks at the dinner where I am the guest speaker for the night. Here are my golden words, unabridged for you to contemplate 'You see before you tonight a man who wants to die young'. At this comment I have a lot of attention... so I pause for effect. Yes, I know Uncle Fred, I am a show off and I talk too fast too!

So after pausing for effect I continue 'Yes, I want to die young... at 95! But I may change my mind when I get to 94!'

This makes them all laugh, but I really want to make them think.

On that point, what do you think of this? People will tell me all about their very own Uncle Fred who has just died, passed away, been lost, gone upstairs and all the other things we say about death. They will comment, 'Well, you know, he was 85, was never ill in his life and just died in his sleep! Isn't that terrible… never a day's illness and died just like that!'

I look at the speaker with astonishment, astounded as anyone could be. 'Terrible?' I say, 'Terrible? Not at all, that is what you are supposed to do!'

And that's right. You are not supposed to have a life punctuated with operations, flushed with lots of chemical drugs, having joints repaired and replaced. You are not supposed to get crippled by age. You are supposed to mellow like a good wine. Too many people you know started off as wine and ended up as vinegar… what a lot of people call old age is really advanced degenerative disease… so what do you think about that then?

The major movers and shakers in your body, the group that influence your health more than anything else are these enzymes. The frightening theory is that we are born with a potential bank of enzymes. We do not have an unlimited supply. We use them up. If we are enzyme spendthrifts we will die sooner rather than later.

An example of this theory can be seen in Nature. Elephants are slow moving, normally eat an enzyme-rich diet. This is because raw foods are like saving banks packed with enzymes. This means the elephant economises on its own enzyme bank. It is always depositing funds, so it doesn't go bankrupt.

Compare this to the tiny shrew that goes at a million miles an hour. Everything the shrew does is done as fast as it can go. This is one very fast little speedster. But its life span is short. It gets burnout fast.

The elephant, slow moving, long life; the shrew. fast moving, short life. According to the enzyme theory the major reason is the shrew ran out of enzymes more quickly because of its hectic lifestyle.

If you would like to know more about this theory I urge you

to invest in Doctor Edward Howell's book, *Enzyme Nutrition.* This is fascinating reading and will open your eyes. Worst of all, for some people, not you of course, it will make them think. I say not you because I know you think all the time.

Your food should be making enzyme deposits... but is it?

When you see the words 'wild animal', what do you see in your mind's eye? I was brought up on a diet of Rudyard Kipling's compelling Jungle books, so I see animals in the jungle. I love the power of the big cats. I envy them... their supple movements, their grace, their ability to change pace, change direction at top speed. I envy their health. These animals usually get sick because of injury. It may be from a trap, from fighting other animals, from human efforts to kill it.

It is thought-provoking to consider that animals of all kinds in the wild tend to live longer and more healthily than we do. Have you ever seen a tiger or any other wild animal needing anti-inflammatory drugs? Sure, you have seen domestic pets who need them. Hip displacement is common in bigger dogs, for example.

But the difference between a domestic dog and a wolf is diet.

Wolves don't get arthritis as a consequence of getting older. Nor do they suffer from hip displacement, but domestic dogs do.

What is the biggest difference in diet? The wolf eats raw food, the domestic dog eats cooked food. The wolf eats enzyme-rich food, the domestic dog eats enzyme-poor food... that's the difference. It is a big difference, believe me.

The wolf, like most wild animals, uses the enzymes present in the animal it has just killed... cleverly conserving its own enzyme bank. Contrast this with the domestic dog who eats cooked meat out of a tin and has to use its own enzymes to digest the food. The wolf saves its enzymes, the dog uses its enzymes.

Now according to the theory by Doctor Howell, and it is an eye opener, we start off life with a finite enzyme bank. The more you use as you go along, the sooner you become sick, age, get degenerative diseases. So by eating enzyme-poor food we use up our reserves too quickly.

Cooking kills enzymes. Repeat that, listen to it, read it again, feel the words sink in. I will give it a line all its own...

COOKING KILLS ENZYMES

What do we live on in the Western world? Cooked food, of course.

How many people do you know who eat a lot of raw food? One of the silliest statements I ever read was that children, left to their own devices, will always seek out nutritionally good food.

Have you ever heard anything so ridiculous? Only someone who has never had any kids could say something so absurd. Unless ice-cream, candy bars, cola drinks and cordials have suddenly acquired nutritional value without us hearing about it.

Just watch kids at a barbecue. What do you see them chomping on? Usually a piece of meat or a sausage between two slices of white bread. It is a rare sight to see them, or their elders, chewing the salads. Everybody loves the cooked stuff. They call the salads 'Rabbit food' in a tone of polite disgust.

But it is the salad that contains all the enzymes. The charred meat of the grill has just had its enzymes destroyed. What this translates to is the eater has to find the enzymes to digest the food and in the process makes yet another withdrawal from the enzyme bank.

The Don't Believe All You Read Department

For years and years it was believed enzymes are not used up. The theory was enzymes are what they call catalysts. Catalysts are things that cause changes to take place. Enzymes somehow speeded things up, which they do. But in the old theory they themselves remained untouched by all this activity.

A bit like an efficient traffic cop on point duty hurrying the traffic along. Mind you, without being unkind, in this part of the world the traffic lights do a better job. Probably because the traffic lights get more experience!

Anyway, whatever, let's go on. Under the old idea, the traffic cop stands there and causes the traffic to flow and to keep on flowing. Tell Auntie Maude it is only a theory we are discussing. I know she has been in lots of traffic waits because some policeman didn't realise she was in a big hurry.

But in the new theory, the hypothetical policeman is carried along by the traffic flow and disposed of. This is fine if we have a load of other traffic cops all standing by to take over. Bad news if there isn't.

So that is the situation in your body. The enzymes do speed everything up but they do not do it by standing idly by. They are involved in the activity they are speeding up. Like everything else, they get used up.

This is fine if you are eating food rich in enzymes. While you do this you are craftily saving your own enzymes. Now remember this, it is important, you have only a limited amount of enzymes. The sooner you run out of them the sooner you run out of time!

The bad news is if you are eating a lot of cooked food then you are like a spendthrift who has won a million dollars. The spendthrift thinks the million dollars will last forever, no matter how much he spends. He is wrong of course. You have heard of people winning huge amounts of money on lotteries and losing the lot in about five years.

If you are eating a lot of cooked food, processed food, packaged food, fried food... you are running out of enzymes. I know you look in the mirror and everything is still there. It perhaps could look better, but what can anyone expect? We talk about aging as though it is inevitable.

We say 'She doesn't look at all bad, **for her age**! Isn't that a real kicker? For her age indeed. Cheek of it!'

People who look younger than their age have plenty of enzymes left in their enzyme bank. For most of us, we rely on plastic surgery!

Some wit once said if you want to stay eternally young the secret is simple, lie about your age! But that is hard to do if you look older than your age!

Have a look at those few societies in our world where people live to over a hundred years and remain active all those years. Look at their diet and lifestyle. Sure, it is true they keep on working and often hard work too. But how is it they keep all their faculties and are able to keep slogging away well into what we call old age?

The secret lies in their diet. If they eat meat, they eat aged meat. They eat meat that has rotted somewhat as the enzymes in the flesh broke it down.

If they drink milk, they drink milk that is going or has gone, sour. They eat an enzyme-rich diet. They have spent their whole lives eating raw foods, many different kinds of raw food. Their diet has always been well supplied with enzymes. Their body did not have to rob Peter to pay Paul in the enzyme stakes.

The fact is if your diet is short on enzymes, your body has to drag them from somewhere else. This is robbery on a grand scale. This means your glands have to work harder to produce the extra enzymes. Because of this extra work the glands get bigger than they would or should be.

And yes, you have cottoned on quickly to what this means to

you. Yep, the sad news is people who cause their glands to work overtime producing enzymes that should have been in their food, die sooner.

Hey! Who wants that?

THE SEDUCTIVE, PURE, WHITE KILLER!

A word about our favourite taste… sugar.

I mentioned to you earlier about sugar being empty of everything but taste. Sugar retards your ability to remember. It also slows down the brain, you cannot think as fast as you could if sugar is a big part of your diet.

Sugar can rob you of up to 15% of your life. What that means in brass tacks language is simple. Instead of reaching three score and ten, 70, you will only get to about 60.

Of course, if you are 30 that seems so far away as not to matter. But let me tell you, time flies. This is so true but it has to be experienced to be believed.

I think one of the saddest things that can happen to a thinking human being is to find oneself on one's death bed. To lie there knowing you are dying and crying out 'Is the race really over? I haven't even started to run!' and realising the awful truth, it is too late. All those great things you were going to do and never got around to doing. All your good intentions now dust in your mouth.

But when it comes to Life we are incredible spendthrifts. We waste time as though we are going to live forever. We slump in front of the television, numbing ourselves with the programme and a six pack of beer.

In Victorian times they used to call gin the 'opiate of the masses'. This was because to escape a life devoid of value the poor sought comfort in the gin palaces. At least there they were warm, there were other human beings in a similar state and they could anaesthetise themselves with gin.

Today, you could describe the television as the opiate of the masses. People use it for the same purpose… to escape from a life without meaning. TV makes conversation unnecessary. We do not have to have human contact. We are losing contact with reality. Which is just what a lot of people unconsciously want. They don't like their reality, so they escape from it with alcohol, television and sadly, drugs.

I often pause to wonder the contribution poor diet is making to this desire to escape reality. An enzyme-poor diet, a diet robbed of the riches of nutrition, saps the will. It is impossible to be vital, full of life and energy if you are eating a castrated diet.

A successful life is not measured in years but in quality.

Quality includes living the span allotted. You remember the guy who reached the pearly gates twenty years too soon and riposted 'I ate it my way'? That is not a sign of a successful life.

I tell my grandchildren, whom I love to bits, the secret of success is simple. It is easy to say, for a lot of people hard to do, but I pass it on to you because I want you to be successful.

'Do what has to be done, when it has to be done… WHETHER YOU FEEL LIKE IT OR NOT.'

The real kicker, the hard part but the part that makes the difference is 'whether you feel like it or not'.

When people find out I am a published writer they will often confide that they too are writing a book. This would be wonderful except for one thing. They only write when they feel like it. And that is not often enough. Eventually, the partly written manuscript disappears into a drawer somewhere. Years later the would-be writer comes across it and regrets not having completed it. Who knows? It could have been a masterpiece!

To be a successful writer you have to sit down every single

day and write. It doesn't matter whether you feel like it or not. Write something every day, without fail… no excuses.

That applies to anything else. I know people who send for correspondence courses. They get a lot of pleasure from dreaming about what they will do once they get the qualifications they seek. They see themselves successful, rich, happy.

Then the course arrives!

At first they attack it with vim and vigour. But all too soon the deadly monotony of study saps their will. They find excuses for not studying, too tired, too busy at work, have to watch a particular TV programme, nowhere decent to study. The excuses we make are endless. Worst of all, we finally get to believe our own internal press officer. And another dream… another opportunity for greatness just went down the plug hole.

I can tell you something with confidence. At the correspondence school they have all the first four lessons ready to send out. There are stacks of them. But as the lessons progress, the piles get smaller. You will find in some schools, the accounts department is even more efficient than the teaching department. This is because people who abandon their studies don't want to pay the balance on their account.

But what a waste… I think the greatest waste in our world is the waste of human potential. We could be great, but we are not. Sad, isn't it?

Diet could have a lot to do with it

I honestly believe with all the passion I can muster that diet plays a huge part in our inability to be successful. How can you have the energy needed to do what has to be done if your diet is energy empty?

How can you study with a brain robbed by sugar? How can you dream dreams and made them real if your food is enzyme destitute?

There is a leak in your powerhouse. Your diet instead of feeding you is plundering your energy.

HERE'S HOW TO PUT ENZYME ENERGY
INTO YOUR LIFE

Regrettably, it is almost impossible to eat a totally enzyme-rich diet. There are a number of reasons for this. A totally raw food diet is something few people in our modern world are equipped to deal with. I know older people who have tried this and had all sorts of stomach and bowel problems as a result. After a lifetime on devitalised food their digestive system could not cope with raw foods.

What about vegetarians? Well, on the whole they do better than most people. But even they eat a lot of their food after it has been cooked and so is enzyme starved.

Remember also a lot of our food is relatively old. It has travelled long distances before we got hold of it. Quite a lot has spent time in a cold store where it loses its value as each day goes by.

However, only raw foods come complete with the enzymes to digest them. Nature is clever in the extreme. She provides everything. It's all there, the nutrition, the enzymes to release the nutrition into our body. So what do we do? We wreck everything. We mess about with the food. What we call food is often a caricature of food.

How can we call something 'food' if we have stripped it of everything of value? It is like saying people live in a 'free society' when only rich people have access to the Law.

Can you call white flour food when it has been stripped of its vitamins, enzymes and anything else of value? We feed the goodness of the wheat to farm animals. Suitably doctored with growth promoting hormones, of course.

It would pay you to have a good look at what you are putting in your mouth in the name of food. Read the labels… an alarming trend is today manufacturers can irradiate food without telling you. They claim the gamma rays go right through the food and are therefore harmless.

How do they know that? Well, it is easy. You see no-one actually drops dead after a few years of eating the irradiated food. But you have to wonder what happens after twenty years of eating them.

Mother Nature keeps deadly accurate books of account. Everything you do, eat, think is recorded. One day we all get the bill, we are called to account. A Judgment Day while still here on earth.

So who knows what is being recorded against our names when we are fed a diet of irradiated foods? And now they have the super soy bean. A man-made strain of soy able to withstand massive amounts of weedkiller without being slaughtered itself.

And they try to tell us none of this pesticide gets into the soy! Who are they trying to kid? If you check the labels, you will be surprised at how many foods have soy added to them. You could be getting these suspect soy beans not just in obvious products like soy milk, but in chocolate bars, biscuits, cake mixes and who knows what else. Do you really want genetically altered soy products in your food?

So now we get genetically altered foods, irradiated foods, and take note, careful note… none of these so-called foods are found in nature.

Can I ask you a question without being rude? Do you honestly believe we can live on food that bacteria can't live in? Irradiated food will keep for months without going bad. Bacteria can't live in it. If bacteria can't live in it, how can we live on it?

What effect do you think eating these concoctions have on our bowel? Do you think they give us strength, add to our span of years? Hard to believe they do, isn't it?

The wonder is we survive as long as we do.

But the word is 'survive', we exist on these foods, but do we prosper?

YOU MUST HAVE ENZYMES TO HAVE ANY HOPE OF A VITAL LIFE

Look around you, where are the people so full of health they radiate joy and happiness? Where are the people who charm you with their jubilant exuberance? Where are the people taking Life in their stride, people to whom obstacles are only challenges to be overcome?

Where are the elderly still having sex like you would find hard to believe? Where are the elderly people free of aches and pain, free of stiffness in joint and muscle? Where are the people whose happy laughter fills the air with sunshine? Where are the people who charge through Life without needing alcohol, drugs or other stimulants?

Where are the people who praise in conversation instead of damning? Where are the people who build up other people rather than tear them down? Where are the people who do not complain but get on with it, confident they have the inner resources to beat whatever Life throws at them?

Well, I can tell you they are not plentiful where I live. It may be different in your suburb, town, city, country… but there are so few here it is a miracle to find one. When you do find such a person they light up your whole day!

If you would like to be one of those people radiating joy, hope, and confidence, get enzymes into your diet.

Raw food is packed with enzymes, so it follows you will have to get a percentage of raw food into your daily diet. You can do this by having salad instead of cooked vegetables. You can do this by having raw fruit for your dessert instead of ice-cream, fruit salad out of can, or packaged pudding.

You can do this by eating plenty of raw fruit, not stewed, not out of a can, but as fresh as you can get. Eat nuts, seeds, get some variety into your diet. Cut down on meat, better still… cut it out altogether. I see advertisements for hamburgers… cooked meat, a bit of lettuce, processed cheese, French fries all washed down with a cola drink. What a recipe for disaster! And this is the staple diet of so many of our kids. Can anyone wonder about crime on the increase? How can anyone perform to the maximum on such a minimum nutrition diet? The answer is they can't, and they don't.

Because of our poor diet, our enzyme-starved diet, our glands have to work overtime to provide enzymes to digest what we have just eaten. As I have said, in a good enzyme-rich diet the food brings its own digestive power with it. In a poor diet the body has to find the enzymes.

This means somewhere else has to pay the price for the robbery. Did you know that an enzyme-rich diet boosts your immune system? It stimulates action to destroy abnormal cells in your body. Enzymes can help reduce arthritic pain, if you have some to spare. An enzyme-rich diet protects your heart and circulatory system…

So it is up to you. Increase the raw food element in your daily diet but take digestive enzymes if you are not on a total raw food diet. By taking digestive enzymes with each meal, you will be providing help for your glands. You will also be spared taking yet another deposit out of your enzyme bank. As I have remarked, you have limited number of enzymes in your enzyme bank, so every time you save withdrawing you improve your immune system and prolong your life!

To find out more, do invest in Doctor Edward Howell's book, *Enzyme Nutrition*. I promise you, it will open your eyes and make you think hard about what you are putting into your body!

But now, let us have a chat about that most exploited section of our modern world, the overweight, the obese, the fat… the unwanted (or so too many of them believe!).

THE TWENTY FIRST CENTURY DISEASE!

It used to be called the twentieth century disease but that is outdated now. This disease affects Candida sufferers because they always have a low immune system. This disease is chemical sensitivity. More people have this problem than you may realise.

We are like in a world dominated by chemicals.

Our fields are soaked in them… superphosphates, weedkillers, grass killers, fertilisers, pesticides to name a few. Then there are the chemicals we use to keep ticks and blood sucking parasites off farm animals. Chemicals to strip old paint, chemicals in the new paint. Chemically treated logs for outdoor use. A lot of these chemicals end up in our water supply.

Scientists have found chemicals like DDT and dioxin in the fat of animals and birds far away from the place where they were sprayed. Even more scary, to folks like me, is these chemicals can sit around for generation after generation! Thus are the sins of the fathers suffered generation after generation.

CAN YOU TRUST YOUR WATER?

I have mentioned this earlier… no you cannot trust the water out of your tap. That sparkling glass of water can be a chemical cocktail. The problem for the chemically sensitive is the chemicals in the water reinforce the problem. It can also excite attacks of chemical sensitivity. This means that every time a sufferer has a drink of water from the tap, or a cup of tea or whatever, their problem is made worse. Your tap water can also have a few other nasties in it such as minute algaes, protazoa, amoeba. This is apart from the stuff the authorities put in like chlorine, which is a bleach, or fluoride which is a by-product from aluminium manufacturing.

What do you think of the notion of loading your drinking water with fluoride? Do you believe the story put out by the authorities that it is to protect our children's teeth?

14

At last! The truth about successfully losing all the weight you want... quickly and easily!

We hear of exploitation. Child labour, poor immigrants, women and other disadvantaged groups. They all cry for help. But the cry for help we ignore or profit from is the cry of the overweight.

People who are overweight are made to believe there is something wrong with them. Big is not beautiful in our modern world, no matter how often some people in the media go on about it.

At one time, of course, women were beautiful if they were big and buxom. Look at some of the old masters' paintings. Big, chubby, happy-looking women, flaunting their ample curves for all the world to see. Men in those days would scorn a woman whose body was more that of a teenage boy than a full-blooded woman.

Men liked broad-hipped women and found them extremely sexy. Skinny Lizzies had no appeal at all... but times change and so do tastes. These days females can kill themselves trying to achieve model matchstick figures. They starve to death in a vain attempt to be something they were never intended to be.

But the truth is, and let's be honest, a lot of men and women are overweight because of poor nutritional decisions. In fact, in our over-abundant era more people eat themselves fat than anything else.

OVERWEIGHT PEOPLE ARE OVERWEIGHT ON THE INSIDE TOO!

We are inclined to forget, that is, if we ever knew, fat people are fat on the inside too. When you see someone who is overweight you must know their liver will be infiltrated with fat, there will be a fatty casing around their heart, their kidneys will be interlaced with fat, their arteries will be coated with fat... and their bowel will be clogged up too!

What is also worthy of your attention is that overweight people who ate themselves into that condition are usually undernourished. They are nutritionally deficient. Their body is labouring with difficulty, trying to perform on inadequate high-octane foods.

Does this set the alarm bells ringing in your brain?

Guess what happens to people with fatty hearts? Go on, have a guess. Nothing nice happens to them because they are a walking heart-attack bomb!

Do you believe these people eat an enzyme-rich diet or one loaded with vitamins and minerals? Do you think their bowel works at peak performance level? Do you think they digest everything they eat with ease? Of course they don't! If they did they wouldn't be overweight!

Look, I know it sounds cruel. I am aware that some people will take offence at what I am saying. That is fine, because to take offence they have to read what I am writing and more importantly, think about it. But believe me, I am not a cruel person, if I am cruel it is to be kind... but as you can see losing weight is not a cosmetic necessity, it is a health necessity!

The actuality is, in the end, we all have to accept responsibility for our own condition. What we are today is the combined result of all the choices we have made in the past.

I know that is not a popular point of view for a lot of folks. It is much more comforting to believe what we are... the state of our life... is all the result of outside forces. People spend fortunes on lucky charms, get-rich-quick schemes, diet programmes that promise the earth, people are into magic and all sorts of things. All these magic spells are an attempt to put responsibility for our future outside ourselves.

No wonder they don't work. Because whether we like it or not, we and only we, are the arbiters of our fate.

On the subject of the abnormal, I have often wondered why it is that when these psychics contact Uncle Fred or Auntie Maude the messages from 'the beyond' are so everyday. We do not hear some striking, earth-shattering revelation that will benefit mankind. No, what we hear are things like 'Uncle Fred is fine, likes it here, a treat and sends you all his love'. It sounds more like something one would write on a postcard when on holiday.

I have read a lot of books and magazine articles on the supernatural, on speaking to the dead and so on. I have yet to hear something of importance. Wouldn't you think that we would hear something of incredible value to humanity? It might cheer up their relatives to believe Uncle Fred is keeping a benign watch over them, but it doesn't do much for the rest of us.

OK, so you think I am a cynic. Maybe I am, but maybe I am just impatient to hear something that will curb our headlong rush into environmental oblivion!

But cynic that I am I think it will be a long time if I am waiting for forces outside our society to remedy the environment. We will have to do it or no-one will, and that's the truth.

Similarly with the condition of our body… if we don't like it we have to do something about it ourselves. There is no genie with a magic wand to do it for us. It would be very warming and delightful if there were. I would love to hand over responsibility to some kind, caring 'other' who would put my interests before theirs. But no such luck.

I heard once that the definition of insanity is doing the same thing again and again… and expecting a different result.

You know, we rarely examine our behaviour patterns to see if they are working for us. We keep on trying to reap crops we have never sown. We want to be loved but have never loved anyone. We want to receive but have never given. We never question our attitudes, why we hold the opinions we do. I hate racism. I cringe when someone tells me that there is a Jewish plot to control the world. What a load of codswallop… and yet to someone who holds these views my attitude is offensive.

Where do people get these opinions? Who told people black people had smaller brains? Who said Asian people had no feelings and were 'inscrutable'? Go through the list of dangerous opinions people hold. Seldom are they based on any reliable data. They are usually inherited opinions handed down like family heirlooms. Except these particular heirlooms are junk and valueless.

What is frightening is people go to war based on these outdated, outmoded opinions. Whole nations are incited to kill their neighbours on something so flimsy as they happen to be different.

Oh there I go again, on one of my hobby horses riding headlong into the distance… let me get back to losing weight!

What it all boils down to is that if you are overweight you have to accept the fact that you have the job of getting your weight down. No-one else can do it for you.

It is very important for you to take time out to have a look at the behaviour patterns that have made you overweight and may be making you even more overweight. If you keep doing what you have always done, you will get what you have always got. In this case, even more overweight!

If you are looking for the magic diet, look no further!

We do believe in magic. Yes we do! We buy lucky charms, we consult psychics at five dollars a minute, and we fall for the magic weight-loss diet… not once, not twice, but time and time again.

The women's magazines sell millions of copies all over the world on the promise of yet another 'wonder diet'. You have seen them all, haven't you? The seven-day diet, the banana diet, the pineapple diet, the eat all you want diet. There must be as many diets as there are people looking for a magic diet.

But look no further.

At last here is the truth. The truth is there is no magic diet.

I am sorry to disappoint you. I know your hopes were built up yet again only to be dashed into the dust. I know it isn't fair. My Dad was so right, Life is not fair!

So it gets back to Lifestyle.

SUGAR! THE MAINSTAY OF THE GET-FAT DIET…

Once again the white knight, sugar, is about to be unhorsed by the black knight, the truth. Sugar causes overweight not only because it becomes excess energy but for another little known reason.

When we talk about weight loss we are really talking about changing shape, not necessarily losing weight. We want to fit into a smaller size dress, or we want to be able to buckle up our pants without puffing and panting.

It is not really weight so much as our size that causes us so much concern. So I would like you to do something for me if you are keen to lose weight, or rather, change size. Chuck your scales out of the window. Make sure you don't hit anyone, but throw it as far as you can. Into the dam if you can throw that far!

Hopping on the scales every day is perhaps the most de-motivating thing anyone trying to change shape can do. Here is this determined person who has gone without everything that makes life worthwhile. Gone without chocolate biscuits, forsworn ice-cream, no more cream cakes, cut down on potatoes, stopped the cola tap... in short, done everything that should be done. And tears, cries of frustration, moans, groans... not only has the person not lost weight, they have gained it!

Is there no justice in this world any more? Does virtue not get its just reward? Aren't sinners to be forgiven? What is going on? Everything that should have been done, was done. Everything that shouldn't have been done, wasn't done. And weight has been put on!

No wonder there are tears of utter despair, no wonder the sackcloth and ashes are brought out of the attic and thrown over the head. But wait fair one, the reason is simple. When you do all the right things you will develop muscle. Muscle weighs more than fat... but muscle burns off fat.

Grab the tape measure. Run it around your waist. The sun will shine again in your life. The flowers will bloom and everything will be rosy, because you have lost size around your waist... Bravo! Your sacrifices were worthwhile after all. Wonderful, marvellous, outstanding, incredible... you are lost for words.

But back to sugar!

People gain weight because of a simple equation. If you put in more calories than you use in energy, you gain weight. So you either cut down on the calories, which is the favourite route, or increase energy output, which most people don't want to do at all if they can help it. Sugar is extra calories, empty calories to be sure, but calories just the same.

Now hold on to your hat, here is something few people know or understand. When your body gets calories it expects to get nutrition as well. In the case of sugar it is disappointed. There is no nutrition with white sugar and so none is coming.

So guess what your artful body does? You will never guess so I will tell you… it makes you hungry. Your body craves nutrition so in the hope you will recognise its cry for help it increases your appetite.

All too often it only gets more of the same. More white sugar in its many disguises… so you are now on the weight cramming roundabout. More appetite because of empty calories, more sugar meaning even more empty calories. So your body pleads for nutrition and you keep giving it rubbish. A bit like the French Queen, Marie Antoinette, who when she heard the mobs of Paris were clamouring for bread exclaimed 'Let them eat cake'.

She was rather unlucky because in the end the mob cut off her head. You are not that unlucky but you are now in that class of people who claim they have a weight problem.

So to lose weight, to change shape, your first step is to hunt down sugars in your diet and eliminate them. Look for sucrose, lactose, maltose, dextrose, fructose. Anything ending is 'ose' has to be ruthlessly eliminated.

And what about artificial sweeteners? What about them? If you want to stay taut, trim and terrific for all time, then you need to lose the sweet tooth you have. For some people it is more than a sweet tooth, it is a mouthful of sweet teeth.

I hate to tell you this about artificial sweeteners, it is not the news of the day you have been waiting all day to hear… but the favourite artificial sweetener aspartame has a nasty downside. Over 30 degrees Celsius it breaks down into methanol and formaldehyde. Methanol is wood alcohol and is not stuff you should be messing with. They preserve dead bodies in formaldehyde, something else you do not want in your body 'cos it is a poison.

If you would like to find out more about aspartame, look it up on the Internet... you will find it very interesting and frightening too!

So leaving your sweet tooth to the Tooth Fairy is a good idea.

This means learning not to crave sugar. If you crave sugar I suggest you re-read the chapter on Candida and the one on parasites. You just could be inflicted with both. So unless you address this problem first, you will have great difficulty getting sugar out of your diet.

I used to like sweet things but I no longer even like the taste. Sugar burns my throat so I know I am no longer a sugarholic. It can be done and you can do it. I have also eliminated any desire for salt. I cannot eat anything with salt or sugar in it. I send it back if I accidentally get some in food or drink.

I am confident you can do the same. It is not willpower, by the way, it is imagination. If it comes to showdown between imagination and willpower then put your money on imagination.

If you are using willpower to change your diet but you dream of the joy of feeling luscious chocolate eclairs in your mouth, you will lose. Your imagination will have triumphed yet again.

Dream of being slim, not of not eating sugar-laden items of desire. If you think about not eating something your subconscious mind will think you want some... so watch out.

You remember how we had a chat about the refrigerator and its seductive contents. I told you how people blame the fridge as though all the goodies got in there by themselves. When I suggest the novel idea that they stop buying the so-called goodies and stop putting them in the fridge, you can see the inner battle going on. The face crumples, the eyes take on a look of desperation, you can see the conflict raging. The thought of a fridge minus biscuits, chocolate bars, cola drinks is almost too much to bear.

One lady told me she had cut a photograph of a very fat lady out of a magazine and substituted a copy of her own head for the one on the photo. So now every time she went to the fridge she saw this image of herself as the very fat person… a constant reminder of what she didn't want to be.

What a drastic error! Just what she should not have done. Oh dear, her intentions were the best… but every time she went to the fridge her subconscious mind saw this photograph and thought it was how she wanted to be. No wonder she was finding it impossible to empty the fridge and stop going in. Mind you, she was emptying the fridge, but through her mouth rather than through the backdoor into the garbage bin.

So I suggested she tear the photograph up and consign it to the oblivion of the waste paper basket. Instead she was to look for a photograph of a girl with the figure she would like to have… and substitute her head for the one on the photograph.

This way, every time she passed the fridge she would be reminded of her goal. Her subconsious mind would also pick up on this and do its part in helping her achieve her ambition.

IF YOU ARE OVERWEIGHT, HOW DO YOU SEE YOURSELF?

The biggest enemy anyone has who is trying to lose weight is self-image. Over the years I have counselled thousands of women who wanted to lose weight. Most of them had tried all sorts of diets and had given up hope of ever losing weight.

One thing so many had in common was low self-esteem.

I remember one young lady who came to see me. Tell you what, she was a stunner! Absolutely gorgeous… blonde, blue eyes, lovely teeth, but she didn't smile much unfortunately. You will be astonished to learn she had no mirrors in her house. When I asked her why, she told me it was because of her ugliness. She could not bear to look at herself.

I couldn't believe my ears. Ugly? She was a corker! And yet in her own mind she saw herself as ugly. Much like the anorexic who is as thin as a lath sees herself as fat. I suggested this young lady came to our house, in our mirrors I am sure she would have seen the truth, her beauty.

Now here is something important for you to think about. Because this pretty young lady saw herself as ugly, she acted ugly. She didn't smile, she walked with her head down so people wouldn't see her face. In short, her whole life was a mess.

And so it is with a lot of overweight people. The myth is fat people are jolly people. You used to see these drawings of fat people with big fat cheeks laughing away like crazy. Now I am sure there are a lot of happy people out here who are overweight. But I can tell you with confidence there are a darn sight more who are not a bit happy.

These people often have the idea that because they are overweight, nobody really loves them. I mean, who could love someone with a figure like that? The answer is, of course, thousands of people could. But the overweight person, deep down, does not believe this.

This can create a problem all its own. If nobody loves me, what does it matter if I pig out on chocolate biscuits or scoff a litre of ice-cream? They don't love me anyway, so what the heck!

This is an unconscious cop out. This is doing just what I asked you NOT to do. What was that again? You mean you don't remember? Gosh, no wonder I have to keep repeating myself. What this is doing is putting the responsibility for the poor diet, the excuse for eating junk, on outside forces. The mysterious 'they' don't love me so why not gorge on fattening foods?

People who take this point of view really believe what their unconscious mind is throwing up. They don't stop to give it much thought because they believe people don't love them.

So they love themselves by eating away as though there are no tomorrows.

The mental angle to changing shape is very important. Without it, you will have difficulty. You have to train yourself to believe it is a good idea to lose weight, you have to be motivated to lose weight, you have to believe it is possible for you to lose weight.

Let's have a look at believing it's a good idea to lose weight. What? Do you honestly think you have to ask that question? Do I WANT to lose weight? What kind of stupid question is that, for heaven's sake? Of course I want to lose weight you clown, why do you think I am reading this chapter of your otherwise excellent book?

OK. I know how you feel. It does seem a stupid question. But let us have a closer look at it. While a lot of people say they want to lose weight they are saying this because they know it is what people expect them to say.

People look at you quite oddly if you are overweight and claim boldly you just love being overweight. You think not being able to get into last year's dresses or pants is the best thing that happened this year… but just try saying that out loud. Goodness, everyone will think you are anti-social or something!

So you proclaim loudly and often your wish to lose weight.

The unconscious mind is just that, unconscious. We all have a problem with that idea. People will affirm strongly they are not moved by unconscious forces. They snort at the idea of something deep down forcing them to behave in certain ways. But the forces are unconscious, that means we do not know about them. We cannot look at them, we are not aware of them. I am sure you get it, but I can tell you, loads of people have great difficulty with that idea.

Let me give you an example you will hate.

There are people who are overweight because they either

want to punish someone or want to repel sexual advances from the opposite sex. Go on, what rubbish! Who would punish themselves to punish someone else? That is ridiculous. And who on earth would want to repel sexual advances? They sell millions of dollars worth of all sorts of things just to encourage sexual advances!

That's just what I thought too. But people punish themselves all day long with jealous thoughts, with thoughts of getting back at people they believe have done them wrong, with thoughts of hatred for other people for all sorts of reasons. The world is not full of light and happiness for a lot of people. That is sad I know, but it is also true.

So deep down we may not really, truthfully, honestly, sincerely want to lose weight or change shape. So we have to question ourselves.

OK, so you do want to lose weight... Here is the equivalent of a bucket of cold water over the head, if you are committed to losing weight, if you are as committed as you say you are, then ask yourself if you are prepared to pay the price to lose weight and change shape.

The price is not money, although that is always involved, but in changing diet, exercising, changing lifestyle, taking the important supplements for a healthy bowel, liver and digestion. Not just the usual slimming potions you have been trying for years.

Do you have faith you can lose weight?

The difference between faith and hope is simple. With hope it is a wish. If everything turns out fine, if nothing goes wrong, you think you will lose weight. You hope so, anyway.

But faith is different. Hope hopes and Faith KNOWS. People with faith know they will lose weight. They don't hope the change in diet, in lifestyle, will help them lose weight... they **know** they will lose weight.

So you must develop faith. This will come as you see the inches falling away. When you have to take in your belt a notch or two, find your skirt slipping down, this will gradually change hope into faith.

Once you have faith, your goal to lose weight, to change shape will most definitely be realised.

So now you believe it is possible for you to lose weight despite all past efforts that have been unsuccessful. Terrific! Because that is the truth. You can! But make sure you really want to.

Keep the image of a slender you in front of you.

You are committed, you know you can do it, so now let's get on with it!

Your last weight-loss programme

I don't mean the programme you were on last time you desperately tried to lose weight. You know the one, it worked for a while but you ended up carrying more weight than you had when you started. No, I want to give you stuff you can use to lose weight once and for all, and never put it back on.

I have told you how to hunt down sugar in all its crafty disguises so that is your first commitment to a new life, a new you. Do this and your energy level will soar. It will go through the roof. You will be a dynamo.

I know you are under the impression that sugar gives you boundless energy. That's what the advertisements say. Eat sugar for energy.

If you believe that you believe in fairies at the bottom of your garden. Tell Auntie Maude I know there are fairies at the bottom of her garden, but she is the exception. Most people don't have them any more!

Sugar causes an instant insulin reaction and that sends your energy plummeting as though it fell off a skyscraper.

By cutting out sugar you will be increasing your metabolism.

Metabolism is simply your rate of burn. Do you burn like a slow, smoky fire of wet leaves? Or do you burn up like a blast furnace? Nearer to the smoky old wet fire if you are overweight. But the exciting news is by cutting out the sugar gang you will move nearer to the blast furnace.

Your rate of metabolism will go up and up and up! It will, believe me. People buy fat metabolising pills in the pious hope they will give them that magic metabolism that burns off fat. Cut out sugar if you want them to have a hope of helping you.

Come on, you did tell me you were committed!

No-one can lose weight if they are toxic!

How can anyone lose weight if they have a digestive system that is only working half time? How can anyone lose weight if they do not digest fat properly? How can anyone lose weight if their tissues are clogged up with waste that has built up over years? How can anyone lose weight whose bowel is not eliminating effectively?

The answer is simple. They can't.

The dangerous truth about most weight-loss programmes is that they appeal to the lazy side of us. The people putting these programmes out know a basic truth about most of us. We are lazy. We want a quick fix. The words 'Quickly, Simple, Easy, No Effort Required' are words that get right in to us and push all our buttons. Boy, no effort required, quick and easy too... just what I want. No commitment, it is easy, it is quick and that doesn't need any sort of commitment. Didn't you love the heading for this chapter... how to lose weight 'quickly and easily'. I wrote that just to get you in! I knew it would appeal to your basic instincts...

But it is always a false promise.

They tell you by adopting some new diet you will lose weight, change shape, become trim, taut and absolutely terrific. You buy the diet, you do not lose weight for ever… once again you feel let down, cheated!

This is because diet alone will not, repeat will not, cause you to lose weight and change shape permanently. I know that is hard to bear but it just happens to be the truth. And the truth will set you free!

It is always a diet that is advertised. The hook to get you in is always the false promise, the siren song, the alluring prospect you can achieve your goal without effort. Just eat a few different foods or take some magic potion or pill. People never give up. You have to admire their persistence. Despite repeated failures they try diet after diet after diet… They do, don't they?

And they almost always end up worse off than they were when they started. You see photographs of before and after… miracles! Wonder of wonders! Incredible! A joy to behold! And you think they are talking about you. Sadly, the people you see are often the exception and not the rule.

They are not typical of the people who try out these diets. Come on, deep down you know they are not. You know people who have spent thousands of dollars on magical weight-loss formulas from slim, slinky advertisements. And you also know most of them have been disappointed. But hope triumphs over experience once again!

If you sincerely want to lose weight you must get detoxed first.

Cut out sugar and detox.

These are the two stepping stones to the new you.

Not only will you look better, you will feel the best you have in years! That is a promise.

So let us have a chat about detoxification…

Oooer! Detoxification, sounds very sinister and complicated. It does, but it isn't complicated at all, very simple in fact…

Detoxification is to clean out. To get rid of accumulated wastes that clog up our system, choke our cells, slow everything down and cause us an amazing number of diseases.

How do you recognise you need a detox?

Your body tells you, the problem is that we seldom listen to our body. When someone has been on the booze and well overdone it, the next day he wakes up with a sick head and a sicker stomach. But does he listen to these cries for help? Not on your life… he insults his body even more by going for the hair of the dog that bit him, as the saying goes.

Here are some of the faint cries for help your body hopes you will notice…

Fatigue, yet again. Dizziness, a common complaint with a lot of people. Low immune system, claimed to be the reason there is so much sickness around these days. Nausea, again a common problem. Gas, we have chatted about this. Bad breath, even your best friend won't tell you about. Depression, more and more people are suffering from depression. A build-up of mucus… you remember the Pathologist who told me most people are glued up inside with mucus. Good old-fashioned constipation, a modern scourge.

Poor circulation, an over-heated body can be a sign of poor circulation. That is a shock for most people… B.O., the romance destroyer.

A lot of skin problems are an indicator of a toxic body. Your body tries to throw out toxins through the skin. If we just treat the skin with lotions, ointments, creams, antibiotic creams, cortisone creams, the toxins can go deeper inside and the end result is serious disease.

Did you ever hear the advice the Professor of Medicine gave to his students when they asked about specialisation? He simply said 'I advise you to become a skin specialist. Your patients never get better and they never die.' I hope that is just a story!

But it is not a story when I tell you again that if you ignore calls from your body for a detoxification you must not be surprised if serious disease strikes you.

How to stop toxins ruining your health

You cannot be healthy and lose weight with an unhealthy colon. Sorry to keep hammering this point. I do it because it is very important and as I know you sincerely desire health, slimness, perhaps lots of money and who knows what else, well it all starts with a healthy colon.

There is an old saying 'Death Starts In The Bowel' and so does overweight, low energy, poor skin tone, bad breath and lots of other things we don't want. What deceives us is that death from the bowel is very slow. It can take twenty or thirty years to show, but the quality of life, while this is going on, is not the best by any means.

Take note that death from bowel cancer is on the increase. Bowel cancer does not happen overnight, it takes years to develop. The bigger problem is so often the cancer migrates from the bowel to the liver or other organs… so taking care of your bowel makes a huge amount of sense, doesn't it.

In my practice as a Naturopath I have noticed over the years that by fixing digestion, assimilation and elimination, it is surprising how many seemingly unrelated health problems disappear…

Like losing weight.

It makes sense when you think about it. If you are not digesting what you eat properly, if you are not assimilating the goodness from what you eat, if you're are not getting rid of poisonous wastes out of your body, how can anyone expect to be well? How can anyone be slim, full of vitality, radiating health? The answer, as you well know, is they can't!

Herbs hold the key to resounding
good health

The beauty of herbs is they work with your body and not against it. Drugs tend to assault your body, which is why you get so many side effects. Herbs have been used since man emerged from the distant mists of Time. Body purification has been a ritual in most religions for centuries.

We seem to have forgotten what a lot of ancient civilisations knew and practised... using herbs to cleanse the inside as well as the outside of the body. And we think we are so smart yet we have forgotten the basic health rules known to the modern man of thousands of years ago.

We work our bodies to death. It's true, think about it. We overload it with junk food. These days with degraded soils, gigantic amounts of chemical overload on crops, water and soil, irradiated foods, genetically altered foods, pollution and all the other sorry penalties we pay for our so-called advanced civilisation our body is being called upon to perform tasks it was never designed for. We pay for this in ill health and slow death!

Now you may think we enjoy good health today. Yeah? Who says so? Look around you, countries are almost going bankrupt because of the enormous burden of so-called health care. Taxes keep on increasing because governments can't keep up with the rising costs of Medicare. How many people do you know who are on medical drugs of one kind or another? Loads of them, heaps of them, whole armies of them...

So getting rid of toxins out of our body makes clear good sense, don't you agree? I am sure you do.

It is not just your bowel. The organs of elimination are your skin, your liver, your kidneys, your lungs, your lymphatic system, your blood stream.

A total herbal detoxification system uses herbs to target these organs.

It has always seemed almost mystical to me how different herbs have qualities to help different parts of the human body. Dandelion targets the liver and kidneys, Blue Flag targets the liver, Cascara targets the bowel, Milk Thistle a brilliant liver cleanser and toner… and so it goes on.

In olden herbal lore it was said the herbs you need would grow wild in your garden. What some people ungratefully call weeds, herbalists recognise as God-given herbs. So as an example, if there are a lot of dandelions round your place, take time to look at your liver…

It might be a good idea to go to the library and get a good herb book out. Then you can identify the herbs growing madly around your home… and draw your own conclusions.

ALWAYS USE THE EXPERIENCE OF EXPERTS

Good advice for anyone who wants to be successful in any area of life is to use the experience of successful experts.

Detoxing yourself is no different.

You can study herbs, you can experiment with different herbal combinations… but the problem with learning from personal experience in any field is it is the slowest and most expensive way to learn.

Far better to let someone else do the work. I love letting other people do the work. I am a bit like the guy who said he loved work, he could watch other people working all day and never get tired.

So what I do at least twice a year is I go on a seven-day cleansing programme. Just a quick word before you dash out and hop in your car off to the health food shop or pharmacy…

I use the QuickCleanse programme and recommend it to my patients. This is in Australia and New Zealand; in other countries ask for advice to get a detox programme suitable for you. This is because I have kindly let someone else do the thinking and research for me. This is what I call a 'labour-saving device'.

It is important to ease yourself into the programme. Prepare your body for the shock it will get when you start doing the right thing by it... the day before have light meals.

A word of warning, not to scare you or anything like that... just to let you know some people go through a healing crisis when on a detox diet. The difference between a medical health crisis and a herbal one is that after the medical one you could be dead, after the herbal one you will feel terrific.

The QuickCleanse herbs will keep your bowel working and that is extremely important. You know why, don't you? Of course you do, it is so the toxins draining out of your tissues can be eliminated. For more information on QuickCleanse see back page.

Keeping your bowel working is very important indeed on any fasting or detoxifying programme. If it doesn't keep working you end up feeling terrible and wondering why people rave about detoxing being so bloody wonderful.

The detox herbals are chosen to target every organ of elimination in your body. However, you have to help them. You do this by watching what you put in your mouth.

The kind of food that will spoil everything for you is sugar, as I have said time and time again. No, I am not sorry for telling you this yet again. Salt. Salt is not your friend. Salt holds fluid in the tissues and fluid is what most people lose when they excitedly tell you they lost seven kilos in seven days. It was the fluid... the fat is still there!

Do not eat animal products. As I pointed out to you earlier, too many animal products are host to adrenaline, female hormones, antibiotics and putrefactive bacteria. Not only that, when you are on a detox you do not want to burden your body with energy consuming foods.

Keep off dairy too. As I told you earlier, there are loads of people who are allergic to dairy but don't realise it. Sinus, mucus, allergies can all be the result of dairy foods in a lot of people.

You remember how I told you we used white flour and water to make wallpaper paste years ago? When you are detoxifying, your body is trying to prize this stuff off your bowel wall, so don't insult it by eating more white flour products, will you?

Lay off processed foods too. This is packaged foods, canned foods, mixes, frozen foods and all the quick meal products staple to modern life.

Go without sugared items (I can't bring myself to call them 'foods'): ice-cream, chocolate and chocolate biscuits, donuts, cakes, pastries, glazed fruit. Anything where sugar is part of the processing... and that means most packaged goods.

What about jams, spreads, peanut butter and suchlike goodies. Leave them alone, for heaven's sake...

No fried food, do not use polyunsaturated oils or saturated fats either.

Do you want to hear more or are you too depressed by now?

No, you are a committed person who has made it a goal to be as healthy as possible... so we will press on.

While you are doing the right thing by your body don't do the wrong thing by drinking caffeine drinks. This is not just coffee and tea... it includes cocoa and cocoa-flavoured drinks, cola drinks too.

Go without alcohol while on the detox diet, give your liver a holiday too. One of the deadliest drinks is the cordial. Just look at what it is made from: water, sugar, colouring and artificial flavouring. Some firms try to make cordial respectable by shoving in a bit of genuine, real, re-constituted fruit juice, but these are no better. If you have an overactive child, deny him or her cordial... no matter how the little treasure performs.

No canned fruit, fruit drinks either. These are concentrated fruit sugar.

So what the heck can I eat, for goodness sake!

For goodness sake, eat sprouted seeds and grains. They are

best eaten when about a quarter of an inch long. Legumes are good food, but soak them overnight, drain off the water and use fresh water to cook them.

Raw food and steamed vegetables are good for you and are an important part of your programme. Fresh fruits are great, eat these as often as you like. Eat nuts and seeds... you know what they say, eat six almonds a day to keep cancer at bay. See how good nuts are for you?

Unsweetened, non-toasted muesli is fine. Being a Scot I recommend porridge oats to you, without sugar or salt by the way. My ancestors claimed that millet builds muscle and wheat builds fat, so millet is fine. I always take note of my Scottish ancestors... they were real tough guys.

I know you are wondering what to do about oil so you will be delighted to hear that pure virgin olive oil or MCT (I will tell you more about MCT later in this chapter) is the way to go.

Drink lots of water, herbal teas, soy and rice milk drinks.

Hey, take it easy on the food!

You may find your appetite increases when you are on this detox diet. Do not overeat. Burdening your body while it is working overtime to get rid of all the accumulations of years of overdoing it is not a wise plan. Resist cramming the food in.

The rule of good eating is have breakfast like a king, lunch like a princess and dinner like a pauper. Of course we do it all wrong, but that is typical, isn't it?

Breakfast can be catch as catch can. Often on the run or eating while we get ready for work. Lunch? I won't go on about it. But come the evening, we try to dine like kings. If we go out for a meal we do dine like kings, never mind try!

And what is the result?

Well, here is something you may not realise. When you go to sleep your systems partly shut down. Your metabolism slows, your heart slows, your breathing slows... everything slows including your digestion.

So just when it is needed most, it goes at half speed. Your food is only partly digested and it takes a lot more effort for your body to do it. No wonder people wake up tired, their body has been struggling all night to do something with the load of food and drink dumped on it.

And if you are on a detox diet your body is grinding away draining toxins and here you are cheerfully adding to its load. Not a good idea so don't do it. Give your digestive system help by thoroughly chewing your food. Take time to crunch your food to pulp before swallowing it.

Follow the directions that will usually be part of the detox herb programme you sensibly invested in from the health food shop or pharmacy. The detox programme I use myself is the QuickCleanse programme.

YOU HAVE DETOXED SO WHAT IS NEXT?

Most modern diets lack enzymes. So apart from eliminating sugar you must have enzyme-rich foods with every meal. Now as you well know, this is astonishingly difficult in this modern world. I am dismayed when I go to a function and see the staff with these hygienic metal tongs placing a white bread roll by every plate. When I ask if I could have a wholemeal roll it is as though I asked for the moon on a plate. It is exceptionally difficult to find a decent vegetarian meal in most restaurants.

So getting an enzyme-rich diet is hard. I shudder when I see a hamburger, a packet of French fries and a coke offered as a meal. I am even more appalled at the vast numbers of people who also believe this combination is a good meal. Dial H for Hamburger and you could be dialling H for Horror!

If you have a busy life and have difficulty controlling what you eat, then it is a good idea to keep a container of digestive enzymes with you. Make a habit of taking one or two with every meal. This way you are sure to get enough to digest your food.

Follow the good rules of chewing well and eating, when possible, in a relaxing, worry-free atmosphere.

We live in a fast-paced world. People pant to me 'I'm getting there'. Where 'there' is they do not say. I usually suggest they slow down, we will all get 'there' soon enough, perhaps too soon! So take it easy… slow down. I am in no hurry to get 'there', are you?

Take time to eat and enjoy, not thrust in, gulp down and get back into the rat race as fast as we can. That way lies big trouble, my friend.

YOU NEED FIBRE TO LOSE WEIGHT…

You need more bulk to lose bulk.

Have an honest look at the food most overweight people put in their mouths. The power we humans have to deceive ourselves is awesome.

Overweight people look at me with innocence radiating out of every pore, wide-eyed with purity of heart they gaze at me… and tell me the most diabolical lies. 'Me? Eat between meals? Very rarely.' A lie. 'I only eat good food, I can't understand why I keep putting on weight.' Would not stand up to a lie detector for two seconds.

'I don't particularly care for sugar, just a bit in my coffee.' How can anyone stand there and mouth such falsehoods? 'I go for brisk walks every day.' The real truth is the walking is in the supermarket car park!

'I play tennis twice a week, so I get enough exercise but I can't seem to lose weight.' In all honesty, have you watched these people play tennis? They stand there and if the ball is out of reach they watch it zoom past. They may make a couple of token steps but their heart is not in it.

Contrast this with the slim person who is leaping about all over the place. In a tennis match between a slim energetic person and an overweight, slow moving person, I would put my money on the slim one.

It all gets back to our colossal ability to lie to ourselves.

These people really believe they eat little sugar, they really believe they have a good diet, they really believe they push themselves to the limit when they play tennis.

We are a funny lot, aren't we? I have seen poor little mothers standing up in court as a character witness for a slob of a son. 'He is a good boy really' they quaver, peering at the judge.

Good boy? The guy has a criminal record as long as your arm. He abuses his poor old Mum… something shocking, yet she stands up there and says he is a good boy really, well really? No he is a lout, but even mothers have the power of self-deception well developed.

So have a serious look at what you eat. No self-deception today… write down everything you put in your mouth right through the day. And I mean every single thing. No cheating.

List your meals, details of what you eat… snacks, tasting if you are cooking, drinking and what you are drinking. Every darned thing. No exceptions. Now be brutally honest, are you on a get-fat diet? Are you doing yourself in on the weight-loss stakes?

The actuality is most people, not just overweight people, are on low-fibre diets. The products advertised the most are usually those with the least amount of fibre. Just watch them and take note. Even ready-to-warm-up foods are high in salt and low in real fibre. There are notable exception, but that is what they are, exceptions.

This diet gives substance but not nutrition. That is why we starve amidst plenty. It fills but does not sustain us. We feel hungry because our body is starved despite the work it is asked to do to digest what we dump on it. We ask our bodies to work overtime on low pay. We expect it to do wonders without nourishment.

Now I am realistic enough to agree that getting a fibre-rich diet in these modern times is not easy. So I recommend all people, but especially those who are overweight, to add fibre to their daily diet.

I have already made the point that dashing out and grabbing a packet of unprocessed bran is not always the best way to go.

To my simple mind the best fibres for a healthy bowel are **slippery elm bark, psyllium husks, oat bran, oat meal, linseed** and **rice bran**. These are without doubt your best friends.

You can buy them all separately from your local health food store but I find it a lot more convenient to use something like QuickFibre Plus. QuickFibre Plus contains all of the above ingredients blended carefully together in precise proportions so you get the maximum benefit. I take QuickFibre Plus every day on my muesli… and I have a good diet.

Everyone's bowel needs bulk to get rid of the wastes from their normal diet. It is bulk that encourages the bowel wall to send ripples along to move things for you. If it doesn't move them they stagnate, they go rotten, they decompose… they do you no good at all!

So to lose weight, take digestive enzymes with a good low fat diet. Make sure you are giving your bowel enough fibre by supplementing.

I told you about transit time, didn't I? Transit time is how long it takes for your system to digest food, assimilate and excrete the waste. For some people this can be days, even years for some of the waste. You don't want too quick a transit time… this is what happens when you have diarrhoea.

A good bulky diet encourages a healthy transit time.

Most people I know have what they call 'dysbiosis' of the bowel. This sounds fearsome but it means the mix in the bowel is wrong. Too many of the wrong type of bacteria. To get back in balance, it would pay most people and especially overweight people, to invest in a good acidophilus programme. How can you be healthy and full of energy if your bowel is overwhelmed with the bad guys? You have to get rid of the bowel mafia by sending in hordes of good guys.

How your liver helps you lose weight…

I know you are different, but most people have no idea where their internal organs are situated. They have only the vaguest notion where their liver sits. I have had patients who told me they had a big ache in their kidneys, but pointed way down to the bottom of their spine.

Same with that poor, overworked, overloaded liver. Boy, is this organ abused by day and by night. Just to remind you, your blood supply goes through your liver every twenty minutes. That is your entire blood supply, the whole river of blood pours in and out of your liver every twenty minutes. And your liver has to deal with it.

Pesticides, herbicides, dioxin, residual chemicals of every kind, lead, mercury… the whole chemical works go through your liver. Your liver has to deal with fat, alcohol, sugar, additives, preservatives, emulsifiers, stabilisers, colouring and mock foods. You can only admire the liver for doing any kind of a job when you appreciate its workload.

No other employer could hope to have an employee to function under such a workload. Your liver does its best every second, every minute, every hour of every twenty-four hours. What an organ? Deserves a gold medal, don't you think?

But your liver is not a machine. We couldn't invent a machine with the staying power and efficiency of your liver. So your liver will show its displeasure by causing you mental problems, as I have outlined in a previous chapter.

Did I hear Auntie Maude whistle 'Tell me again, I forgot what he said'? Well, we're friends so shout to Auntie: irritation (don't show yours to her!), tearful, lacking energy, depression, sick headaches, nausea… and weight gain.

Your liver processes fat. If it is not doing a good job then fat accumulates. The problem with fat cells is as you store more and more fat the number of cells grows. This is obviously due to the fat having to be stored and needing containers. But the lousy thing is, you can lose the fat out of the cells but you can't lose the cells themselves.

It's shocking to think that fat cells are like little sacks that sit there waiting… You lose fat, the sack empties but stays where it is, waiting for you to fill it again. If this were in the outside world you would need a string of warehouses just to hold the empties, never mind the full ones!

There is just no justice anymore! So when the slim, thin, slender, waif-like person starts to put on weight they add fat cells that may empty but will never ever go away again. And that is sad, isn't it?

So you have to be on your guard to keep the fat out of those cells waiting to slurp up the fat and change your shape for you.

THIS IS WHERE YOUR LIVER STRUTS ITS STUFF!

Your liver is vital in the fat department. It pushes out bile to emulsify fat. It mixes with the fat and turns it to liquid. Clever little trick! Mind you there is a limit to how much fat your liver can process in one go.

Your liver manufactures cholesterol as we have discussed already. To get your cholesterol back in balance you have to address your liver. Give it some tender loving care, be charitable and help your liver. You can use the amino acid methionine, use herbs like Milk Thistle, Dandelion, Blue Flag and so on.

It is wise to look for a liver herbal already made up by a reputable manufacturer. You can get such combination in your local health food store or pharmacy.

Your liver is a powerhouse of energy when in good shape. A lot of people these days complain about low energy. If you are one of them, have a look at helping your liver. Could make a big difference for you.

It is my humble opinion that any weight-loss programme must attend to the liver if it is to have any real hope of success.

BLOOD SUGAR… GET IT RIGHT OR NOTHING CHANGES!

You will recall we had a little chat about low blood sugar in a previous chapter. I would hazard a guess and say that overweight people would have a blood sugar problem.

You remember how I told you sugar eating makes people want to eat all the time because the body is desperate for nutrition, not just calories?

Low blood sugar is a very real problem standing in the way of successful weight loss. Unless you get this problem sorted you will have Buckley's chance of keeping your weight down.

Just to remind you, no sugar at all, no sweets of any kind (only sweet words), eat little and often but eat high-fibre snacks. You can get what they call 'sucrose formulas' at your health food store or pharmacy. These are designed to help you cope with sugar.

Help your pancreas by taking a pancreatic enzyme formula. Showing my origins, eat porridge before going to bed to keep your blood sugar level constant during the night. You will wake up a lot more lively if you do.

In the olden days, we Scots were a very lively race because in those days we lived on porridge. Nowadays, sad to say, Scottish diet is pretty dreadful so the Scots are not as healthy as they were once. It's a good thing they don't have to charge up and down the hills and dales, leaping along the glens, dashing about flashing claymores all over the place. On today's diet, all that the

Scots can do is to keep up with the weather. Scottish mists are legendary, so is the arthritis that goes with them. That is why the Scots invented whisky, simply to keep the cold out, and for no other reason, no matter what Uncle Fred may say!

I can be critical of Scots because I am a Scot, but don't let anyone else criticise Scots near me, could be dangerous!

Lecithin is very helpful for your liver and weight loss. This is because lecithin emulsifies fat in the bowel. Lecithin is also useful for brainpower. When you think (something most of us avoid because it requires so much effort), your brain uses something called 'acetylcholine' to transmit the message along the track. Lecithin is a rich source of acetylcholine.

EVEN MORE HERBAL HELP TO GET THE SHAPE YOU HAVE ALWAYS WANTED!

If you have been on the detox programme you will have been delighted to wake up and find you are slimmer than you were when you started. There are other herbs to help you make your slim dream come true.

Brindleberry has the ability to suck fat out of those containers I told you about. A sort of herbal liposuction without the high cost.

To help you cope with your incredible sweet teeth there is a herb to reduce sugar craving. For a joke we gave some of this to a bloke who loved his pint of beer, just before he partook. He was very annoyed to find his taste for the golden brew was perverted. He did not enjoy it because this herb affected his taste buds, so he swore. The herb is called **Gymnema**. You will find it in some of the better weight-loss products. Gymnema is a small shrub growing in India… the locals call it the 'sugar destroyer'. I guess that says everything.

Carnitine is an amino acid very useful in a weight-loss programme. I will tell you why and you will be amazed. Carnitine has the ability to take fat out of the fat cell containers, take it to your muscles where it is used for energy. The extra energy speeds up your metabolism and helps you even more.

Chitosin is also unique. This is made from shellfish shells and listen to what it does, it absorbs fat. They use this stuff to mop up oil slicks. It binds to fat. Empty some Chitosin into cup of white coffee and it will turn black. This is because the Chitosin binds to the fat in the milk, rolls it up and holds it. It does the same in your body. It does not move fat already there but it does bind to fat in your diet and make it unavailable for depositing.

Do not take Chitosin with any fat-soluble vitamins such as Vitamin E or A, the Chitosin will roll them up and out too. If you are taking Evening Primrose Oil or Omega 3 fish oil, no, no, no… they will be taken out too! Same with Cod Liver Oil, the Chitosin will do the same to it, out!

STICK TO YOUR DETERMINATION TO WIN THE WEIGHT WAR!

When I was a kid my Dad used to tell me that the world was full of starters and what the world was desperate for was a lot more finishers. I have noticed this to be a major obstacle for a lot of people who are trying to lose weight. They are constantly looking for the magic formula, the 'holy grail' of weight loss. They hop from diet to diet, always hoping, seldom achieving.

The trick is to stick to basics and STICK TO THEM.

The basics are cutting out sugar, eating fibre-rich foods, detoxing your body at least twice a year, keeping a healthy bowel, and keeping a well-toned liver. Eat enzyme-rich foods so you can digest what you eat. Supplementing with herbs to help your cause along… and sticking at it, making it a way of life.

You will not win the weight war without fibre!

Get this firmly into your mind… you will never win the weight-loss war on a low-fibre diet. It is impossible.

Tell Uncle Fred and Auntie Maude I know I am going on about fibre yet again. I know I am, and the reason makes sense to me. When I briefly explain, I know it will make sense to you too. We learn by repetition. That is why I suggest to people that they read my books three, four and more times. Don't lend them out because people honestly steal books. If someone else is reaping the benefit of your financial outlay, you do not have the book to refer to... and you are encouraging non-commitment, so there!

Fibre blocks the absorption of fat, and thus calories. It does this in the intestines. See, I told you how important your intestines are to you. They are vital to health in so many different areas of your life.

If you have no or low fibre in your diet, you cannot help but put weight on. So it isn't clever to try to lose weight on a low-fibre diet, is it?

ENTER THE STARVATION ENZYME...

Now here is something you need to know. And you need to know it NOW...

Lurking in your fat is an enzyme. Not your everyday enzyme either. This one has a special job to do. It is full of self-importance and is convinced it is there to save your life!

It sees its role in life as saving you from starvation.

So as soon as you lose some weight, guess what this party pooper does? It sends a sneaky message to your brain to increase your calorie consumption. No matter that the message is more suitable to prehistoric times and is out of date today. Your brain responds! And you know what happens? You've seen it happen, it could even have happened to you. The luckless dieter ends up with more weight than ever before!

You stifle this enzyme by eating a high-fibre diet and cutting down dramatically the fat absorption from your intestines.

A diet low in fibre tends to be high in carbohydrates and that means too much sugar, baby. Dumping sugar causes an insulin reaction and too much insulin also triggers off the ever-watchful anti-starvation enzyme.

Seems sometimes that you can't win!

I know, I know, I know, sometimes you can't get enough fruit and vegies because of your hectic lifestyle. You have to dine out for a million good reasons and most restaurant food is low fibre. You have to take the kids to the fast food factory or your life is hell on earth. I know how it is!

So how are you going to get enough fibre to block off the fat and the sugar? How are you going to choke off that ever-ready enzyme just dying to send starvation bulletins to your brain?

By taking a high-fibre supplement, that's how!

There are advantages to you taking a high-fibre supplement. For example, finely ground fibre is far more easily digested.

Another advantage is when you take finely ground fibre with your food the transit time of your bowel speeds up. As I have mentioned, when waste loiters in your bowel, the devil finds mischief for idle waste. Cancer being the ultimate mischief, but Irritable Bowel, Diverticulitis, can also be the result of slow transit time. And, of course, weight gain!

Using a good formula fibre supplement guarantees you will be getting finely ground good quality fibre. And what is more, the essential fibres so necessary for good health and losing weight. Eating lots of fruit may be a problem for someone with low blood sugar… but a fibre supplement helps people with low blood sugar. Wonderful when you know what to do, isn't it?

The other great thing is when you invest in a top fibre supplement you are getting variety. And as we all know, variety is the spice of life.

Tell Uncle Fred before he gets too worked up we are talking about weight loss, not girl friends!

The other advantage of a good fibre supplement is it makes you feel full. It is a health supplement that is an appetite suppressor. Now that is great, isn't it?

And if you are pulling out your calorie counter, you can put it away. There are no calories at all in fibre! There is no fat either... and no cholesterol. What a boon and a blessing to weight-conscious people!

Mind you, most people I know could take a fibre supplement with great health advantages.

Taking QuickFibre Plus as part of a weight-loss programme makes more and more sense doesn't it? You have to shut that darn enzyme up and taking extra fibre is the way to do it.

Has it ever occurred to you why diet plans are so successful? Why women's magazines are always coming up with new and better diets that promise wonderful results?

Because they don't work!

That's what I said, they don't work. If they did they would publish just one weight-loss diet, the one that worked...

No folks, you know the sad story, you have seen it often... people go on this incredible low calorie diet, lose it and then end up fatter than ever... and start looking for yet another wonder weight-loss diet or programme.

Hope always triumphs over experience in the weight-loss stakes!

There is one fat that doesn't digest like a fat!

Hey! Tell me about a fat that doesn't digest like ordinary fats. This fat is called MCT; it stands for Medium Chain Triglycerides, and is dealt with by your liver just like carbohydrates. It doesn't get treated in your bowel so it will not excite that underhanded enzyme I told you about earlier.

You can cook with MCT oil, use it for energy. What about this for smart thinking? MCT can even do something to help you burn off the fat that is bothering you at this very moment! It does not store well in your fat bags either. What an oil!

Where can you get your greedy hands on this oil? At your health food store but not usually in the food department where you would expect to find it. You will usually find it in the body building department because athletes use it for energy. A little goes a long way with MCT, so use it sparingly,

THE OXYGEN CONNECTION TO WEIGHT LOSS

Here is an interesting theory for you… in all your searching, all your reading, all your hoping, I bet you never thought lack of oxygen could be part of your weight problem.

One reason people put on weight is fluid accumulates around the cells. The other factor is increase in the fluid density of the cell wall, the membrane. This can be due to a lack of oxygen available for cell combustion. This can also lead to inflammation of the joints and muscles. Lack of oxygen can also be a factor in high blood pressure.

WHY ARE WE SHORT OF OXYGEN?

It has been calculated that the oxygen supply in our atmosphere is well down to what it was fifty years ago. And no wonder!

We can't go on bulldozing the rain forests of the world as though there is no tomorrow. In fact, if we keep it up, there will be no tomorrow! Trees breathe out oxygen and breathe in carbon dioxide. Because there are now millions of hectares fewer trees in the world, the balance between oxygen and carbon dioxide has been upset.

We have the 'greenhouse' effect because of too much carbon dioxide in our air. We blame industry, fossil fuels and so on… but hacking down the trees is a BIG factor.

So now we have international tiredness, increasing diseases and a never-ending battle being fought to combat mightier and stronger bugs.

I told you about cooked foods being devoid of enzymes, well cooking and processing also oxidises foods. That means we use up the oxygen before we get to use it. High fat diets, low exercise levels, alcohol, cigarettes, fungal overgrowth... these all use up precious oxygen.

CANCER CELLS HATE OXYGEN!

Cancer cells detest oxygen. They loathe it. This is because they find it hard to survive in an oxygen-rich environment. Cancer cells thrive in an oxygen-poor environment. Another reason to keep your cells well oxygenated.

Just by taking ten to fifteen drops of oxygen formula in a glass of water two or three times a day will intensify cellular uptake of oxygen. This will improve detoxification, and reduce excess fluid round your cells... the end result being a loss of weight.

The good news is this will improve your body's ability to burn off excess fat.

You can get a good oxygen formula in liquid form from your health food store or pharmacy.

AH, FOR THE GLOW OF YOUTH!

Oh, how we long to have the suppleness, the energy, the joy of being young. If only I could be young again, I would not squander it... I would treasure it. It was George Bernard Shaw who remarked wistfully that the tragedy of youth is it is wasted on the young!

But cheer up, help is here!

One of the reasons we age and put on excess weight is because our production of growth hormone does a nosedive. Young people produce growth hormone by the bucketful. They have heaps of the stuff.

But as we mature (not age, mature!) our supply of growth hormone gets less and less… and we lose that glow of youth. Once again, my Dad was right, Life is not fair. What more proof could anyone need?

The answer does not lie in the false promises of drugs. Anabolic steroids are a trap, an illusion, givers that takes away what they promise to give.

But I want you to be youthful. I want you to bloom and blossom. I want you to lose weight and be tight, taut, slim, slinky… in short, desirable!

So how the heck are we going to do this without the help of nasty, smelly drugs?

I have a plan, trust me, I am a Naturopath!

First up, eat more cereals, nuts and seeds. Try taking potassium in liquid form if you can get it. Low potassium equals low-growth hormone. If you are a hero, you can get potassium from raw foods. Another golden rule to remember is high processed foods mean low potassium. High processed foods also mean high sodium… and we all know what excessive sodium does to us, don't we? If you are one of the many who are not sure what excess sodium does, just keep in mind it ain't that good for you!

BEDTIME SNACKS NOT THE BEST WAY TO GO!

Sitting there watching the TV quietly munching away. I bet most people would get a bit of a shock if they realised how many calories they manage to tuck away while watching the telly.

When it comes to growth hormone, eating before bedtime is a disaster area. The time you pump out growth hormone is after you have been asleep for a couple of hours. But if your slowed-down metabolism is having a fight with all the high carbohydrate chokkie biscuits, pizza and you know what, it will do the dirty on you and cut down the growth hormone.

That way lies skin like a prune, sagging muscles, sagging

stomach and sagging everything else that gravity can pull down!

I have told you before that sugar is white, pure and deadly. I have told you how it will reduce your IQ (Intelligence Quotient, not quota, Auntie Maude!). It does something else pretty rotten to you too... it reduces the output of youth-giving, energy-promoting growth hormone.

Who knows, you could see bumper stickers proclaiming 'Win The Race To Old Age... Eat Lottsa Sugar'.

The amino acid Arginine acts on that part of the brain that produces growth hormone releasing hormones. I wonder if that is why Arginine is so helpful in impotence, it makes things grow?

EAT MORE OFTEN TO LOSE WEIGHT!

What is this, the promised land? Eat more and lose weight, are you hearing things, is your eyesight failing? Is your comprehension level dropping?

No, not at all...

But, there is always a damned 'But', isn't there? I love you, but... I don't want to hurt your feelings, but... I don't want to be rude, but...

Funny how people tell you what they don't want to do, then use the 'but' word to clobber you verbally.

So you snack a lot, but... the snacks have to be low sugar and downright healthy foods. None of this snacking on the odd chocolate biscuit, 'One little biscuit won't do me any harm, will it?' This said wistfully like a child asking for the moon to play with.

But you cannot win without exercise!

You can read all the false promises about losing weight quickly and easily on this or that wonder diet. But the hard truth is to lose weight you have to get some muscle.

It is amazing what we humans believe. When I suggest to some nice but overweight person exercise might be a good idea, they will look at me and say seriously, 'I don't want to look like one of those people in the body building magazines. But you have to be careful don't you, muscle turns into fat.'

Heavens above, have you any idea how dedicated these bodybuilders are? The average Jane or Joe would not go through the torture day after day; these people go through to look the way they do. They train for hours: pushing weights, sweating, forcing themselves to keep going even though every cell, every nerve, every fibre is crying out in pain. Most of us find it hard to keep walking never mind pushing weights hour after hour.

I use weights at least three times a week because I believe weight training is excellent for a healthy body. Sure, I am not dedicated, I am not huge, but I do have well-toned muscles and I am slim. Perhaps not as slim as I was when I was in hard training for Judo contests, but slimmer than a lot of grandfathers. In fact, my grandson, Ben, was involved in a discussion with some other kids about grandfathers, of all things. The other kids were complaining that their grandfathers were all fat, overweight and had big bellies. Ben emphatically rejected this saying firmly 'MY grandad is very muscley and his belly is flat and hard!'. What a great PR agent he is for me, bless him.

Weight training is excellent to prevent osteoporosis. This is because weights cause your body to build up calcium in the bones to strengthen them to cope with the weights. However, weight training is not possible for everyone, so other exercises are needed.

By the way, it is biologically impossible for muscle to turn to fat. The day I can bear children is the day muscle will turn to fat. That means never. Fat and muscle are totally different, like chalk and cheese, Samson and Delilah. One cannot change into the other.

What sometimes does happen is when an athlete stops being athletic but keeps on eating as though the daily workouts were still part of the daily routine, fat overlays the muscles. The muscle has not changed to fat, it has simply disappeared under the coating of fat.

Muscle will only burn off fat as long as you are not piling fat into yourself. It is a bit like trying to empty a bath full of water. No use just pulling out the plug to drain the water if you have a hosepipe going full bore pumping gallons of water into the bath at the same time.

So what exercises can a lazy person do?

The first one is what I call 'push aways'. You have probably heard of push ups. You lie face down and using arm strength push against the ground causing your body to lift. Sounds easy but very hard especially if you weigh a ton or two!

Push aways are a lot easier physically. You sit in your chair at the dining table and placing your hands firmly on the edge of the table you push yourself away. You do this well before becoming red-faced and gorged on all the goodies you usually tuck away at meal times. Doesn't take much strength, but it does take a lot of willpower!

Walking is great exercise. But I mean walking, not ambling along being passed by snails in a hurry to find shelter. Really stepping out. People tell me they walk for exercise but they are like the tennis player, slow. So really give it stick when you go out walking. Get a sweat up, feel your heart pound just a little...

Another handy little exercise is in the kitchen. Whenever it is convenient, lean against the breakfast bar and push yourself away. Do this as often as you can.

Take a can of beans (a can of anything will do), one can in each hand and swing your arms round like a windmill. This will tone up your muscles. You don't have to do a lot of these exercises but you do have to do them as often as you can.

Hold on to the breakfast bar or table and bend your knees. Bodybuilders call this squatting; in our case, it is knee bends with support. As your muscles strengthen you will be able to do these without support. Later you may even be able to do them holding a can of peas in each hand. Keep at it, the end will make all your work worthwhile!

The body part causing most concern is usually the stomach. A huge, bulging stomach is not usually a turn on. More likely a turn off. However it is not just the appearance of a sloppy tum, with weak stomach muscles a person is more likely to be constipated. This is very noticeable. So getting some sort of stomach tone is vital not only for losing weight but for internal health, which is our main concern in this book.

Don't do sit ups. Lying down with your feet under a chair or similar and sitting up or trying to sit up, could wreck your back. It is better by far to anchor yourself and lean back. Just lean back far enough to feel the pressure in your gut, no matter how slight. Hold it. Then come back up. Repeat this as often as you can without killing yourself! Take it easy but not too easy.

A lot of women complain especially of lower back pain. Now this could be from the uterus; if you have a womb like a tomb expect trouble. A lower back pain is only one problem. It could be an overloaded colon pressing down and causing back pain.

A very common problem is sloppy buttocks. I watch some women waddling through a shopping centre, sucking away at an ice-cream, and their buttocks wobble like a water bed. I know these people have a bad back just by watching their buttocks flop. Not a pretty sight… so don't call me a pervert, please!

If the buttocks, known as gluteals, are sloppy, they do not give the spine any support. This in turn will cause a bad back because it has no support and is constantly strained.

So practise contracting the buttocks. You can do this anytime anywhere. Just contract them, do it for ten goes, rest, and try again. This will also strengthen the pelvic floor which is another good reason to do the exercise. Weak pelvic muscles not only cause constipation but can also be responsible for a weak bladder.

I suggest you go to your public library and ask the Librarian to suggest a good mild exercise book to help you lose weight.

This book is not long enough to give you a full diet schedule or exercise programme, but there are good books out there which will do both for you.

Keep thinking slim and build up your self-image. On this point, you are a worthy person with unique qualities; you have your own place in the universe, so claim it! Take the herbals, detox every six months, keep away from demon sugar, take a good herbal formula for weight loss, keep your liver in good condition… and above all, stick at it.

There is everything to gain by looking after your health. To radiate health outside you have to shimmer with health inside. You may not live longer, who knows? But you will have a great quality of life.

Living longer is not much of a goal unless that life is full of vitality, love, energy and achievement. A friend of mine used to give wonderful motivational speeches; to make people think, he would ask his audience a question. As I recall it, he asked them 'When you die and I come to write your epitaph, and all I can find to write about you is that you were born and you died… I have to ask you this very personal question "Why were you born at all?"'

Heavy stuff indeed, but a question to make us think. A successful life is one full of good things done. To be able to say we have realised our potential is marvellous, what a great life. It is quality that counts. You need energy to have quality of life and for energy you need health.

Read this book five or six times, don't argue with me, try what I say, give it a fair go… you will be pleased with the result. Most of us are like people living in a crowded valley at the bottom of a snow-capped mountain. We don't look up so we don't notice the mountain. But one day we get a nudge, look up and see the mountain. We are moved to climb a little way up and when we see the marvellous view we are motivated to climb higher and higher. The higher we climb the better the view.

The mountain is awesome good health. Start your climb today…

Would you do me a favour and read the next chapter carefully. I would like to tell you why I am a vegetarian. I am not seeking to convert you… I would simply like you to know why so many people these days are changing their minds about the meat and potato way of life.

15

Vegetarians live longer and have better sex!

Vegetarians definitely live longer and have fewer degenerative diseases. Whether vegetarians have better sex than non-vegetarians, I shall leave to your imagination. Certainly, the healthier you are the better your sex life can be.

I am proud to be a vegetarian.

This is for three basic reasons. Firstly, the vegetarian way of life has been proven time and time again to be the healthiest road to take in this life of ours.

Secondly, people who eat a lot of animal 'products' tend to get more degenerative diseases than vegetarians.

Thirdly, I cannot stand the cruelty we inflict on animals. The way animals are treated in our society is shameful. If there is such a thing as Karma, then we have piled up a massive Karmic debt.

VEGETARIANS HAVE MORE FUN...

Well if you are healthy you tend to enjoy life more. It is difficult to have the energy to have a real good time if your body is clogged up with decaying dead body products. Difficult to be one hundred and ten percent joyful if your body is suffering from creeping log jams of animal-sourced antibiotics, growth hormones, adrenaline and other degeneration-causing goodies.

Meat eaters tend to get a greater whack of bowel cancer, high blood pressure and all the familiar ills we blame on our modern life style.

Ah, but contrast this with dedicated vegetarians. They get a lot less of the degenerative diseases than meat eaters. They get plenty of enzymes with their salads, raw vegetables, fruit, nuts and seeds. They eat a lot closer to Nature.

Eating plenty of vegetables, salads and fruit brings real nutrition. The old-fashioned idea that meat, roast potatoes and boiled vegetables make a wholesome meal is outdated, outmoded and bad for your long-term health.

This has been shown in a real life context. Seventh Day Adventists are vegetarians and their frequency of degenerative diseases is much lower than that of the rest of the community.

So for greater staying power and glowing good health I have chosen the vegetarian way. I smile when dedicated dead animal eaters make fun of my diet. They call salads 'Rabbit food' as though these foods are no good for real men. The thought occurs to me that a lot of men would just love the sexual energy of a rabbit! The message they seem to put out is that real men chomp on big steaks washed down with a mug of beer.

Real men lead a destructive lifestyle, if you believe these people. In reality they are trying to justify the way they eat. I can tell you that plenty of real men and real women are vegetarians and don't have to justify themselves.

Have you noticed how we try to sanitise our slaughter of millions of animals? I find it hard to walk past a butcher shop. The smell of blood revolts me as does the sight of all those bloody corpse parts displayed in the window. I see the jolly butcher hacking away at some dead animal's leg or shoulder, up to his elbows in blood.

Imagine if they were human corpses! If the shop was full of human bodies and we saw the butcher hacking away what would we feel? But we are only meat too when you get down to it.

We wrap the animal parts in plastic on neat styrene plates. This way we can pretend we are buying products and not parts of animals slaughtered for our culinary delight.

Now and again we see on the television horrific pictures of the cruelty of modern-day animal factory farming. Did you know a pig has similar intelligence to a chimpanzee? They are bright animals. We abuse them in our language, we portray them as dirty animals. They are only dirty because we force them to be by keeping them in unnatural surroundings.

A pig is a natural forager. In the wild they spend their days on the move. They shove their snouts into the ground looking for roots and other culinary delights. In the animal farm they are confined to narrow metal cells. There is no room to move. They stand on a metal grill, not earth. They are fed diets not natural to pigs. The diet is to fatten them up for killing in the shortest time possible.

Sows are strapped to boards so the boar can rape them. Sows in the natural state choose a mate just as we do. This is denied in the animal production line. The look of misery on the faces of these poor animals is heartbreaking.

But there is no mercy in pig farming.

Hens are by nature scrabblers. They scratch and dig for food. They walk about; they are social creatures. But in the chicken and egg business they are kept in cages called batteries. They stand not on Mother Earth but on wires. They peck at themselves and their neighbours out of desperate boredom.

In their food they put antibiotics. Because of the unnatural way they are kept and fed, disease would run through the flocks like the plague. So to prevent this they are fed antibiotics… and then so are you as you eat the chickens.

Turkeys are bred so the breast is the largest part of the bird. This is because humans prefer turkey breasts to the rest of the bird. So they are bred to the stage where the birds cannot mate, their breasts are so overdeveloped they cannot make contact with each other. Chickens collapse on legs too weak to support unnaturally large bodies.

This is all taken as part of the 'cost of manufacture'. The animals are not seen as living creatures but simply as items of production. As I said, there is no mercy in factory farming.

If you have the stomach to face the truth of what we do to animals in factory farming you cannot do better than to read the book, *Silent Ark* by Juliet Gellatley, published by Thorsons Books.

This book made me very angry. My mind had difficulty taking in what I was reading. Human cruelty seems to know no bounds. Read this book and I doubt if you will ever eat meat again.

SHOCKING NEWS… MEN TURNING INTO FEMALES!

There is a world-wide crisis no-one wants to talk about.

More and more boy babies are being born with deformed penises, also showing female characteristics. The sperm count has dropped by almost 50% in the men of today. Perhaps that is why we are seeing so many women seeking intro-fertilisation as the only means of having a child.

Science fiction could become reality when the only male sperm is in cryonic vaults controlled by politicians, not medical people. You have to wonder where our mad chemical dash is taking us.

WHY IS MACHO MAN NOT SO MACHO ANYMORE?

Why is this happening? What has gone wrong?

One reason is that the dead animals are unwittingly getting their own back. As macho man chomps cheerfully on his huge T-Bone steak, little does he realise he is eating a chemical feast. Of course, few people are really aware when chewing at meat that they are chewing at a part of once living animal. And that once living animal was part of the great factory farming system.

Now listen to this, if you were factory farming producing beef cattle, how would you like a method that would fatten the animals up in record time and on less feed? You are in business so a chance to make more money in less time would make your eyes glisten.

The way this is done is to add female hormones to the cattle feed. These have the desired result, fatter animals in shorter time on less feed.

A great commercial success... except for one thing! The female hormones get into macho man. As he is chomping away, he is taking in small amount of female hormones. But these pile up over time. No-one has measured the effects of adding these hormones to animal feed over twenty or thirty years.

The way drugs are tested is really mind-bogglingly simple. You get a laboratory animal, say a white rat, and force-feed it the drug. Never mind that any resemblance between a white rat and human would have to be coincidental. So they pile loads of the drug into the animal until it drops dead. They take careful note of how much of the substance they got into it over what period of time. Now they gradually reduce the dose until the rat survives. They then say that a percentage of that amount in human terms should be safe.

But there are no long-term tests on humans. By long term I mean twenty or thirty years. Can't wait that long? Of course, not. But they have found giving women birth control drugs have had unwanted effects after years of taking them. They are now investigating the incidence of cancer in people who were vaccinated forty or fifty years ago. It seems the vaccination may have something to do with the cancer so many of those people have today.

So chucking female hormones into animal feed may not be so smart after all. Incidentally, the poor animals get their own back in other ways. Heavy meat eaters tend to be prime candidates for bowel cancers, heart problem, by-pass surgery and all the other joys of modern life.

THERE IS ANOTHER SINISTER PROBLEM FOR YOU!

There is another sinister problem looming up. Another reason for the feminisation of the male is our agribusiness farming methods.

We pour chemical fertilisers on the land, we drench it with herbicides, pesticides without which we could not reap a crop. Did you know that in some types of farming it is impossible to use the land for anything else for about fifty years? This is because the land is so poisoned! That should make any sensible person pause to think.

But there is something else. Something we are not told about… something that could, one day, spell the end of the human race. You think I am exaggerating? You think I am making a mountain out of a molehill?

Well, let me tell you what is happening and then you can judge for yourself. A lot of these chemicals we throw at the land end up in our water supply. You cannot see them, you cannot smell them, you cannot taste them. But they are there!

Now here is the part to make your hair stand on end… in the human body they act like estrogen. Estrogen is the female hormone!

Before somebody writes and tells me all farming chemicals are not like that, don't bother. I know they are not all like that. But enough of them are to cause a problem and to wonder why nothing is being done about them.

Here is an experiment that took place a couple of years ago… see what you think. Researchers put some male fish in a wire basket and placed it near an outfall where domestic water waste went into a river. The fish were left there over a period of time.

Now just listen to this, get the picture… when the researchers went back the male fish were all showing female characteristics! How does that make you feel, eh? Made my hair stand on end, I can tell you.

What is really quite terrifying is nothing is being done about the problem. Have you read anything about it in your newspaper? Have you seen anything on television? Have you heard anything on the radio?

No you haven't. So the problem can only grow.

Where are we going with our so-called civilisation? Don't you ever wonder?

One thing is clear. If you are serious about your health then detoxifying, keeping your bowel working well, internal cleansing is more important now than it ever was.

WHAT ABOUT THE REAL COST OF FACTORY FARMING?

On the surface, factory farming may seem to make economic sense, regardless of the pain and suffering of the millions of God's creatures murdered every day.

But does it really make economic sense?

Is it sensible to bulldoze the lungs of the earth, the once mighty rain forests? Is it good economics to poison the water… to poison the air? Does it make economic sense to empty the seas of fish? You will see more and more 'exotic' fish in your supermarket because the usual breeds of fish are getting scarcer and scarcer.

Is it sensible to so rob the sea of its natural life and balance that we now have a problem with killer whales? Killer whales? What have they got to do with anything? Well, because the waters where the killer whales hunt have been emptied of fish because of our wasteful fishing ways, there is very little for the killer whales to eat. So they are eating sea otters by the score.

The result is the sea otter population is diminishing. So what? So what if the sea otters used to keep the sea urchins in check and now they don't. So the entire balance of Nature has been upset and the sea urchins are now a major problem.

These are just a couple of examples of the invisible mayhem humans are causing. The end of all this is inescapable. We cannot keep on destroying natural resources and survive. True, we are smart enough to make three blades of grass grow where one grew before. This is why world starvation with out-of-control population growth would not pose a problem… so we were told by experts. I worry about some experts, don't you?

However, we have increasing famines; the increased production cannot match increased demand for food. The three blades of grass now growing where one grew before do not have the same nutritional value the one blade had.

There is a song that goes 'When will they ever learn' and the same thought strikes me quite often. When will we humans ever learn?

The end of the world will not be a spectacular blaze of fire and thunder. No, we will disappear because of famine, thirst, diseases immune to our so clever drugs. Unless people stand up and make a noise we will inevitably, inescapably lose everything.

There is no visible political will for change. The comforting thought is great changes were seldom made by politicians until they were forced on them. Women did not get the vote because politicians over their cigars and brandy chuffed 'I say, old fellow, don't you think it's time we gave the gals the vote?'

It was dedicated women like Mrs Pankhurst who forced the changes on the politicians of the day. Do you think slaves were given freedom because the white cotton planters said over their mint juleps, 'Hey guys, don't you agree it is time we gave these black fellows back their human dignity and did away with slave labour?'

Not a chance. It took someone like Mr Wilberforce to raise public awareness. And like so many far-seeing visionaries he was persecuted… something shocking. The familiar cries went up. 'If we abolish slavery, economic ruin will follow… Without cheap labour we cannot compete in world markets… The cost to America of freeing slaves is incalculable.'

You will notice that not a word was said about the human face of slavery, only the money side. But Wilberforce prevailed and eventually the slaves were freed.

In our modern day things haven't changed all that much. When visionaries draw attention to the damage being done by our wasteful farming methods, the great cry is 'Jobs'. Any change will cost jobs.

Stopping meat eating will cost jobs. Stopping destroying the rain forests will cost jobs. We simply cannot afford to change our ways.

The real truth is we simply cannot afford not to.

The rain forests are disappearing to provide poor quality grazing for beef cattle destined to end up in a hamburger palace. Never mind that we are changing the weather patterns of the planet. Never mind we are reducing the oxygen content of the air we breathe and increasing the carbon dioxide levels.

Never mind that Macho Man is turning into something a lot less than macho. Never mind that we could feed the world's poor and hungry in a fraction of the landmass devoted to beef raising.

The sad thing is the jobs are self-limiting. Once we have destroyed the world's natural resources, as we are bound to, there will be no jobs. There will be no life either.

So those are the reasons why I have chosen to be a vegetarian.

I do not want the death of the planet on my conscience.

From a selfish point of view, I have been a lot healthier since becoming a vegetarian.

Oh, on that point, I hear a lot of clamour about becoming a vegetarian is harmful to health. This is utter rubbish! All the available evidence says vegetarians as a group enjoy better health than meat-eaters.

People plead 'Where will I get my iron, my B12?' Fact is, men rarely need extra iron, your body conserves it. Lots of vegetables have iron. Women can get iron from a good diet of vegetables, salads, fruits, nuts, seeds and legumes. As far as B12 is concerned, your body usually has at least five years supply tucked away. You don't need very much and meat is certainly not the only source.

Doctor Vogel, the Swiss doctor credited with inventing muesli, was a vegetarian from the age of 17 and his blood count was excellent. This is because dark leafy vegetables and herbs such as parsley are rich sources of B12. So don't take any notice of these people who trot out medical myths such as vegetarians are unhealthy because of lack of B12.

You will enjoy greater energy, a lot less sickness and a greater joy from living if you are a vegetarian.

Sometimes I see extremely overweight people who assure me they are vegetarians. They may not eat meat or meat products, but they do eat lots of sugar-laced products. They eat cakes, biscuits, packaged food, frozen foods and the usual stuff you see in so many supermarket trolleys.

In our home, the greatest weekly expense is not from the supermarket, it is from the greengrocer. It is money spent on vegetables, salads and fruit.

If you would like to lose some weight, if you would like more energy, if you would like to protect your health for the present and the future, then consider becoming a vegetarian.

You will notice in so many cancer programmes the emphasis is on a vegetarian way of life.

I once told one of my grandsons, our Jamie, 'to be truly successful, do one thing, look at what every one else is doing... AND DON'T DO IT'.

That is because most of humanity is struggling. Struggling to pay off debts because their tastes rise just ahead of their income. Struggling because of doctor's bills. Struggling because their lifestyle and eating habits are robbing them every day of energy. Struggling to make a living. Struggling just to survive.

If most of humanity is struggling could it just be because they are doing the wrong things? Could there be a remote possibility that people are to a great degree the result of their choices?

Look at what most people eat. Look in the shopping trolleys, look at the lifestyle, the lack of exercise, the influence of television.

How many people do you know who realise the importance of internal cleansing? How many people do you know who realise the importance of supplementing their diets given the impoverishment of so much modern food?

More to the point, how many people do you know who are jumping out of their skins with the sheer exhilaration of being alive?

Sadly, not many, I guarantee you!

But now you have read my book you have a road map to excellent health. You have a map leading to hidden treasure, to glowing health and vitality.

All you have to do is use the information I have given you.

Hopefully what you have read has given you food for thought.

The choice is obviously yours and yours alone. You can keep on doing what you have always done and nothing will change.

You can embrace internal cleansing, good bowel management, improve digestion with enzyme-rich foods and enzyme supplements, the choice is yours.

Let me tell you yet another story...

When I first started off in Naturopathy I was a white knight on a snow-white charger. I intended to help everybody. I had all this knowledge to help people get rid of their troublesome health problems...

But I found that human nature is such that quite a lot of people chose to ignore my sound advice. I found this hard to accept.

How could people who were sick, who had come to me for help, how could they continue with a lifestyle that was killing them?

Well, quite easily, thank you!

It really bothered me. I used to get quite upset about it.

Then one day God took me on one side and spoke to me. Tell Auntie Maude that I am not some nut who hears voices, but God does speak to me. Well, believe it or not, here is the conversation...

'Er, Ron, I think there is something you seem to have overlooked?'

'What ME, overlook something?'

'Yes, a very important thing too.'

'Oh really, what on earth could that be?'

'I know this will come as a great shock to you, but think about it, I run the universe and not you!'

That was a bit of a shock because I was behaving as though the universe were my responsibility. But that wasn't the end of the lesson, there was more...

'Yes, and something else you seem to have overlooked.'

Now what? But when God talks I listen!

'I also gave people free will. And what that means is they can please themselves what they do. If they want to go to hell in a bucket, that is their free choice... and it has nothing to do with you!'

'But... but... but...'

'But nothing! They can choose what they do because they must bear the cost of whatever they do, not you. They have free will but they must also pay the price for exercising that will… so BACK OFF!'

So I backed off and have stayed off ever since.

So here we are, just you and me, and I want very much for you to be healthy. I really desire for you to claim your birthright, which is your glowing health. But to do this, you have to pay the price.

The choice is yours… think about it and read this book again a couple of times before you make any decisions. This is because your whole life depends on the decisions you make…

And I passionately want you to be truly well…

Let us now go to the next, and final, chapter… In the next chapter I want to pull everything together. I want to make it easy for you to grasp the principles of internal cleansing and the importance to your future health and happiness… so what do you say? Let's go!

16

Would you like to feel wonderful for the rest of your life?

Answer the question, would you like to feel wonderful for the rest of your life? If you are like me, the answer is a resounding YES!

The secret lies in internal cleansing because the truth is this is the real key to vibrant health and vitality.

We have been told the truth will set us free and that, in itself, is true.

But first we have to get the facts, and you have the facts about internal cleansing in your hands.

All the evidence screams out 'Internal Health is THE key to eternal youth and vitality'. There can be no doubt about it. None at all!

Only with good digestion, good assimilation, a healthy liver, bowels in tip-top condition and working effectively, can anyone be truly healthy.

We humans function way below our true capacity. We accept less than we can have. But the grim fact is we think it is all we are capable of being. We fall for the three-card health trick that drugs will fix our problems. They can't fix them all, they don't fix them all, but as hope springs eternal we keep on keeping on.

This book is a wake up call.

Internal health is the key to eternal youth and vitality. Let me ask you a question, would you rather be full of joy, full of energy, radiating vitality? Or would you rather limp through a life where too many things are too much of an effort? It is important to note that being free of disease does not mean a person is healthy.

We both know lots of people who are symptom-free thanks to drugs, but would you honestly describe them as healthy?

Of course not...

So let us now get into the herbs and supplements you may need to get your internal systems running beautifully...

DIGESTION, THE FIRST STEP TO VITALITY

Your digestion is the engine that drives everything else. It is impossible to be well if your digestion is not running properly.

Why don't we digest as well as Nature intended?

The reasons are straightforward, we don't chew our food. Life is taken on the run, everything has to be instant... everything has to be now. We do not want to 'waste time'. We are oh so often late for things. We must hurry. A bit like the White Rabbit in Alice in Wonderland, constantly looking at his watch as he hurried along.

So the first step to good health is slow down. Take time to chew your food. Give your stomach a break, send down food ready for the next step; don't give your stomach all that extra work.

WATCH OUT FOR DIGESTION BLOCKERS!

Be on your guard for the other reasons we don't digest as well as we should. Drink a lot more water, filtered of course. You would be surprised to find out just how many human ills are caused by insufficient good water.

Here is something else to drop at parties… who realises that well before the time you feel thirsty you are dehydrated. Your body is crying out for water long before you feel thirsty.

No matter what the advertisements promise, alcohol creates thirst, it does not quench it. Alcohol is drying. You know how you feel the next morning after a night on the town. Thirsty!

Eating too much makes it hard on your digestive system to cope. So stop eating before they have to get a crane to lift you away from the table. The golden rule (apart from the one that says 'them wot has the gold makes the rules) is always leave the table feeling you could have eaten a little bit more.

Lack of exercise and floppy stomach muscles make for poor digestion. This business of driving home, eating a meal and crashing in front of the television with a couple of beers is not a way to good digestion.

Watch out for lactose intolerance. I told you, you remember, how a lot of people who walk about complaining of sinus, are really lactose-intolerant. Lactose intolerance can give you the guts ache, diarrhoea, bloating and other conditions you would rather be without.

Eat enzyme-rich foods to help digestion. These are foods that have not been cooked, roasted, toasted and generally been done in by heat. Raw vegetables, salads, fruits, nuts are rich in enzymes. Try to include some with every meal.

If this is impossible, and for a lot of people it is impossible, take a good slow-release digestive enzyme supplement. Eat your meal free of stress, taste it before mindlessly showering it with salt. Laugh a lot, laughter is wonderful for digestion. Try it, you will love it…

NOW FOR THE 'CLEAN' BOWEL...

Can we get one thing out of the way? Emptying the bowel is not the be-all and end-all of internal cleansing. It is like the house I told you about with all the rubbish left lying about. Simply keeping the garbage bin empty would not solve the problem of all the garbage lying about in every room.

So it is with internal cleansing. Our goal is to draw into the intestines all the impurities, the toxins, pollutants and wastes from every part of your body. We want tissue cleanliness, cell cleanliness and we want an efficient bowel so all these impurities are sent on their way out of your body.

So first, we cleanse the stomach.

As I said, the first job is to help the stomach digest and we do this by eating enzyme-rich foods or helping with a digestive enzyme formula. A well-working stomach is a real joy. It makes for a happy life. It causes the sun to shine through the clouds on the dreariest overcast day.

In short, a good stomach is a boon and a blessing. Ask anyone who does NOT have a good stomach. Ask the antacid walloper. Ask the person with gas, bloating... a good stomach is indeed one of the joys of the world.

Here are the stomach herbs. I always look on herbs as friends. They are friends who will work away gaily for me. Don't you just love anything that works away happily for you? I know I do!

Paw Paw otherwise known as Papaya. This is a splendid gift from Nature. In Africa, where I once lived, the locals wrapped food in paw paw leaves to cook. They had found the paw paw sort of pre-digested everything and made it easily digestible. So paw paw is a good herb to have in your formula.

Have you heard of **Psyllium**? This is pronounced 'silly-um'. This is a marvellous herb to give bulk to the bowel. It has often been used as part of weight-loss programmes because of its ability to mop up fluid and to swell, giving the feeling of having eaten.

Peppermint has been used by Herbalists since heaven knows when to settle down unsettled stomachs. It is a great help for digestion. Ginger has also been used for the settling stomachs. It is a very popular remedy for travel sickness because of its settling effect.

Fennel, the herb with the aroma of aniseed, is another great stomach herb I recommend to you. **Gentian, Slippery Elm**, these all soothe the savage membranes. **Magnesium** has been used commercially for years to too-acid stomachs, so a little magnesium would be a good thing too.

You don't have to go searching the world for the stomach herbs, you can get them in most health food shops. I can't be bothered getting all the herbs separately and mixing up my own remedy. I am basically quite a lazy sort of person.

I get QuickCleanse because their stomach formula has all those herbs and more already there, ready for me to take when I need them. There are other herbal formulae and if you can't get QuickCleanse ask for advice.

A DIVERSION TO THE LIVER…

The liver makes a big contribution to digestion and elimination so perhaps we can make a detour and chat about liver herbs.

We have chatted about the liver at length already. Some people may even say 'ad nauseum', which means until we are sick of it. Good point! So many liver complaints have nausea as one of the symptoms.

I have told you how important the liver is in getting high cholesterol levels down to manageable proportions (whatever that means!). I have found **methionine** excellent for this.

It is a good idea to tone up your liver regularly. We go on about toning up our muscles, quite rightly of course, but little attention is given to toning up our internal organs. I know body builders who have built themselves up to astonishing proportions (same word again!). These guys walk into a room and it is just as though the light went out, they are so enormous. But when it comes to their insides, they are not all as well informed as they need to be. Their focus tends to be totally on size. They will buy almost anything to boost size but little to tone up inside.

For top level, outstanding, remarkable health it is vital to spend time and money on the inside. You get the inside right and the outside will look after itself! True! A beautiful skin depends on a good liver function. Clear eyes need liver support. Need top-level, awesome energy? Look at your liver!

Convinced? Or should I keep on at you? OK, I know you are convinced so I will summarise the good herbs and vitamins you need for a well-toned and well-behaved liver.

In all good liver formulas and this includes fat metabolising formulas because they are liver-active too, you will find **Inositol** and **Choline**. These two are lumped in with the B group of vitamins. Their role is helping fat absorption. So look out for them when choosing a liver-toning complex.

The next are the amino acids, **taurine** and **methionine**. You may find you will get one or the other in the complex you are looking at. One or the other is fine, to get both may be difficult.

Taurine is a vital amino acid for good liver function. Taurine is necessary for the liver's production programme for bile salts. You will remember bile is that stuff needed to absorb fat. The liver calls on Taurine for detoxification work. People with what is called the 21st Century disease, which is chemical sensitivity, need Taurine. This wunderkind in the amino acid family is an important part of the steps to take toxic metals out of your body. You know these by-products of our advanced civilisation, lead, mercury and so on get into all of us whether we like it or not.

This hard working, unrecognised amino breaks down drugs and gets them out of your body in bile. I bet you didn't realise how important Taurine is to your health and well-being, did you?

Now for the traditional herbs, weeds to some, miracles to we Herbalists... God's gift to suffering humanity, in my humble opinion.

If I repeat myself, please encourage me because this is the only way we humans ever learn anything, but I am awed by the cleverness of herbs. Don't you agree it is remarkable how certain herbs are beneficial to particular human organs or conditions? These little wonders have in them special ingredients that target specific human systems.

Dandelion is great for the liver and helps the kidneys too. Dandelion is a world wide star in the herbal theatre. The benefits have been sung for centuries all round the world. It used to be the favourite remedy of old-fashioned doctors. Maybe you didn't know this but all doctors were once herbalists. That's why I find it strange when doctors asked about a herb, will often respond: 'Well, it might not do you any good, but it won't harm you, so take it if you want to'. Sort of denying their own heritage in a way, don't you think?

Milk Thistle is so good for the liver it is said it can help reverse cirrhosis of the liver. This is when the liver starts looking like a well-worn old boot. This distinguished herb has even reversed fatty degeneration of the liver. Milk Thistle protects the liver against modern day assaults by elements in our toxic world. It also rushes in to repair damage done by the pollutants we innocently take in almost every single day.

Milk Thistle is a must-have herb for anyone who has, or has had, hepatitis. Hepatitis is a modern-day scourge. I have never seen so many people with this problem in my life as I see these days.

I believe every liver formula needs Milk Thistle in it.

Berberis is another traditional herbal for the liver. Berberis is also known as Barberry. Eating the berries off the bush is a great tonic for the nerves... shows how versatile Mother Nature is, doesn't it? Barberry keeps popping up in different herbals for different problems. It helps to relieve diarrhoea, it has been used to help menopausal women.

Berberis was used by the American Indians for ulcers, as a tonic, for heartburn, for the stomach and liver, as an appetite stimulant. So as you can see, this is a traditional herb with a long history of helping suffering humanity.

But our concern is the effect of Berberis on the liver. Like so many liver and stomach herbs, Berberis (remember it is also called Barberry) is a bitter herb. It is a tonic herb and one I would expect to see in any self-respecting liver formula.

Now here is a herb that is not very well known at all. It is called **Bupleurum**. Whilst we may never have heard of this herb other people have. The Chinese call it Chai Hu; it has lots of helpful qualities and has been used since ancient times for complaints like asthma, bronchitis, diarrhoea, dementia (interesting for a liver herb, eh?). It is used by Herbalists for hepatitis, jaundice, skin disorders (another sign of an under-active liver).

So as you can see, Bupleurum is a good herb for anyone who want their liver to be one hundred percent on the ball!

Here is another splendid liver herb, it is called **Schizandra**. This herb is also known in Chinese medicine and rejoices in the name Wu wei tzu. This is not a well-known herb but that doesn't mean it isn't a great liver herb. In human nature we tend to dismiss things we don't know much about.

'All right in theory but no good in practice, mate.'

We use this handy grab bag of a sentence to debunk any plan, scheme or strategy we are not comfortable about. But the truth is if anything IS 100% in theory it should be pretty reliable in practice. If the theory is wrong, the practice will be wrong…

Sorry about that diversion… I sometimes worry that I am too easily distracted.

Getting back to Schizandra, this herb has an impressive list of benefits. It is used to relieve chronic diarrhoea. Can I be rude and explain the way I use the word 'Chronic'. A lot of people use chronic to mean bad. They will tell you the pain is 'something chronic' or they have a 'chronic cough'.

The correct meaning is 'of long standing'. So when I say chronic diarrhoea I mean some poor soul is spending hours, perhaps weeks perched on a toilet seat wishing they were dead or something while they pour their guts down the toilet. As I remarked earlier on, we learn something new every day, if we are not careful. But I am sure you already knew the meaning of chronic. Take comfort in the thought that someone to whom you lend this book may not… they may not return your book either!

Schizandra is a liver cleanser, good for indigestion and as a free gift, is wonderful for excessive perspiration.

So make sure it is in your liver formula!

Moving on, **Dong Quai** is a herb I usually associate with female complaints. However, versatile herb that it is, it has been used successfully for hepatitis, stomach ache, Candida and also for constipation.

There are lots more liver herbs but I think we have enough in our armoury to guarantee our liver is fine and is up to scratch.

Now I know what you could be thinking (a touch of arrogance here), but you are wondering where on earth you are going to get these herbs. Even more worrying is how the heck are you going to blend them in the right proportions, will it be messy, do I have the time, is it worth it and all those other little worry demons that just love to batter our self-confidence.

But not to worry yourself, you can get them all in one box. You will find all these herbs in the QuickCleanse Lipid Clear… Most health food shops carry liver complexes so have a look at the labels and choose the one you think is the best for you.

AT LAST... WE TOUR THE BOWEL!

I know you have been gasping with suppressed excitement waiting for me to get down to the bowel... so no more suspense.

Your bowel is vital, I repeat VITAL, to your health. To get you back to good health or to make sure you stay vibrantly healthy... if your bowel is off, so are you.

You cannot be healthy with a sick bowel.

Burn this with letters of fire into your brain. No matter what you do to improve your health, no matter how hard you try, if your bowel is up to maggots, so are you. No argument here!

Bowel problems dog the footsteps of so many excellent people. These superb people, the salt of the earth, are plagued with Constipation, Irritable Bowel, Diverticulitis, Crohn's Disease... most of the ills that flesh is heir to. All because of a bowel that is not performing.

FIRST, SOME GENERAL COMMENTS ABOUT YOUR BOWEL...

Let me first talk about the bowel generally before getting into specific complaints.

It is essential, vital and fundamental to good health to realise the importance of a bowel with the correct balance of bacteria. Do not take your bowel for granted.

Most people have a less than adequate bowel, that is the reason for so many health problems these days. The word 'biosis' means life, so guess what dysbiosis means? Yep, life crippled or something similar. What it boils down to that most people have dysbiosis of the bowel.

Their bowel is not populated by wonderful bacteria breaking down waste, helping digestion, manufacturing vitamins and boosting the immune system. These people are seldom full of fun unless full of some stimulant.

ABSOLUTELY ESSENTIAL TO REPOPULATE THE BOWEL REGULARLY

Our little friends down there are under constant attack. There is a war going on in your bowel you are not aware of. Unfortunately, all too often we are on the side of the bad guys.

Sounds crazy, doesn't it? We are on the side of the bowel hoodlums, the vandals and the crazies instead of supporting the good guys. We take antibiotics for anything. A bit like those people who have chips with every meal or tomato ketchup on everything, even their breakfast cereal. We are given antibiotics for the most trivial complaint. No wonder we have succeeded where all else failed to promote the growth of the 'superbugs'.

So restoring your bowel is your number one priority. This is particularly the case if you are unlucky and have Irrritable Bowel, Diverticulitis, Crohn's Disease, Constipation, Low Energy, Candida, Parasites or anything else you can think of!

Many years ago I was lucky enough to learn Iridology from Doctor Bernard Jensen. Doctor Jensen is one of the world's premier nutritional scientists. He has been a pioneer for zonks pushing, pleading, persuading people to do something about their bowel.

Doctor Jensen told us that one of the seldom recognised and least known keys to glorious good health is the flora in the gut. Intestinal flora are those micro-organisms which live in the dark depths of human bowels.

Listen to this, it may be news to you, without a good mix of these micro-organisms you could not keep your food down, you could not digest it properly, you could not get any nourishment from the food you eat. You think that's all? No way, listen a bit more, read on my friend… without these friendly little guys you could not evacuate your bowel and get rid of waste matter. Your energy level would be zero, nix, nothing. Your zap would be zapped before it could even zip!

WHAT AM I DOING TO MYSELF FOR HEAVEN'S SAKE?

You might well ask. What do we innocently do to screw up our bowel? You know what I am going to say, wrong foods, wrong food combining, alcohol in excess, powerful prescription drugs (not your doing!), eating too fast, too much stress and worry. All these combine to make a mess of our bowel flora.

When this happens nothing seems to work out as we would like. We have no energy, we are prey to anything going around, we get severe Constipation, Irritable Bowel, Diverticulitis and all the other misery-makers a bowel can whack us with!

So it is essential, vital, important, crucial and any other words you can think of to stress the importance of doing something about it.

ALL ACIDOPHILUS COMPLEXES ARE NOT EQUAL

You walk into your health food store or pharmacy, you ask for Acidophilus because you are now health conscious. You are handed a bottle, pay your money and depart. You have a warm fuzzy feeling you have done the right thing at last. You are going to repopulate your bowel with the good guys.

But wait! All Acidophilus complexes are not the same.

Are there enough of the bacteria? The amounts can vary significantly. What strains are in it? There is more than one strain. The best known is Acidophilus, but there is Bifida, Bulgaricas and other members of the family too.

How is the formula presented? Why I say that is sometimes the Acidophilus never gets to the bowel, it is hijacked on the way through your stomach. You have to have a formula that can send the reinforcements where they are needed. You don't want one that allows the little troops to be ambushed along the way!

HERE IS THE CRÈME D'LA CRÈME OF ACIDOPHILUS FORMULAS

Let me introduce you to what is, in my opinion, the best of the Acidophilus formulas. Tell Uncle Fred I know the plural of formula is really formulae, but who cares? Most people say formulas, so we'll go with the masses for once!

When buying an acidophilus formula is it easy to be mislead… you read on the label the formula contains 10 million, 20 million, a 100 million bacteria or even more.

'Wow', you say to yourself, 'That's cooking with gas! All those millions of little bacteria just waiting to get down there and get to work! Will wonders never cease?'

Woah, wait a blooming minute, there is a question you need to ask. Of all those millions or billions of bacteria, how many will actually get down into your bowel?

This can vary alarmingly from brand to brand. While they tell you how many are in each capsule they very often cannot guarantee how many survive the trip.

There is another thought to ponder. If the environment in one's bowel is pretty dreadful, as it is in a lot of people, the bacteria may get a hostile reception. This will take its toll too. It makes you sick when you consider all the obstacles in the way of a healthy bowel.

Imagine planting rows and rows of healthy seeds in your garden. Sorry, but very few come up and they are pretty wimpy looking. What was the matter? Defective seeds? No, the answer is poor soil. Even the best seeds will not prosper in poor soil. They need rich, fertile soil.

Same with your bowel… the bacteria need good nutrition, a rich environment to encourage them to go forth and multiply by the billion. So a formula that provides boosters for the bacteria is the best.

If you can guarantee that TEN BILLION active bacteria can get right to the bowel, if you include more than one variety, if you include the stuff that guarantees the right food to boost the bacteria by the billion… you have something worthwhile.

FLORAMAX, THE KEY TO BRILLIANT BOWEL HEALTH!

This has to be the superdooper formula in bowel management.

Just have a look at what is in it and stand, sit or fall down, amazed. I was astonished when Ross Gardiner revealed the formula.

Listen to what is in it, you judge for yourself, and if you are like me you too will be overawed…

It has Acidophilus, it has Bulgaricus, it has Bifidus… a **minimum** of TEN BILLION in every capsule.

And it is guaranteed every single one will get right down into your bowel.

But that is not all, not by a long shot, there is more!

Here is a word to get your tongue round 'Fructooligosaccharides'. Isn't that a beauty? Imagine saying to someone 'How are your fructooligosaccharides today?' They would be overwhelmed by your extraordinary grasp on things unknown to the average mortal.

You may not believe it but this substance is the food of the gods as far as acidophilus, bulgaricus and bifida are concerned. They love it, they lap it up, they thrive on it. Hey, and guess what? The bad guys in the bacteria community hate the stuff!

And **FloraMax** brings with 200 mg of FOS (saves me typing fructooligosaccharides) in every capsule. So the billions of bacteria come supplied with their own field rations.

For the good bacteria this has to be the promised land. They arrive in a warm, dark place with a packed lunch. A lunch crammed to overflowing with growth factors. Picture them gobbling away, crunching and munching, slurping and slobbering. You can almost hear them!

And they show their devotion by multiplying at a mind-staggering rate.

Billions upon billions. All good. All working for you!

So look for **FloraMax** by Ross Gardiner; this has to be the best in my opinion… I take it myself because I honestly believe it is the best you can get.

LET'S GET DOWN TO BRASS TACKS…

Not that your bowel is full of brass tacks, although for some poor people it feels as though it is…

Let us now get to specific complaints. Let us discuss how to ease the misery of Constipation, Irritable Bowel, Diverticulits, Crohn's Disease, Gas Bloating.

It is remarkable but because your body is not in watertight compartments helping one complaint helps others. When we talk about the various things that go wrong with the digestive system, getting certain basics right can go a long way to fixing other problems.

You help Irritable Bowel, then you help Diverticulitis. You help Diverticulitis then you do something to relieve Crohn's Disease. And so it goes!

So first let us have a little chat about **constipation**.

I will summarise the earlier chapters on these important matters. Whatever the official definition of constipation may be, if you don't go regularly you could be in trouble. Once, twice even three times a day is healthy. Big dumps are the order of the day. Reluctantly parting with little bits, round balls, narrow strips, slim tubes is constipation. You must part with heaps. What goes down your throat must keep on going down.

Don't be a waste hoarder.

Laxatives are big business but they are not your friend. They promise they will help you. They promise to relieve you. False promises! They do little to help the cause of constipation.

Fibre is the answer. You must get fibre into your diet. Do this by eating enzyme-rich vegetables (not boiled), salads and fruits, nuts and seeds. For most of us getting a fibre-packed diet is difficult. Remember, unprocessed bran can be too rough for a lot of people. It may be cheap but for some it can also be nasty.

The best fibres are **linseed, oat bran, oat meal, slippery elm bark, rice bran**. For the best results these fibres must be finely ground into a powder. This means they will be easily absorbed and will not irritate.

You can get excellent fibre formulas from your health food shop or pharmacy. My own preference is for QuickFibre Plus in Australia and New Zealand.

It is important to realise that constipation starts in the **mouth**.

Digestion begins with the enzyme amylase that breaks down starches as you chew them. Poor chewing equals poor digestive breakdown. Eat slowly and chew well without stress. TV eating is not the best way to go.

If I repeat myself, which I know I do, it is because I sincerely want to impress on your mind the utmost importance of internal health.

If your bowel is packed tight with ancient wastes hardened to the status of concrete, you will need either an enema or colonic irrigation. Make sure you go to a trained and registered colonic clinic. Be prepared for a mind-shaking shock when you see what comes out!

Fresh cabbage juice before breakfast is great to get things moving. Lots of folk take a spoonful of blackstrap molasses in warm water first thing in the morning to shock the bowel into expelling waste.

A favourite for years has to be figs. A very popular natural laxative used to be Syrup of Figs. I don't know if this is still around. It was very popular when I was a kid. But cook up some figs and eat them.

Honey and bee pollen is another old remedy. Mix them together and spread them on good old black bread, or the nearest you can get. Gives the bowel bulk. But chew well first!

THE FAMOUS ASCORBIC FLUSH!

For some people taking a vast amount of ascorbic acid, Vitamin C powder in water, can cause the bowel to move in a big way. We used to call it the 'ascorbic flush'. Once your body gets to saturation with Vitamin C, diarrhoea can set in.

When treating patients we often suggest they take enough Vitamin C to bring on diarrhoea. Then we know we have tissue saturation. At that point we suggest they reduce the dose until the diarrhoea eases up.

If you find you take massive amounts of Vitamin C and nothing happens, could be your body has been waiting for Vitamin C for a long time. So persevere. Keep it up. And sooner or later you will get the big flush.

CASTOR OIL POULTICES…

If you have severe constipation and do not like the idea of a colonic irrigation, try a castor oil poultice. What you do is soak a cloth in castor oil and place it over the bowel area. You can lightly tie a crepe or elastic bandage round to hold it in place. Leave it on overnight and you should see a result when you go to commune with yourself on the toilet first thing in the morning.

These are for chronic constipation cases. But the same advice holds for everyone. Make constipation cracking foods a way of life.

Take a course of **FloraMax** or its equivalent (if you do not live in Australia)... you cannot win unless you have a healthy bowel.

Remember what I said 'Death starts in the bowel'?

Even more important, LIFE starts in the bowel too.

No matter what disease, no matter what illness, no matter how trivial or deadly, good bowel management is a major consideration if you want to get well. So there!

IRRITABLE BOWEL SYNDROME...

Irritable bowel, colitis, spastic colon, no matter what you call it this complaint is almost as widespread as the common cold. For some reason this problem hits three times as many women as it does men. Not fair at all.

The symptoms are unpleasant:

- abdominal cramping
- diarrhoea alternating with constipation
- bloating
- gas by the train load
- nausea and fatigue
- pain
- mucus in the bowel

You can often pick someone with Irritable Bowel. They have a drawn look on their face. They look unhappy, and no wonder.

Watch out for stress as this is a common trigger. If you are stressed try **Hypericum**. This herb is wonderful for easing anxiety. In Germany Hypericum is prescribed by doctors at least as often as Prozac. How wise they are. You can get Hypericum from your health food store or pharmacy.

Another thing to watch out for is **allergies**. Allergies can often be the hidden cause of Irritable Bowel Syndrome. If you find your symptoms get worse at certain times put on your

Sherlock Holmes hat and track down the cause. Could be something you ate!

Watch what you eat. One of the common causes of allergies is eating the same food all the time. Try to vary your diet. Keep a diary of what you leave out and see if it makes any difference to your symptoms.

Eating too much sugar is bad for anyone with Irritable Bowel. So is excessive cow's milk. Cow's milk is wonderfully nourishing for calves but doubtful for human health.

GENTLE SOOTHERS FOR THAT INFLAMED PULSATING BOWEL!

If you have Irritable Bowel you will be looking for quick relief.

Take a **digestive enzyme** with each meal. Let's make sure we break down the food before it gets into the bowel.

Next, flood the bowel with **acidophilus**, **bifidus** and **bulgaricus**. Take a course of **FloraMax**. This way you will be sure you have a large, healthy population of good bacteria working for you.

Get plenty of gentle fibre into your bowel. I recommend QuickFibre Plus, but there are other good formulas around. Ask the staff at your health food store or pharmacy for advice.

Essential Fatty Acids are essential to ease your Irritable Bowel. These acids are not the burning kind of acids. They do not irritate; they soothe.

It has been discovered that people with Irritable Bowel are very often short on Essential Fatty Acids.

These are mainly Omega 3 and Omega 6. You get Omega 3 from fish oil, flaxseed oil. Omega 6 is usually from Evening Primrose Oil. It is a good idea to take 100 i.u. of Vitamin E with your Essential Fatty Acids to make sure they do not go rancid in your body. Vitamin E also helps you to absorb the Omega 3 and 6.

Herbal help. Herbs are tiny powerhouses. They can have a tremendous effect when taken properly.

Cascara Sagrada is a herb that conditions the bowel. It encourages a natural peristalsis. Peristalsis is the word used to describe the gentle muscular contractions that propel matter along the bowel.

Chamomile, **Ginger** and **Peppermint** are herbal teas that can help relieve the symptoms of Irritable Bowel.

Golden Seal sometimes called 'The Prince of Herbs' is used for allergies, and you recall I suggested that allergies may be part of your problem. It has been used traditionally to ease Colitis, which is another word for Irritable Bowel. Golden Seal is used to relieve inflammation of the mucosa. This means the linings of your organs. In olden days Golden Seal was used to relieve Constipation.

So you can see this is a useful herb for you to think about.

Rhubarb is a favourite ingredient of pies in Europe. I loved rhubarb pie when I was a child. Especially if it was a bit 'tart', acid tasting. However, rhubarb as a herb has been used, since the year dot, for abdominal pain, biliousness, constipation and diarrhoea too. Obviously, an excellent bowel remedy.

The amino acid, **Glutamine** helps to lessen the effects of colitis and iron is also useful.

Grapefruit juice should be avoided by anyone with an irritable bowel.

PARASITE INFESTATION...

When dealing with Irritable Bowel, or any bowel problem, do not forget the possibility you are a walking diner for parasites.

I suggest you consider taking Colloidal Silver along with special herbs.

Elcampane is one herb that sees its life work as eliminating worm and parasite infestation in the bowel.

Wormwood, the name gives the game away, another excellent parasite and worm fighter. This herb has been used for hundreds of years to fight parasites. Yeah, parasites are probably a lot older than we are in the scheme of things. Wormwood has been used for constipation, gastritis, liver disorders and getting rid of pin worms and roundworms that have taken residence in your bowel (without your permission or knowledge).

Sage is an interesting herb. It got its name because it is believed to clear the mind. A clear mind is essential for wisdom and sagacity, hence Sage.

But Sage does more. It is excellent for flatulence… better than saying wind or gas. It too is renowned for helping Colitis, which you know is another word for Irritable Bowel. It too does a job on parasites in the bowel.

Isn't it fascinating to find out these herbs do so many worthy deeds for we poor humans? Such a variety of complaints dealt with…

And some people have the nerve to call them weeds!

Calcium and Magnesium can help to calm down a spastic colon. Persuade it to stop going into spasms all over the place. Taking a good quality **multi-vitamin/mineral** supplement is a practical idea. This is because if you have an Irritable Bowel there is a good chance you are not absorbing vitamins from your food.

HAVE YOU HEARD OF 'SITZ BATHS'?

I prefer to think of Sitz Baths as 'Sits Baths' because that is what you do. You sit in a bath of warm water filled to below your belly button. Jazz the water up with apple cider vinegar, Epsom salts, baking soda or salt.

You may rather add delightful herbs: Chamomile, Comfrey or Lavender to the water.

Here comes the clowning around bit. Stick your legs up on

the sides of the bath. Do this without falling over backwards, of course. If they are long enough, let them hang over the sides.

Have a good soak, enjoy yourself.

If the Sitz bath routine is all too much for you try soaking a warm towel with hot water containing Epsom salts. Hold this on the painful area for as long as it takes to ease things for you. Keep reheating the towel with hot water. Keep this up until you feel things are getting better…

It took a long time for your Irritable Bowel to get that way, so it won't get better overnight. The days of miracles have long gone. So do it the natural way, with patience and perseverance.

Realise you have to move out of your comfort zone and try things that may seem odd to you. But follow the advice I have given and not only will you ease the agony, your bowel will work sweetly and without complaint! Which is more than you say for some people we both know!

IS IT DIVERTICULOSIS OR DIVERTICULITIS SENDING YOU CRAZY?

What's the difference? Tell Auntie Maude to stop showing off. We know she knows but lesser mortals like you and me need reminding…

Diverticulosis is when you have these little pouches sticking out of your bowel all over the place. There is no pain. Half the population have this condition but do not know it.

Diverticulitis is a different kettle of fish.

With this condition the little pouches are full of inflammation. And inflammation causes pain. Food is trapped in there and the bad bacteria have seen this as a golden opportunity to cause mischief. They have gone in and caused the trapped food to go rotten. This causes the inflammation and pain.

This Is Why You Get Diverticulosis…

You will not be surprised to find it gets back to diet.

In our modern world we tend to have lousy diets. We think they are wonderful, we don't like people telling us they are terrible. But they are!

Full of fat. Low on fibre (that fibre word again), high on sugar. We love fast foods, we love processed foods out of packets. We leave the salad, we seldom think to eat an apple or other fruit at mealtimes. Some of us don't ever think of eating an apple.

We pour coffee, tea, milk, alcohol down our throats with gay abandon.

And we wonder why we have troubles!

The miracle is we don't have a lot more than we do. End of penny lecture!

So you must get Fibre with a capital 'F' into your diet. I have gone on about this before, so you can look back and take notes.

Fibre absorbs moisture to produce soft, bulky and quite delightful stools. The kind everyone with Diverticulitis would welcome.

Chew your food even more thoroughly. This is to make sure seeds, nuts, popcorn and anything else doesn't end up in those little bowel pockets.

We don't want to feed the bad bacteria and add fuel to the inflammation already causing so much pain, do we?

WATER, WATER EVERYWHERE… BUT WHO IS DRINKING IT?

It doesn't look like it, I know, but at least 80% of your body is water.

This water has to be replenished. You use it up. Your cells cry out for water. They are dried up and gasping for a drink… especially if you suffer from Diverticulitis.

It is essential to drink around eight glasses of water every day. Drink filtered water, not that stuff coming out of your faucet or tap, whatever you want to call it.

Water helps the fibre to expand giving your bowel the bulk it craves. Water prevents stool drying out. You know what happens when you have dried up stools. Usually nothing. But if something does happen it is painful.

Soft, easy-to-pass stools are what we want! Water is what you need to make them happen.

BETA CAROTENE TO HEAL BOWEL LININGS...

Beta Carotene is turned into Vitamin A by your body. While it is possible to overdose with Vitamin A, it is most unlikely you will with Beta Carotene.

It is Beta Carotene that makes carrots red, pumpkins yellow. Take 25,000 i.u. a day. This will do wonders for healing your bowel wall. Vitamin A is part of your immune defences too. A Vitamin B complex will reinforce the good work the **FloraMax** is doing in your bowel. It is also helpful for stress... and Diverticulitis is stressful.

Vitamin E is very handy because it protects the lining of your bowel.

Diverticulitis can cause constipation, but you know what to do about that...

The herbs I told you about for Irritable Bowel are just as useful for Diverticulitis. **Alfalfa** is a great herb for healing the bowel. Don't forget to take plenty of **FloraMax**. A well-populated bowel is essential if anyone expects to get rid of Diverticulitis. A healthy bowel is the foundation of health.

Eat small meals often and chew, chew and chew again!

If you think digestive system problems are small fry, think again. The digestive system cluster of diseases puts more Americans in hospital than anything else. I don't imagine other western countries are any better as a percentage of the population.

Almost half of Americans suffer from one or another of these diseases. Makes you stop and think, doesn't it?

Keep in mind cancer often starts in the bowel before migrating to other parts of the body. What should make us think even harder is these diseases of the colon were almost unheard of 100 years ago. So much for our progress!

It is a brilliant idea to take **digestive enzymes** with each meal. I have discussed this with you earlier. Most important if you suffer from Diverticulitis!

Garlic in capsules is also a good idea. Garlic has been called 'Nature's antibiotic'. Which gives you a reason for taking it.

If there is one substance people with any form of digestive system disorder should be on, it's **Aloe Vera**.

Aloe Vera is soothing to the bowel, prevents constipation, alleviates heartburn. Aloe Vera can even help some kinds of peptic ulcers. If you rub it on your skin, it can penetrate into the blood stream.

Aloe Vera helps wounds to heal in record time. It is a stand by for helping scars to heal. It has to be one of Nature's wonder herbs.

It may be you have to take antibiotics because your diverticulae are so infected. That is fine. You have to do what you have to do.

But, it is vital you take a course of acidophilus after your have finished taking the full course of antibiotics. Get **FloraMax** or the nearest you can to it. You know what antibiotics do to your bowel, so it is up to you to put it right.

Let me reinforce the message. Eat a low carbohydrate diet, eat more fibre, take QuickFibre Plus or its equivalent. Eat fruit. Do not eat seeds, nuts or grains. Drink at least eight glasses of filtered water every day.

Take the supplements and herbs I have told you about...

This way you will beat it... and then by reforming your diet and taking bowel-enhancing supplements you will be free of Diverticulitis once and for all.

PITY THE DEADLY CROHN'S DISEASE VICTIM

Crohn's Disease is nasty. The poor soul with Crohn's has ulcerations on his gastro-intestinal tract. This ulceration can be in limited parts of the colon or intestine, but in really bad cases it can be the whole tract, from the throat to the anus.

Someone with Crohn's looks ill and is ill. It often makes it impossible for the victim to go to work. They look pale, drawn with a pinched, pained expression. They can also lose weight because they are not getting nutrition from what they eat. They are not absorbing nutrients. Crohn's patients can get anaemia, as though ulceration were not enough of a cross to bear.

Diarrhoea is common too…

As I said, bad news!

The good news is I have had success with Crohn's patients. Yep, I have seen them put on weight, lose that pale, drawn look. I have seen their energy levels rise. All good news.

HERE ARE THE SECRETS OF HOW I HELP CROHN'S PATIENTS

If there is one health drink that is bad for anyone it is orange juice. People slurp this down by the glass. I wonder if they would sit down and gobble the number of oranges it takes to make a glass of juice?

Orange juice is bad for arthritics, it is bad for people with diabetes and it is poison for people with Crohn's.

If you suffer from Crohn's throw away your orange juice… sorry about that. It is never nice to find out that something you were doing which you thought to be good, turns out to be bad for you.

People with Crohn's tend to be short of **Folic Acid.** Folic is from the word 'folate'. And folate has the same origin as foliage. This is more ammunition for you to use in conversations. By the time you have absorbed all this information you will be in demand at dinner parties all over the place!

Most of the Folic Acid in foliage is in the dark outer leaves. You know the ones. They are the ones we usually throw away! So it might be a good idea to take Folic Acid as a supplement. It is inexpensive and you can get it from any health food shop or pharmacist who sells vitamins.

If you are a female of child bearing age then taking Folic Acid is a must. Do not do what so many do. That is come in for Folic Acid when they are pregnant. You have to take Folic Acid before you get pregnant.

Why Folic Acid? Because it reduces the chances of having a baby born with Cystic Fibrosis. But it is no use taking it to prevent Cystic Fibrosis once you are pregnant. It is too late then.

Another element missing in a lot of Crohn's patients is zinc. Zinc is great for healing. Zinc is needed in over 80 different activities inside your body. And if you are male, it is imperative, urgent, critical, important and any other adjectives you can scrape up, to take zinc. Your prostate depends on zinc. Prostate cancer is now the biggest killer of men. If that doesn't scare you then your instinct for survival is damaged.

My book, *How to Fight Prostate Cancer and Win* should be compulsory reading for every man over 30. It could save a life!

But getting back to Crohn's... **Aloe Vera** is marvellous for this problem.

Aloe has an enviable record for healing. The wounded membrane respond gratefully to Aloe Vera. Take at least an egg cupful three or four times a day. I give all my Crohn's patients Aloe Vera. The results have been outstanding. If you get diarrhoea then reduce the amount. Aloe Vera is a mild laxative, but in severe Crohn's Disease I have noticed that diarrhoea does not always show.

Slippery Elm Bark has been used in English Folk medicine for generations for hundreds of years. It used to be given as a restorative for sickly patients. It was seen as a food for delicate digestions.

Today we use it to soothe the inflamed mucus membranes. To heal them… to cover them with a gentle balm and give them a chance to calm down.

Rather get the powder. I know capsules are more convenient, but the powder is better. You put a spoonful in a glass, cover it with warm water and stir it up into a paste. Then fill the glass with pure water. Add some cinnamon to taste because a glass of Slippery Elm has all the charm of a glass of mud. Nonetheless, it is great stuff to drink down to ease the suffering of Crohn's. So take it!

I give my patients **Homeopathic medicine** too. If you know any Homeopaths they can make up remedies to help Crohn's and Colitis.

LET US NOW CONSIDER OTHER ANNOYING PROBLEMS!

Let us now look at the other annoying problems: heartburn, flatulence and acid reflux.

Heartburn is also called Pyrosis or Reflux Oesophagitis. I think we'll stick with heartburn! Heartburn and Acid Reflux are different degrees of the same problem… so my remarks will cover both.

I am sorry to tell you but alcohol is no good for anyone with heartburn problems. Alcohol relaxes the lower Oesophageal Sphincter. 'Gee', I can hear you say, 'Who would have guessed that?'

What it means is alcohol causes the little muscle at the bottom of the tube going into the stomach to relax. When it relaxes guess what happens? Yep, you're right, the contents of the stomach can come rushing up the tube into your mouth. Burning all the way!

IMPORTANT NOTICE!

If heartburn worsens before meals, or if it occurs regularly over three or four weeks, it could be an ulcer. So see your doctor and see what the official opinion is.

STEPS YOU CAN TAKE TO EASE THE PROBLEM

I have never believed in suffering if I don't have to. And you don't have to keep on getting heartburn and acid reflux either.

Chew **magnesium** tablets. Magnesium-coat damaged tissue and prevent further heartburn. This would be a good idea for anyone with Crohn's to do.

Once again **Zinc** is called for. I will repeat myself and tell you zinc is an essential healing agent for skin and mucus membranes (linings).

Most of the problems we humans suffer with our guts respond to the same medications, herbs, supplements and vitamins.

Heartburn and reflux are no exception.

Aloe Vera is great, take it.

I told you about **Barberry** earlier. A wonderful herb for the liver and good for heartburn and reflux.

Diluted potato juice is great stuff for heartburn and reflux. Very good for arthritis too. Cut up a potato into small pieces, cover with pure water, simmer on the stove for twenty minutes or so. Strain off the cooked potato and let the juice cool, then drink it. Mmmm, good stuff!

Slippery Elm Bark powder is good for heartburn and reflux too. Use the powder and not capsules.

Peppermint oil is excellent. You will find this in good antacid formulas.

In Australia, I can recommend **QuickCleanse 'Intestinal Clear'**. This formula contains finely ground Psyllium Husks, Slippery Elm Bark powder, Linseed powder, Fennel Seed powder, Dandelion root, Sage, Oat Bran, Rice Bran, Soya bean and Carob. All in one easy-to-take powder.

As I said earlier, these ingredients are best taken finely ground so your system can use them. Intestinal Clear uses only the most finely ground products,

This formula, or one similar if you don't live in Australia, can help a lot of gastric, intestinal, stomach problems.

Most of these problems have a common cause, but different reactions in different people. As you may have noticed we are not all the same and we react differently to different health problems.

GETTING THE GAS ATTACK UNDER CONTROL

Gas, wind and flatulence are not usually life threatening unless you let go at some terrorist meetings. But it is an embarrassing social problem for a lot of genteel people.

Breaking wind noisily can disrupt sales meetings, presentations, spoil a romantic moment, or cause people to collapse in laughter or frown dismally.

The reactions are varied, the problem the same… how to get it under control.

We can all be forgiven for the occasional lapse. Even the most civilised among us, even the best bred, the most proper can fart noisily at the least appropriate moment. And if it stinks the place out it is even more embarrassing. But this is not the person I am talking to.

No, it is the inveterate, the constant, the let-go-anytime-anywhere person… the one who seems to have lost control. Whose farting exploits are the stuff legends are made from. That is the one who needs my help the most.

This may not be you, but read on anyway. At times we all need help in this department!

IT ALL START IN YOUR MOUTH!

I must admit that a lot of people, except you and me of course, do a lot of damage with their mouths. I am not talking about the gossiping, the backbiting, the boasting, the slander… not at all, I am talking about the way we eat.

People do not chew enough. They take in air as they chew. If you take in air when you chew you are going to get gas.

If you do not digest your food properly, you will get gas. Partly digested food ferments. Fermentation produces gas in large amount. That is what fermentation is all about.

So the first steps are chew more thoroughly. Take a digestive enzyme with your meals.

Undigested starches in the bowel are manna from heaven for the putrefactive bacteria. They love and thrive on it. And they create a lot of gas from it!

Smelly gas tells you a lot about the state of someone's bowels. If you think the stink is bad, imagine what it must be like down in the darkness of that person's bowel. I don't want to think about it!

The next step is to get the bowel in good shape. You do this as I have mentioned, take a good acidophilus formula. In Australia and New Zealand I recommend **FloraMax** by Ross Gardiner. This is a wonderful formula.

So by chewing food properly, taking a digestive enzyme and getting the bowel really healthy, you have gone a long way to beating the problem. And if you have a healthy bowel at least your farts won't stink the place out!

Charcoal helps to reduce gas. Charcoal absorbs toxins from the digestive tract. Charcoal has been found more effective than some drugs given for wind, gas, flatulence, call it what you will…

Ginger can give temporary relief from a gas attack. Ginger is a great settler of the digestive system. It is a good remedy for travel sickness.

The formula by Totally Natural called 'Stomach Clear' has in it a lot of the herbs recommended for getting rid of gas.

Here is a list for you to look at. If you are like me, you will be impressed. Here goes: Paw Paw (Papaya in some areas), Psyllium, Peppermint, Fennel, Slippery Elm Bark, Gentian, Bioflavonoids, Magnesium, Artichoke, Black Walnut and Cats Claw.

This would be an excellent thing to take if you suffer from gas.

Would you like another item to drop into a flagging conversation? Did you realise in your wildest dreams that the average person produces two gallons of gas every day? That is one heck of a lot of gas.

Thankfully most of it is reabsorbed but around two cups of gas is released each day usually via the rectum. Silent, innocent, non-smelling emissions, farts! Most of the time for most of the people this gas is creeping out unnoticed.

If you don't want gas problems, don't overeat. Don't eat a lot of gas-forming foods… the cabbage family, beans and other foods you have noticed that constipate you.

If you are on medical drugs be warned that some of them cause gas. Tranquillisers, laxatives, cholesterol-reducing drugs, can all cause gas in some people. Check with your doctor if you have a problem.

Apple Cider vinegar is good to take to prevent gas.

Vitamin B5 after each meal can help too.

Gas can cause symptom reminiscent of a heart attack. Pain in the heart region, a pain going down the left arm. This is caused by bubbles of gas causing the transverse colon to expand. It then pushed up against the diaphragm and this in turn can constrict the heart.

In the end, at the end of the day, in the final analysis, the bottom line and all the other clichés come to one thing... If you don't want gas, get a good digestion and bowel system.

You are responsible for your well being. If you sincerely want to feel wonderful for the rest of your life... DO SOMETHING ABOUT IT!

Let us now go to the final chapter for some last thoughts...

17

A few thoughts to cheer you on your way…

I hope you have enjoyed my book. I sincerely hope you have obtained valuable information to help you to a joyously healthy life.

We are often reminded about personal hygiene. We are told to clean our teeth. Wash our hands after going to the lavatory. Keep our fingernails cut short and out of mourning. That means no black edges!

But who tells us about Internal Health? Unless you are extremely fortunate, no-one does.

If you have the choice, would you rather have a feeling of excitement coursing through your veins or would you rather be lethargic?

Surely hopping and skipping through Life is the way to go. Limping through life, plagued by disease, crippled with pain is not an option.

Boost your immune system. Build an immune system that makes disease-bearing organisms cringe in fear!

Take LactoMax, find out all about Lactoferrin in *How to Fight Prostate Cancer and Win.* Take the maritime bark, the grape seed, get the immune system boosting benefits of green tea. You can get the three of these in a product called 'TriGenol' made by Ross Gardiner. It is part of my daily routine.

Take QuickFibre Plus every day. Every six months do a detox.

Get plenty of fibre… plenty of enzyme-rich food in your daily diet.

Read this book at least three times. Keep it. Refer to it…

And don't lend it to anyone!

There is a good chance you won't get it back. My point is that if someone is serious about helping themselves, then investing in my book is small potatoes. You bought this book with your hard-earned money. Let others do the same.

I know you are kind-hearted and want to help. So do I. But I can only help people who are committed to helping themselves. You invested in my book… that shows real commitment.

Drink lots of water. Most people are dehydrated and don't know it. If you are thirsty you have gone too long without water.

Think positive thoughts. Say good things to people. Do not say bad things. Be a builder, not a destroyer.

Your thoughts shape who and what you are…

Thank you again for investing in my book, I sincerely hope it helps you become part of my dream. My dream is a world full of healthy, joyous and happy people. I want to hear laughter ringing down our streets. I want to see people smiling.

I believe the first step to a better world is the step you, me and thousands of people take towards radiant health… and that first step is to make internal cleanliness a way of life.

QuickCleanse. This is a total internal cleansing system that contains 31 (that's right, 31) active herbs. These herbs cleanse, strengthen and support your entire digestive system. The QuickCleanse internal cleansing programme consists of FOUR amazing herbal, multi-fibre and nutritional products. These are: 1 Stomach Clear, 2 Lipid Clear, 3 Bowel Clear and 4 Intestinal Clear. The exact formulas are stated on their labels.

When you use these formulas together they act just like a powerful internal washing machine, quickly flushing out and getting rid of unwanted wastes and impurities from your body.

Remember, if symptoms persist or if you are pregnant or breast-feeding, seek medical advice. Always drink plenty of pure water when you are on a high-fibre diet.

QuickFibre Plus. This is a delicious 100% natural high-fibre nutritional formula. It contains Slippery Elm Bark, Psyllium Seed, Oat Bran, Linseed Meal and Rice Bran... all micro ground for easy assimilation. They have been blended carefully in precise proportions to give you maximum nutritional benefit. Just one serve gives you a combination of both insoluble and soluble fibre and this equals over one-third of an adult's daily dietary fibre needs.

Every single serve of QuickFibre Plus gives you a rich source of Omega 3 and Omega 6 Essential Fatty Acids, a combination of insoluble and soluble fibre plus Calcium, Potassium, Protein and heaps of complex carbohydrates. QuickFibre Plus is available in either Chocolate or Carob flavours... I recommend this formula as a great nutritional addition to any meal for you and your family.

Lactoferrin... surely one of nature's miracle food! This has to be one of my favourite nutrients because I am awed by what it does to help suffering humanity! It works WITH the body to create a battle-ready immune system helping your body to fight like an elite SAS unit. Lactoferrin fights disease-causing bacteria that are always trying to attack us.

Lactoferrin is on guard at all your body entrances stopping these nasties from getting a foot in the door. The beauty of LactoMax is the whole family can take it from infants to their grandparents!

As you now know, for your bowel to be healthy, it should be swarming with good bacteria. If your bowel bacteria are out of balance, you may suffer from Gas, Bloating, Constipation, Thrush, Diarrhoea and have the perfect environment for parasites (and who wants that?).

The good news is there is now FloraMax… got to be my favourite formula for healthy bowel bacteria by the billion. Why take two or three capsules to get the balance right when ONE capsule of FloraMax will do it for you? Imagine getting 10 BILLION good guy bacteria in one capsule… all GUARANTEED to get right down into your bowel plus all the food they need to get them breeding like crazy! FloraMax Pro will do this for you with one easy-to-take capsule, just one a day…

You can get all these products from any good Health Food Store or Pharmacy… If you have a problem finding a stockist in Australia please contact Totally Natural Products on 1800 240 917 for QuickCleanse and QuickFibre Plus, and Ross Gardiner on (02) 9905 5250 for LactoMax and FloraMax… If you live in New Zealand please phone Crombie & Price on 0800 118311.

Before anyone asks… NO, I do not have a financial interest in either of these companies… although I admit it would be nice if I did. I offer you this information in friendship hoping to help you to vibrant good health… naturally.

Your friend,
Ron Gellatley ND

Flora-max.
omega 3- 6. Vitam E
flaxseed oil
Depression; liver overwork

Carol
Drenan